8-SESSION COMPANION STUDY GUIDE

Make Me a Blessing

YOUR ORDINARY LIFE CAN HAVE ETERNAL IMPACT

Cassia Elder

Copyright © 2019 by Cassia Elder

Published by Oran & Oscar Wordsmiths

All rights reserved. No part of this work may be reproduced, stored in a retrieval system, or transmitted in any form or by any means—for example, electronic, photocopy, recording—without the prior written permission of the author. The only exception is brief quotations in printed reviews.

Printed in the United States of America

ISBN 978-0-578-52394-1
Library of Congress Control Number: 2019906543

Unless otherwise noted, all Scripture is taken from: The Holy Bible, New International Version®, NIV®. Copyright © 1973, 1978, 1984, 2011 by Biblica, Inc.® Used by permission. All rights reserved worldwide.

Scripture marked (ESV): The Holy Bible, English Standard Version. Copyright © 2001 by Crossway Bibles, a publishing ministry of Good News Publishers. Text Edition: 2016. All rights reserved.

Scripture marked (NLT): The *Holy Bible,* New Living Translation. Copyright © 1996, 2004, 2015 by Tyndale House Foundation. Used by permission of Tyndale House Publishers, Inc., Carol Stream, Illinois 60188. All rights reserved.

Cover Design by Cori Horvath
Author Photo by B+N Photography

Cover Photograph is a detail from *Mosaic with Imago Clipeata of Bacchus*: Roman, from Tunisia, Floor Mosaic, about 140 – 160 A.D., polychrome marble and glass tesserae set in grouting, width 9 ft. 10 3/8 in., length 9 ft. 9 1/2 in., Toledo Museum of Art, Purchased with funds from the Libbey Endowment, Gift of Edward Drummond Libbey, 1990.73

Contents

Welcome! 5

SESSION 1 The Heart of Blessing 7

SESSION 2 To Don't List 19

SESSION 3 Pray: Ask God to Meet Needs 29

SESSION 4 Encourage: Meet Emotional Needs 41

SESSION 5 Give: Meet Material Needs 51

SESSION 6 Serve: Meet Physical Needs 61

SESSION 7 Share: Meet Spiritual Needs 71

SESSION 8 Inspire: Compel Others to Meet Needs 79

About the Author 87

Connect with Cassia 89

Welcome!

Hello, friend! I am so glad you have decided to link arms and join me on this journey. In this 8-Session Bible Study, we are going to dig deep into God's Word together. We will discover what it means to be blessed, why we are blessed, and the practical ways to live out being a blessing to others. My prayer is that you will come away from our time together encouraged that what you do really matters and inspired to be a blessing more and more.

—*Cassia*

What You Need

Each participant will need her own:

1. *Make Me a Blessing* **8-Session Bible Study Guide**. The Bible Study Guide includes memory verses, Bible reading, questions for review, deeper discussion, and personal reflection. Additionally, you will find suggested reading for more information on specific topics.

2. *Make Me a Blessing* **Book**. The Bible Study Guide is a companion to the book *Make Me a Blessing*. Many questions are a review of material found in the book.

3. **Bible**. The Bible Study Guide will frequently point you back to Scripture. Be sure to have a Bible handy in whatever translation you prefer. Some fill-in-the-blank questions have been created from the New International Version (NIV). If you do not have that version available, you can look up verses on Biblegateway.com.

Study Format

Homework for each session, although not specifically split into days, is meant to be broken up over the course of the week, not necessarily completed in one sitting.

Each session includes practical activities for exercising the principles discussed in that chapter. (Example from Session 1: "Schedule a 'Date Night with Jesus.' Share your experience or your plans.") You may not be able to put all of these activities into practice before gathering for your next group meeting. Time will be given in future sessions to share your experiences.

Memory Verses

Each session of the study includes a memory verse. Memorize the verse in whatever version you prefer. Share your memory verse with another group member before or after the session. Set a goal to share all eight verses on the last week of the study. (TIP: Write each week's verse on a note card. Punch a hole in each card, and place all eight verses on a key ring or tie with a ribbon to keep them handy.)

Leading the Group

Set aside time for participants to recite memory verses at the start or end of each session. For session 8, include time for group members to recite all eight memory verses.

Give participants the opportunity to share any experiences or activities from previous sessions that they put into practice this week.

Look ahead. The last page of sessions 3, 4, 5, 6, and 8 include Bonus Group Activities. Be prepared in advance to provide the group with time and materials to complete or discuss these.

STUDY GUIDE SESSION 1

The Heart of Blessing

Read:
Make Me a Blessing- Introduction: *Uniquely Unqualified* and Chapter 1: *The Heart of Blessing*

Memorize:
"And I will make of you a great nation, and I will bless you and make your name great, so that you will be a blessing," Genesis 12:2 (ESV).

Memorize the above verse in whatever version you prefer. Share your memory verse with another group member before or after the session.

A Favorite Quote from *Make Me a Blessing*:
"Blessing is not a contest where the one with the most toys wins. A person with more material goods is not more blessed than someone with less. Blessing is every good thing in our lives."

1. Do you wonder if what you're doing really matters? Tell how you are encouraged by the statement: "Ordinary people can have eternal impact while living out our everyday lives."

2. What is our common, singular, one-and-only purpose? (See page 9.)

2a. In what two ways can we execute that purpose?

3. Do you relish those quiet, solitary moments? Schedule a "Date Night with Jesus." Share your experience or your plans.

4. Who makes your Top 5 List of Most Influential People? How did those people encourage and inspire you in your faith?

1.

2.

3.

4.

5.

5. Read Genesis 12:1-3. What song, verse, or message has been planted in your heart? (Time permitting, if you are comfortable, sing or recite the words for the group.)

6. When have you sensed a wink from your Father? Do tell!

7. Read James 1:16-18. Why is it difficult to recognize every gift is from God and belongs to God?

7a. Why is it even harder to remember that everything still belongs to Him?

8. In what ways have you seen God use the seemingly small and mundane for his glory?

9. How have you noticed the word "blessed" being misused?

9a. In what ways can we act to redeem the meaning of the word "blessed?"

10. Share part of your Count Your Blessings List. Try to come up with a few more.

> For more on Gratitude check out:
>
> *One Thousand Gifts*
>
> by Ann Voskamp

11. Draw a picture of one of your favorite blessings below.

12. When have you found yourself practicing "thanks-stating" instead of thanksgiving? Share your experience with pausing to express your thanks.

13. How will you continue to count your blessings?

14. Complete the Blessing Cycle chart below. (See page 21.)

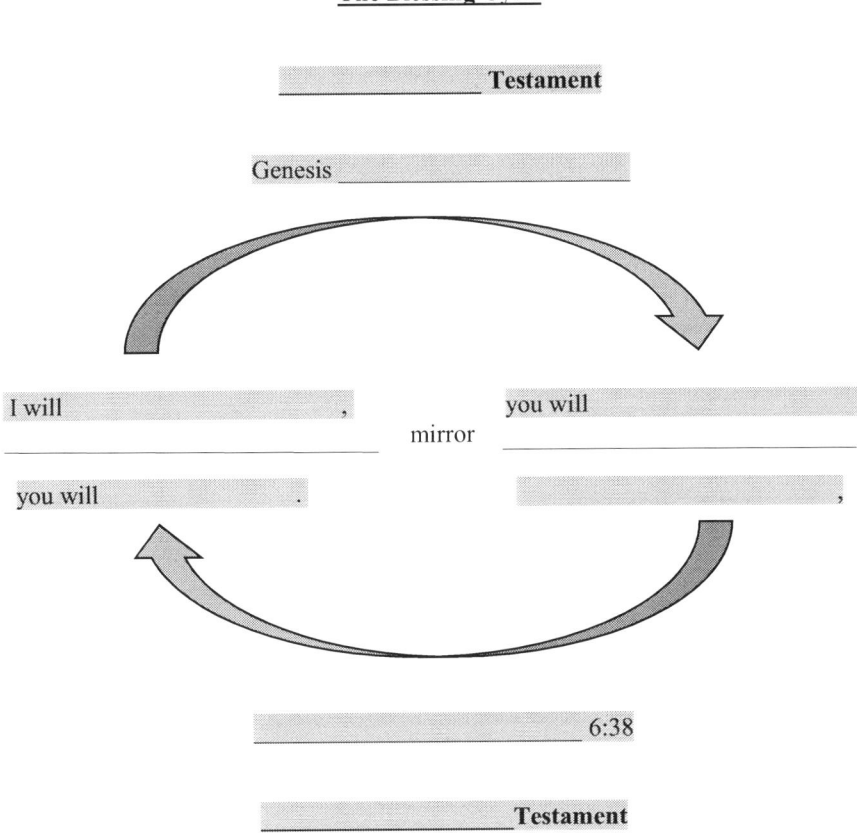

15. Read Matthew 6:19-20. Is there something you've been hoarding? I'll go first. I hoard craft supplies. I rarely use them, but I'm certain that I will someday, so I keep acquiring more. I also hoarded my gift of teaching for many years. Your turn.

16. Why is it difficult to allow others to bless us?

16a. In what ways can we gracefully accept blessing?

17. List the six Blessing Packages. (Try from memory, then see page 25.)

        _____ – ask God to meet needs.

        _____ – meet emotional needs.

        _____ – meet material needs.

        _____ – meet physical needs.

        _____ – meet spiritual needs.

        _____ – compel others to meet needs.

17a. Circle the Blessing Packages you are actively implementing. Share how.

17b. Put a star next to the Blessing Packages you would like to grow in. Explain.

17c. Draw an X next to the Blessing Packages that scare you a little bit. Why?

18. I talked about how my toddler loved to watch "Robots" and "The Incredibles." What movie have you seen more times than you can count? Name the theme or principle that stuck with you.

19. Do you remember the wise advice from Big Weld on getting started in blessing? Fill in the blanks:

_____ a need; _____ a need.

20. Knowing that your home is the epicenter of your circle of influence, how can you be intentional about being a blessing in your home this week?

21. Respond to the idea "Your position has not already been filled. You are not redundant."

22. Who is in your Circle of Influence? Fill in the acronym FRANKS next to the letters. (See page 28.) List two people, one per line, in each category.

F _____

_____

_____

R _____

_____

_____

A _____

_____

_____

N _____

_____

_____

K _____

_____

_____

S _____

_____

_____

23. Do you currently see a need within your circle of influence? Jot down any known needs next to the names on your FRANKS list. Pray about ideas to fill those needs and add them to your list. Make an effort to fill one or more of the needs this week.

24. "Jesus says the whole of the gospel can be summed up in two things. Love God. Love others. *Make Me a Blessing* is the call to action produced by love for others."

Read Matthew 22:34-40. Meditate on this passage as you spend time in prayer. Ask God to reveal to you any need for lifestyle change in the area of loving others. Pray for a heart that looks at each person you encounter as the potential recipient of the many gifts with which you've been entrusted. Write out a prayer below.

STUDY GUIDE SESSION 2

To Don't List

Read:
Make Me a Blessing- Chapter 2: *To Don't List*

Memorize:
"He must become greater; I must become less," John 3:30.

Memorize the above verse in whatever version you prefer. Share your memory verse with another group member before or after the session.

A Favorite Quote from *Make Me a Blessing*:
"Every time we say 'No' to our self and 'Yes' to Jesus, we grow weaker in our flesh and stronger in our spirit!"

1. Read the story of the Good Samaritan in Luke 10:29-37. Who in the story kept scrolling? Who stopped?

2. List three or more ways we keep scrolling. Give a reason or excuse next to each.

3. Name a few problems that seem too big. Take time this week to pray and ponder, "What could I do?"

4. What is the #1 enemy of blessing?

For more on Overcoming Self-Focus check out:

Free of Me

by Sharon Hodde Miller

5. Read 2 Timothy 3:1-5. Where do you see the sickness of self most prevalent in our society?

6. What opportunities to bless have you missed or almost missed?

7. "So God created mankind in His own image," Genesis 1:27a. Throughout the week, look people in the eye, remembering: "God's face. Give grace." Write about ways this affected your interactions.

8. What are the three indicators we are self-focused in attempts to be a blessing? (See page 38. Hint: they all start with "E.")

9. Place a check next to the "To Don't List" items you have practiced. Circle the one you struggle with most. Give examples beside the item.

- ○ Don't be obligated.

- ○ Don't feel superior.

- ○ Don't complain.

- ○ Don't brag.

- ○ Don't take rejection personally.

- ○ Don't expect reciprocation.

- ○ Don't expect gratitude.

- ○ Don't try to buy happiness.

- ○ Don't try to buy God's love.

10. List some of your current obligations. How can these be redeemed into blessings?

11. Read Philippians 2:1-5, 14. What are we commanded to do? To don't?

    To Do: **To Don't:**

12. Read Matthew 6:1-4. What distinguishes sharing from bragging?

13. Why do we tend to take rejection so personally?

13a. How can you shrug your shoulders and move on?

14. Luke 6:34-35 tells us to give without expectation. What are some ways we can practically apply this instruction?

If you prayed the salvation prayer for the first time while reading this chapter, Congratulations! Welcome to the family! Share with your group leader, another trusted group member, or the whole group if you feel comfortable. Ask for prayer and help learning to grow in Christ.

If you have never prayed a prayer of salvation and have more questions about relationship with Jesus, reach out to your group leader or another trusted group member.

15. "God's unconditional love is difficult to wrap our minds around." In what ways have you found yourself trying to earn God's love?

16. Name the five P's of Self-Denial? (See page 51.)

                        P _____

                        P _____

                        P _____

                        P _____

                        P _____

17. State some practical ways can we live out "MORE HE. less me."

18. It can be helpful to have a visual reminder of our commitments. I used a picture, a note, a necklace. What visual reminders will you use? Describe or draw a picture below.

19. What happens when we take on someone else's assignment? Share your experience.

20. Write the three options for how to apply the examples and ideas of being a blessing. (See page 55. Hint: they all start with "A.")

_____: Use it as is.

_____: Change it up and make it your own.

_____: Start from scratch; come up with an original.

For more on Choosing Your Own Assignments check out:

The Best Yes

by Lysa TerKeurst

21. "Let us not become weary in doing good, for at the proper time we will reap a harvest if we do not give up," Galatians 6:9.

Meditate on the passage above as you spend time in prayer. Ask God to keep you from growing weary in doing good. Pray to see others as God sees them and for opportunities to be a blessing. Write out a prayer below.

STUDY GUIDE SESSION 3

Pray
Ask God to Meet Needs

Read:
Read *Make Me a Blessing-* Chapter 3: *Pray*

Memorize:
"Therefore confess your sins to each other and pray for each other so that you may be healed. The prayer of a righteous person is powerful and effective," James 5:16.

Memorize the above verse in whatever version you prefer. Share your memory verse with another group member before or after the session.

A Favorite Quote from *Make Me a Blessing*:
"Prayer is not the equivalent of fingers crossed or sending good feelings out into the universe. Prayer is not passive; it is warfare."

1. What are the four prayers of blessing? (See page 60.)

Pray to bless—_____ and _____.

Bless through prayer—_____ and _____.

2. "But God won't draft us into service; we must enlist." I challenge you to begin praying, "Make me a blessing." Pray it every day, throughout the day. Write below how you feel about taking this step. Are you excited? Intimidated? Do you have any concerns? Reservations? Expectations? Please explain.

3. Fill in the blanks. James 1:5 "If any of you lacks _____, you should _____ _____, who gives generously to all without finding fault, and it will be _____ to you." (I used NIV.)

3a. Name one specific situation for which you need wisdom. Take a moment to pray for wisdom in that area.

4. Read Romans 7:15-19. Restate the main principle in these verses.

4a. How do you see this principle working in your own life?

5. Write out Ephesians 2:10.

5a. What stands out to you about this verse?

6. In what areas do you need to concede? Spend time in prayer, asking God to show you.

7. Why do we tend to believe prayer is passive?

8. According to James 5:16, what two words describe the prayer of a righteous person?

8a. How would really believing this change our prayer lives?

9. Consider the problems that seem too big. Ask God to give you a compassion for one of those problems and commit to praying for it this week.

10. Explain in your own words how prayer is Limitless and Unstoppable.

11. What is the difference between praying *for* and praying *about* another person? How have you experienced both?

12. List some of the needs within your circle of influence. Commit to praying for one or more of these needs each day this week. Choose at least one person to TELL specifically what you prayed, and ASK another how you can pray for them.

Friends _____

_____

Relatives _____

_____

Acquaintances _____

_____

Neighbors _____

_____

Kids' Connections _____

_____

Strangers _____

_____

13. Colossians 4:2 "Devote yourselves to prayer, being watchful and thankful." What one step can you take this week to be more devoted to prayer?

14. Pray this Scripture, replacing the underlined words with the name of a person in your circle of influence. Ephesians 1:17-19a, "I keep asking that the God of our Lord Jesus Christ, the glorious Father, may give <u>you</u> the Spirit of wisdom and revelation, so that <u>you</u> may know him better. I pray that the eyes of <u>your</u> heart may be enlightened in order that <u>you</u> may know the hope to which he has called <u>you</u>, the riches of his glorious inheritance in his holy people, and his incomparably great power for us who believe."

15. While reading *Make Me a Blessing* Chapter 2: *Pray,* did you pray Ezekiel 36:26 for a lost person in your circle of influence? How did this exercise affect you? Commit to praying for each other's unsaved loved ones.

16. Find your own promise or passage of Scripture, and use it as a guide to write an intercessory prayer below.

> **For more on Praying Scripture check out:**
>
> *Praying God's Word*
>
> by Beth Moore

17. Consider your circle and beyond. Commit to praying each day for one person or in general for all members of each group.

Ministers _____

_____

Authority _____

_____

Believers _____

_____

Enemies _____

_____

Lost _____

_____

18. Name some delightful experiences that often come with a little risk.

19. BAM! Have you ever experienced a Blessing Appointed Moment when God clearly put you in the right place at the right time to be blessed or to be a blessing?

20. On the 1-5 scale below, where is your current comfort level with public prayer? Circle the box that best describes you.

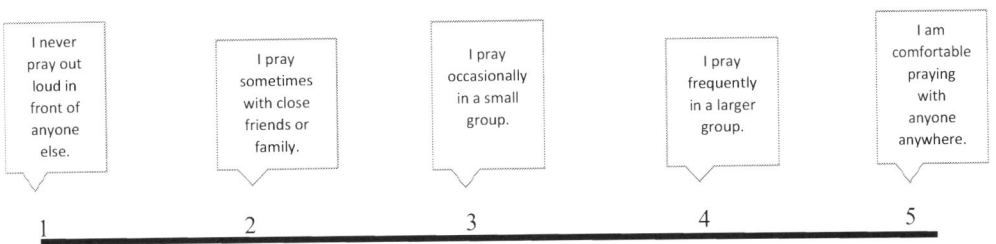

21. Spend some time in prayer before answering: Where would you like to be on this scale? Place a box around the number on the line. What action steps can you take to get to the next level in your comfort with prayer? Write down one thing you plan to do this week.

If you circled 5 on the prayer comfort scale, thank God for the boldness He has given you. Pray for your eyes to increasingly be opened to opportunities to bless others by praying with them.

22. What is one area in your circle of influence that you can create a culture of prayer?

23. What "Just a…." labels have you found yourself wearing? Fill in the nametag below.

> **Hello. My name is….**
> **Just a….**

24. Ask God to break that "Just a…." mindset. Put a bold **X** through the "Just a…." label. Make a new nametag that reaffirms—your prayers are powerful and effective.

> **Hello. My name is….**
>
> **How can I pray for you?**

25. Read Jeremiah 29:12-13. Meditate on this passage as you spend time reflecting on how to bless through prayer. Write out a prayer below.

"Again, truly I tell you that if two of you on earth agree about anything they ask for, it will be done for them by my Father in heaven. For where two or three gather in my name, there am I with them," Matthew 18:19-20.

Bonus Group Activity:
Close your group time by dividing into pairs and agreeing together in prayer.

STUDY GUIDE SESSION 4

Encourage
Meet Emotional Needs

Read:
Read *Make Me a Blessing*- Chapter 4: *Encourage*

Memorize:
"Therefore encourage one another and build each other up, just as in fact you are doing," 1 Thessalonians 5:11.

Memorize the above verse in whatever version you prefer. Share your memory verse with another group member before or after the session.

A Favorite Quote from *Make Me a Blessing*:
"Everyone within our circle of influence needs a fresh dose of encouragement every day. She is in a constant battle. The enemy fights to tear her down. The world fights to tear her down. Her own negative self-talk fights to tear her down. We must wage the war to build her up."

1. I hope you have you been praying "Make me a blessing." How has this caused a shift in your heart? In what way have you already seen God answering this prayer? Share the impact of this simple prayer.

2. Look up "Encourage" in a dictionary, thesaurus, or internet search. Share your definition with the group.

3. According to Proverbs 18:21, what power is in the tongue? How does Deuteronomy 30:19 relate to this concept?

4. Share a moment when encouragement made an impact on your life.

5. Respond to the idea "None of us get a pass on any of the blessing packages." Which Blessing Package did you hope you would get a pass on? Why?

6. "Put. It. On." In what practical ways can we bless in areas that do not come naturally?

7. Your personality is who God created you to be. Explain in your own words the difference between personality and character.

8. Read 2 Corinthians 12:9-10. What weakness will you choose to boast about as you receive God's sufficient grace?

9. Define appropriate transparency. What sets this apart from over-sharing?

10. James 4:17 says, "If anyone, then, knows the good they ought to do and doesn't do it, it is sin for them." Prayerfully consider if there is a good you've known to do but omitted. Ask God to show you how to correct the situation.

11. Read Exodus 17:8-13. Who has been Aaron and Hur in your life by holding you up when you grew weary? Share how. If possible, thank that person for being a blessing. Consider a hand-written note of gratitude.

12. Write Psalm 19:14.

12a. How can we ensure our words are pleasing to God?

13. Seize the opportunity this week to be a positive pointer-outer. Share your experience.

14. Read the verses below and fill in Paul's "Compliment Sandwich."

> Philippians 1: 3-6—Compliment:

> Philippians 2: 3-4, 14—Correction:

> Philippians 4:10—Compliment:

15. Look up 1 Corinthians 12:26-27. (I used NIV.) Fill in the blanks.

"If one part _____, every part _____ with it; if one part is _____, every part _____ with it. Now you are the _____ of _____, and each one of you is a _____ of it."

16. Which is more difficult for you, to rejoice with those who rejoice or to mourn with those who mourn? Why do you think that is?

17. Who could use encouragement within your circle of influence? Commit to encouraging one or more of these people each day this week.

18. List practical ways to bless with encouragement. (Example: Send a card or note.) As the group shares, write down new ideas presented by others.

19. "Let the redeemed of the Lord tell their story," Psalm 107:2a.

What is your story? Consider your experiences good and bad. What part of your story have you been holding back? How has God used your story to encourage others?

He will use your happiness to bring hope.

He will allow your celebration to invite expectation.

He will take what nearly broke you and break chains for someone else.

He will use what bound you to set others free.

He will turn your misery into ministry.

20. Which "He will" statement resounds with you right now? Why?

21. Write a prayer below. Thank God that He doesn't waste a thing. Offer up the broken pieces you have viewed as crumbs, and ask Him to show you how they can be used to encourage others. Ask God to let your story bring Him glory.

Bonus Group Activity:

Give each participant a sheet of paper and have them write their name at the top. Pass the sheets of paper around, each person writing a word of encouragement for the person named.

STUDY GUIDE SESSION 5

Give
Meet Material Needs

Read:
Read *Make Me a Blessing-* Chapter 5: *Give*

Memorize:
"Each of you must bring a gift in proportion to the way the LORD your God has blessed you," Deuteronomy 16:17.

Memorize the above verse in whatever version you prefer. Share your memory verse with another group member before or after the session.

A Favorite Quote from *Make Me a Blessing*:
"I know we've heard one man's trash is another man's treasure, but giving trash and expecting it to be treasured is not blessing. Despite the popular adage, it is not the thought that counts; how we give and what we give matters."

1. How have you witnessed God answering your "Make me a blessing" prayer this week?

2. Fill in the blanks. (I used NIV.) Matthew 6:21 "For where your

_____ is, there your _____ will be also."

2a. Explain this verse in your own words.

3. What is your "such as I have?" If you need help getting started, go back to your growing Count Your Blessings List.

4. "God not only supplies all of our needs but also some of our wants." How have you found this to be true in your life?

5. Read 1 Chronicles 29:6-16. (I used NIV.) What adverbs describe how the leaders gave?

_____ly (verse 6), _____ly (verse 9),

_____ly (verse 9), _____ly (verse 14)

5a. How did David describe the source of everything given (verse 14 and 16)?

6. Have you seen real poverty first-hand? Share how the experience affected your life?

7. Write Romans 12:2.

7a. How can we impact the world without being influenced by it?

8. In what practical ways can we give God our "firstfruits and not our leftovers?"

9. Read 2 Corinthians 9:10-15. What is the reason God provides increase? (Look for the "so that" statement.)

9a. What is the result of obedience in generosity?

10. Ask God for help defining want versus need in your own life. Are there luxuries deemed necessities that inhibit your giving?

11. "Jesus was not impressed by the one who gave the largest sum, but the one who made the largest sacrifice." How does this truth encourage or challenge you?

12. Why is the phrase "it's the thought that counts" not always true in giving?

13. What are the three ways we can be sure to Give Good? (See page 120.)

14. How have you been blessed by someone who practiced Giving Good?

15. Read Matthew 25:14-30. How did the master respond to each servant?

15a. What is your key takeaway from Parable of the Talents?

16. What is the practical application of being a good steward of God's blessings?

17. List ways we can plan ahead and be prepared to give. Write down any new ideas shared by others.

18. Fill in the three attitudes that can affect our giving. (See page 130.)

_____ mindset

_____ mentality

Attitude of _____

18a. Circle any of the above attitudes you have had in the past.

18b. Draw an arrow pointing to your current attitude towards giving.

19. If we aren't feeling like "it is more blessed to give than to receive," what weapons in our arsenal will help us to give with joy? (See page 130.)

19a. How can these three concepts help us?

20. Consider your circle of influence. What material needs do you see? Commit to meeting one or more of these needs this week.

21. "Give generously to them and do so without a grudging heart; then because of this the LORD your God will bless you in all your work and in everything you put your hand to," Deuteronomy 15:10.

Meditate on the verse above as you write a prayer asking for opportunities to bless others through giving.

Bonus Group Activity:
Plan a giving project to meet a material need in your community.

STUDY GUIDE SESSION 6

Serve

Meet Physical Needs

Read:
Read *Make Me a Blessing-* Chapter 6: *Serve*

Memorize:
"Each of you should use whatever gift you have received to serve others, as faithful stewards of God's grace in its various forms," 1 Peter 4:10.

Memorize the above verse in whatever version you prefer. Share your memory verse with another group member before or after the session.

A Favorite Quote from *Make Me a Blessing*:
"What we see as an interruption may actually be an intervention to get our plans in alignment with His."

1. Share how God has answered your "Make me a blessing" prayer this week.

2. How have you labeled yourself and limited God?

3. Understanding a broader definition of service, in what ways are you already serving?

4. What experience have you had with "not every good work is my work?"

5. "Our hearts lead us with emotion, but our heads lead us to ambition." Circle the one you tend to be led by:

Heart/Emotion

Head/Ambition

5a. Give an example of being led by your heart or head.

6. What should lead us as we choose our own assignment in service?

7. Read John 13:1-17. Jesus said to follow His example. What would "washing feet" look like in today's terms?

8. In your own words, explain Matthew 20:25-28.

9. What is the difference between gifts, talents, and skills?

9a. What is the common Source of gifts, talents, and skills?

10. Consider your own gifts, talents, and skills. What is your bailiwick of blessing?

11. Read 1 Corinthians 12:4-7. Circle the words "Different," "But," "Same," in this passage. How does this emphasize the importance of each person's gifts?

11a. For what purpose are the gifts given?

12. In what practical ways can you "not neglect your gift," and "fan it into flame?"

13. "Our people must learn to devote themselves to doing what is good, in order to provide for urgent needs and not live unproductive lives," Titus 3:14. How do we devote ourselves to doing good in our daily lives?

14. "'Let me know if you need anything' doesn't usually mean much; it's small talk." What are some ways we can sincerely inquire? Write down any new ideas shared by your group.

15. Fill in the blanks. (See page 144.)

"Do what's _____ because it's _____ to do, and do it _____ with the _____ attitude."

16. When have you gone through the motions of meeting needs without having a heart to bless?

17. How does Ephesians 6:7 instruct us to serve?

18. While doing seemingly mundane acts of service this week, practice intentional gratitude. How does this cause a shift in your heart?

19. Where do you currently serve in your church? If you do not, find out what current needs can be met.

20. "What we see as an interruption may actually be an intervention to get our plans in alignment with His." What presumed interruption was actually your assignment?

21. Do you have a Big Dream? Write about it.

21a. What are the small things that make up your Big Dream?

22. List some of the physical needs in your circle of influence.

22a. How might God be calling you to meet those needs?

23. Write out Luke 16:10.

Meditate on the verse above as you write a prayer asking God to help you to choose your own assignments and bless others in your circle of influence by serving.

Bonus Group Activity:
Plan a service project to meet a need in your church or community.

STUDY GUIDE SESSION 7

Share

Meet Spiritual Needs

Read:
Read *Make Me a Blessing*- Chapter 7: *Share*

Memorize:
"But in your hearts revere Christ as Lord. Always be prepared to give an answer to everyone who asks you to give a reason for the hope that you have. But do this with gentleness and respect," 1 Peter 3:15.

Memorize the above verse in whatever version you prefer. Share your memory verse with another group member before or after the session.

A Favorite Quote from *Make Me a Blessing*:
"Through Jesus' sacrificial death on the cross, we as believers enter into restored relationship with God. This unmerited gift, like every other, is a blessing not to hoard, but to give away. The free gift of salvation is given to us so that we may know God and make Him known."

1. This week, in what way has God answered your prayer "Make me a blessing?"

2. Write out Matthew 28:19-20.

> For more on **Evangelism** check out: *Tell Someone* by Greg Laurie

3. Fill in the blanks. (See page 156.)

The Great Commission is two-fold:

Be a _____ to the _____.

_____ up _____.

4. Explain why "improving people's outward status" is not "fulfilling the Great Commission."

5. Take an honest introspective look. How often do you consider other people's eternity?

6. Find a "fear not" verse that speaks to you. Write it below.

7. Respond to the idea that fear of sharing is cleverly disguised self-focus.

8. What are some practical ways you can "start small" in sharing your faith? Write down any new ideas shared in the group.

9. How have you seen others use their platform to share Jesus?

10. Read 2 Timothy 2:24-26. What was on Paul's "To Don't List"?

10a. How should we behave instead?

10b. What might be the result?

11. Your Heart Speaks. What do you love that flows naturally from your mouth?

12. Your Story Speaks. Consider your personal testimony. What was your life like before Jesus? How did you come to know Jesus? How has He changed your life?

13. God's Word Speaks. If you have never memorized John 3:16, I challenge you to add that to your memory verses. Find one or two additional verses or passages that communicate the Gospel message and write them below.

14. The Spirit Speaks. When have you experienced the Holy Spirit giving you words to speak?

15. Your Actions Speak. "Our best witness is our walk." How have you found this to be true?

16. None of us is promised another day. Is there someone you have put off sharing with?

17. Our urge is to say, "Don't follow me; follow Jesus." But Paul said, "Follow my example, as I follow the example of Christ." How does this idea challenge you?

18. What are the practical ways we can promote the growth of newer or less mature believers?

19. What four characteristics distinguish authentic Christian community? (See page 183.)

    C_____   C_____

    C_____   C_____

20. Where are you now or have you been a part of authentic Christian community?

21. How can you help others to experience community?

22. "My mouth will tell of your righteous deeds, of your saving acts all day long—though I know not how to relate them all," Psalm 71:15.

Meditate on the verse above as you write out your own prayer asking God to embolden you to Share.

STUDY GUIDE SESSION 8

Inspire
Compel Others to Meet Needs

Read:
Read *Make Me a Blessing*- **Chapter 8:** *Inspire*

Memorize:
"And let us consider how we may spur one another on toward love and good deeds," Hebrews 10:24.

Memorize the above verse in whatever version you prefer. Share your memory verse with another group member before or after the session.

A Favorite Quote from *Make Me a Blessing:*
"If we bless the people within our circle of influence and they are compelled to bless those around them, we create a ripple of blessing. As blessing is inspired to the third and fourth and fifth generation, more stones are cast, more ripples are created. The potential reach is limitless—all peoples, all nations, blessing and being blessed."

1. How has God answered your "Make me a blessing" prayer?

2. Over the course of this study, how have you seen blessing become a lifestyle?

3. Read Genesis 12:3, 22:18, 26:4, 28:14. What is God's promise to Abraham and his descendants?

3a. As followers of Christ, we are "the seed of Abraham." How does God's promise to Abraham apply to our lives?

4. Fill in the blanks. (See page 186.)

"Our circle of influence is finite. But the good news is, where our circle _____, someone else's circle _____."

4a. How does this truth encourage you in blessing?

5. When have you witnessed or experienced a ripple of blessing?

6. What are the four ways to Inspire? (See page 188.)

E _____   E _____

E _____   E _____

7. Read Matthew 5:16. What are practical ways to live out this verse?

8. Who has inspired you to bless because of their example? Explain how.

9. How do you plan to express the message of *Make Me a Blessing* and compel others to bless?

10. "Just like you and me, our children have a Right Now Purpose." How can you incorporate "present talk" in your life?

11. Consider the Six Blessing Packages: Pray. Encourage. Give. Serve. Share. Inspire. How have you been blessed by a child in your life?

12. When has another person engaged you in blessing?

13. How will you engage someone in your circle of influence in your own blessing activity?

14. Who has empowered you to be made a blessing? Explain. Write a note to thank that person.

15. Read Philippians 3:12-14. Paul tells us he has not arrived. What does he do?

16. How will you continue to keep blessing a priority in your life?

17. "We are God's masterpiece," Ephesians 2:10a (NLT). Tell about your favorite work of art or spend some time researching art. Share your thoughts on your experience.

18. Read 1 Corinthians 13:12. Respond to the idea that your life is a mosaic.

19. Read Philippians 1:6. What good work are you trusting God to be faithful to complete in you?

20. Write out Numbers 6:24-26.

21. Read Matthew 25:34-40. Write out a prayer below. Thank God for using you in His Blessing Cycle. Ask Him to continue the good work of *Make Me a Blessing* in your life and to help you do this more and more.

Bonus Group Activity:
Break into pairs, speak the Numbers 6:24-26 blessing over each other.

About the Author

Cassia Elder is an author, speaker, and women's ministry leader. It is her joy to connect with an online audience through her website and social media where she has conversations about real life, engages with Scripture, and navigates the practical application of how those two things fit together. What fills her cup most is to have these authentic conversations with women in person—to hug their necks, hear their stories, and share the truth of God's Word.

Cassia lives in Southern Indiana on a nearly-off-grid microfarm with her husband Chris, their son Asa, and a porch-sittin' hound dog named Moonshine. Their days are spent restoring a rustic log cabin on the creek and exploring nature. Most mornings you'll find Cassia rocking in her Grandma Phyllis's hand-me-down glider on the back porch with a mug of coffee in her hand and a Bible in her lap. She is a nerd for God's Word who enjoys gardening and has been passionate about crafting with words since joining the Young Author's Club in the fourth grade.

Connect
with Cassia

- CassiaElder.com
- Cassia Elder-Author
- @cassiaelder
- @eldercassia

Made in the USA
Middletown, DE
25 June 2019

The Foreign Policy Priorities of Third World States

Also of Interest

† *Change in the International System,* edited by Ole R. Holsti, Randolph M. Siverson, and Alexander L. George

† *From Dependency to Development: Strategies to Overcome Underdevelopment and Inequality,* edited by Heraldo Muñoz

† *The Third World and U.S. Foreign Policy: Cooperation and Conflict in the 1980s,* Robert L. Rothstein

† *The Theory and Structures of International Political Economy,* edited by Todd Sandler

† *Transnational Enterprises: Their Impact on Third World Societies and Cultures,* edited by Krishna Kumar

The Foreign Investment Screening Process in LDCs: The Case of Colombia, 1967–1975, Francois J. Lombard

† *Debt and the Less Developed Countries,* edited by Jonathan David Aronson

The New Economics of Less Developed Countries: Changing Perceptions in the North-South Dialogue, edited by Nake Kamrany

Technological Progress in Latin America: The Prospects for Overcoming Dependency, edited by James H. Street and Dilmus D. James

The Military and Security in the Third World: Domestic and International Impacts, edited by Sheldon W. Simon

African International Relations: An Annotated Bibliography, Mark W. DeLancey

† *Africa's International Relations: The Diplomacy of Dependency and Change,* Ali M. Mazrui

U.S. Foreign Policy and the New International Economic Order, Robert K. Olson

† Available in hardcover and paperback

Westview Special Studies in International Relations

The Foreign Policy Priorities of Third World States
edited by John J. Stremlau

Despite the growing economic interdependence that binds industrialized and developing countries—as well as the risk that regional conflict in the Third World could escalate into a major confrontation between the United States and the USSR—relatively little has been published on how governments in Asia, Latin America, and Africa pursue their international interests. This collection, especially intended for university courses in international relations, is designed to fill that gap by highlighting the changing foreign policy priorities of the diverse group of 120 developing nations.

The authors identify and analyze key factors in recent trends in the international relations of Third World countries. Each chapter is problem oriented and reflects an appreciation that Third World governments face real, if very limited, choices as they seek to enhance simultaneously their national security and their economic well-being.

John J. Stremlau is associate director of international relations at the Rockefeller Foundation and an adjunct professor of political science at Columbia University. One of his recent publications is *The International Politics of the Nigerian Civil War.*

The Foreign Policy Priorities of Third World States

edited by JOHN J. STREMLAU

WESTVIEW PRESS / BOULDER, COLORADO

Westview Special Studies in International Relations

All rights reserved. No part of this publication may be reproduced or transmitted in any form or by any means, electronic or mechanical, including photocopy, recording, or any information storage and retrieval system, without permission in writing from the publisher.

Copyright © 1980, 1982 by Trustees of Columbia University in the City of New York

Published in 1982 in the United States of America by
  Westview Press, Inc.
  5500 Central Avenue
  Boulder, Colorado 80301
  Frederick A. Praeger, President and Publisher

Library of Congress Cataloging in Publication Data
Main entry under title:
The Foreign policy priorities of Third World states.
   (Westview special studies in international relations)
   "Initially published in 1980 as a special issue of Columbia's Journal of international affairs"—Pref.
   Includes index.
   1. Underdeveloped areas—Foreign economic relations—Addresses, essays, lectures.   2. Underdeveloped areas—Foreign relations—Addresses, essays, lectures.   I. Stremlau, John J.   II. Title.
HF1413.F67   327.1'11'091724   81-22004
ISBN 0-86531-374-1   AACR2
ISBN 0-86531-383-0 (pbk.)

Printed and bound in the United States of America

Contents

Preface ix
List of Contributors xi

1. The Foreign Policies of Developing Countries in the 1980s,
   John J. Stremlau 1
2. Developing States and the International Security System,
   Edward A. Kolodziej and Robert Harkavy 19
3. OPEC and NOPEC: Oil in South-South Relations,
   Bijan Mossavar-Rahmani 49
4. Atomic Diplomacy in Developing Countries, *Rodney W. Jones* 67
5. External Financing of Development: Challenges and Concerns,
   Roger S. Leeds 97
6. Industrialization, Trade and the International Division of Labor,
   Luciano Tomassini 117
7. Multinational Corporations and Developing Countries,
   Joseph LaPalombara and Stephen Blank 133
8. The North-South Dialogue: The Political Economy of Immobility,
   Robert L. Rothstein 151

Index 169

Preface

This volume originated in a graduate seminar on the foreign policies of developing countries at Columbia University's School of International Affairs. The seminar encourages students to seek a better understanding of how governments in the Third World have adapted to the unprecedented international diffusion of political and economic power that affects their self-determination and national welfare in new and complex ways. The enthusiastic response to this collection, when it was initially published in 1980 as a special issue of Columbia's *Journal of International Affairs,* suggests that it could serve to fill a gap in international relations curricula as well as being of use as a general reference for scholars engaged in more advanced research on contemporary foreign policies of developing countries.

Few international relations instructors have the time or background to adequately introduce students to the difficult foreign policy choices that confront the diverse range of 120 countries that compose the Third World. Despite the many dramatic examples of economic interdependence that bind industrialized and developing countries—as well as the risk that regional conflict in the Third World could escalate to a major confrontation between the United States and the Soviet Union—relatively little has been published on how governments in Asia, Latin America, and Africa develop and pursue their foreign policy strategies. The contributors do not analyze the foreign policy priorities of particular governments; rather they attempt to provide the reader with an appreciation of recent trends in the international behavior of Third World countries.

Each chapter is problem oriented and encompasses both security and economic issues. The first four chapters fall in the domain of political science; the rest cover topics usually dealt with by economists. Such disciplinary distinctions, however, have little relevance for analyses of contemporary international relations. The selection of topics reflects our collective desire to question whether the "North-South" issues that feature so prominently in debates and in Western journals and newspapers are, in fact, of vital concern to policymakers in developing countries.

Although we tried to accurately reflect the perceptions of elites in developing countries, it should be noted that most of us are not nationals of these countries; our views are doubtlessly influenced by our Western education and by our particular experiences in the handful of nations in which we have had the privilege to be temporary residents. We hope future case studies that analyze the foreign policy priorities in important Third World capitals will test the assumptions that shaped the scope and content of this book.

I am grateful to David Chaffetz and his colleagues on the editorial board of the *Journal of International Affairs,* who invited me to develop this collection. Mary L. Ryan's patient editorial assistance is also warmly acknowledged.

John J. Stremlau

About the Contributors

Stephen Blank is a partner in Multinational Strategies, Inc., a New York–based research and consulting organization. Formerly a professor of political science at the University of Pittsburgh, he has written several books on European politics and multinational corporations.

Robert Harkavy, professor of political science at Pennsylvania State University, is the author of books and articles dealing with the military aspects of the Arab-Israeli conflict.

Rodney W. Jones, currently a staff associate at the Georgetown Center for Strategic and International Studies, specializes in U.S. foreign and national security policies and international energy problems. His most recent works are *Next Steps After INFCE: U.S. International Nuclear and Nonproliferation Policy* and *Nuclear Proliferation: Islam, the Bomb and South Asia.*

Edward A. Kolodziej is professor of political science and former head of the Department of Political Science at the University of Illinois. He recently edited a volume (*American Security Policy and Policy-Making*) with Professor Harkavy, and they are currently working on another dealing with the security policies of developing states. Professor Kolodziej is also completing a study on French arms-transfer policy.

Joseph LaPalombara, Arnold Wolfers Professor of Political Science at Yale University, is a distinguished writer in the fields of European and international politics. He has served as chairman of the Political Science Department at Yale and recently was cultural attaché at the U.S. Embassy in Rome.

Roger S. Leeds is an investment officer at the International Finance Corporation, an affiliate of the World Bank, and also teaches courses in international finance at the Johns Hopkins School of Advanced International Studies. He is the author of a number of articles on international political and economic affairs.

Bijan Mossavar-Rahmani is an Iranian energy analyst and consultant currently based in Cambridge, Massachusetts. He was a Visiting Research Fellow at the Rockefeller Foundation in New York between October 1978 and October 1980, prior to which he worked in Iran in a number of capacities, among them as a member of his country's delegation to OPEC. Mr. Mossavar-Rahmani, who holds degrees from Princeton and the University of Pennsylvania, has published widely on energy issues and is the author of *Energy Policy and Iran: Domestic Choices and International Implications.*

Robert L. Rothstein has taught at Columbia and Johns Hopkins universities and is currently an international consultant in Washington, D.C. His most recent books are *Global Bargaining: UNCTAD and The Quest for a New International Order, The Weak in the World of the Strong: The Developing Countries in the International Order,* and *The Third World and U.S. Foreign Policy: Cooperation and Conflict in the 1980s.*

John J. Stremlau is associate director of international relations at the Rockefeller Foundation and an adjunct professor of political science at Columbia University. One of his recent publications is *The International Politics of the Nigerian Civil War.*

Luciano Tomassini is on the staff of CEPAL, the UN's Economic Research Bureau for Latin America. He had contributed scholarly articles on the subject of Third World trade and development.

1. The Foreign Policies of Developing Countries in the 1980s

JOHN J. STREMLAU

Developing countries will continue to face domestic and external constraints that will severely restrict the range of options and the authority of their foreign policies. The further diffusion of political and economic power within and among nations, however, will produce new opportunities for international cooperation as well as new dangers of conflict. How these governments choose to order their foreign policy priorities and how they decide to deploy their limited political, economic and military resources in pursuit of these objectives could have a cumulative impact on the shape of world order in the 1980s that will be as important — if less dramatic — as decisions that are taken in Washington and Moscow.

The articles that follow indicate the changing scope and complexity of important international relations that currently engage the interests of many governments in the Third World. A detailed analysis of the foreign policy processes and shifting agendas of developing countries with shared or common interests was beyond the scope of this volume.[1] These essays on broad functional issues and multilateral negotiations should inspire further research that will bring to light the changing nature of foreign policy formulation and implementation by Third World governments and their relative successes and failures in dealing with the asymmetries of interdependence.[2]

Foreign policy in both developed and developing countries tends to concentrate only on relations with a few of the major powers. Successful adaptation to complex interdependence, however, will require all governments not only to manage a lengthening agenda of national interests with international dimensions, but also to anticipate and adjust to the decisions of a greater number of developing countries with the unilateral or collective power to affect those interests.

At the broadest level, the foreign policy of any government simultaneously will seek two interrelated objectives: enhanced national security and greater economic development.[3] The formulation

---

I am indebted to Carolyn C. Stremlau for her many helpful suggestions.
1. For a brief introduction to comparative foreign policy analysis of developing countries within and among the regions of Southeast Asia, the Middle East, Sub-Saharan Africa, the Commonwealth Caribbean, and Latin America see: *Foreign Policy Making in Developing Countries,* edited by Christopher Clapman, New York, 1977.
2. For the theory of "complex interdependence" see: Robert Keohane and Joseph Nye, *Power and Interdependence,* Boston, 1977, Chapter 1. As the vulnerabilities of developing countries change, the possible consequences of alternative foreign policy options available to each government need to be analyzed issue by issue. For some of the methodological strengths and weaknesses of an issue-oriented approach see: William Potter, "Issue Area and Foreign Policy Analysis," *International Organization,* Vol. 34, Summer 1980.
3. Among the many variables that may be salient in shaping a developing country's foreign policy the

of national security policies in developing countries usually begins with judgments of what is necessary and possible to protect the physical safety and political tenure of a particular leader and his regime. Economic development policies can contribute to this sense of well-being or threaten it, but such decisions rarely take first priority. Recent trends of rising debt and energy prices, expanding trade of conventional arms and nuclear technology, a deepening world economic recession with the threat of new trade barriers, plus growing concerns about the political implications of overpopulation and food scarcity, have blurred distinctions between national security and economic development policies, as well as between their foreign and domestic dimensions.

This short essay turns on seven propositions that have been derived more from intuition than from systematic empirical research:

1. The primary and prevalent concerns of Third World governments are with the threats to their security that are domestic in origin or emanate from conditions in neighboring countries; the international dimensions of these local issues will typically determine the core of the foreign policy of these countries.

2. Most developing countries continue to be ruled by highly personalized authoritarian regimes which generally pursue consistent, cautious foreign policies that reflect a limited capacity to wield international influence but seek maximum freedom to deal with internal security.

3. Developing country elites prefer to rely on regional collective security arrangements to isolate and resolve local conflicts or to strengthen their freedom to deal with domestic insurgents, rather than to resort to appeals to the United Nations or, except in cases of grave military threats, to enter into bilateral security arrangements with a major power.

4. Problems associated with the quest for rapid economic development are increasingly perceived by developing country elites to be interrelated with problems of internal security and the international dimensions of these economic issues have become increasingly germane to domestic tranquility.

5. The international economic policies of most

---

following checklist is suggested. At the domestic level the analyst needs to consider: political/ethnic/religious cleavages; economic disparities; resource endowment; the stage of industrial development; the effectiveness of governmental institutions — civilian and military; the country's size and location; and the personal characteristics of key members in the ruling elite. Regionally there are important relations among states and ethnic groups that need to be carefully identified in terms of: the historical record of conflict and cooperation; the prevalence and intensity of civil strife; interstate disparities of political/military/economic power; the extent of major power involvement in regional affairs; special issues such as the liberation of black South Africans or the fate of the Palestinians; and the degree of authority of regional norms and organizations. A developing country's foreign policy also may be strongly influenced by special bilateral relations beyond the region that are based on: the legacy of colonialism; trade, aid and investment interests; ideological affinity; or military ties. Finally, there are numerous more subtle variables related to how a developing country elite perceives and reacts to: the current state of the world economy; trends in the US-Soviet global balance; the institutional capabilities and intentions of the United Nations, its many agencies, and other large multilateral organizations; the role of transnational organizations including manufacturing, financial, communications, educational, and religious organizations.

developing countries give higher priority to bilateral relations than to regional economic cooperation or the North-South dialogue.

6. Conditions of local instability in the Third World and heightened tensions between the United States and the Soviet Union have created the need for closer coordination of domestic and international security policies among developing countries.

7. Over the longer term, shared and common security concerns could provide the impetus and legitimacy for closer economic cooperation within and among Third World regions.

Foreign Policy and the Security of New States

When more than eighty territories became independent following World War II, indigenous elites typically inherited what William Zartman has called "state-nations," in recognition of their cultural heterogeneity, narrowly based political institutions, and economic underdevelopment.[4] Foreign policies of these new states initially reflected a need to consolidate local authority and affirm the identity of the state internationally while reducing — or at least diversifying — foreign influence at home.[5] Successful foreign economic relations became politically significant when aid, foreign investments, and important trade concessions could be allocated to key constituencies.

Establishing an international identity for a new state could be accomplished with relative ease by joining the United Nations and many of the nearly two hundred intergovernmental organizations that existed by the mid-1960s.[6] Ruling elites might occasionally shade the political/ideological characteristics of their new states to reassure neighboring states or, more importantly, a major power; the international environment was, however, hospitable to decolonization following World War II and the objective of establishing the identity of new states was quickly achieved. The diplomatic efforts by newly independent states to give further momentum to decolonization, unilaterally and through the nonaligned movement, may have hastened the decline of the imperial powers and perhaps enhanced the domestic stature of some Third World leaders. But the developing countries obviously lacked the resources to materially assist liberation struggles, although their diplomacy occasionally helped to legitimize Soviet or other outside support. The persistence of Portugese colonial rule in Africa was, for many years, a poignant reminder of the limited foreign policy options available to Third World governments wishing to influence that decaying imperial power.[7] Furthermore, the

---

4. I. William Zartman, "Characteristics of Developing Foreign Policies" in *French Speaking Africa: The Search for Identity*, edited by William H. Lewis, New York, 1965.
5. Robert Good, "State Building as a Determinant for Foreign Policy in New States" in *Neutralism and Nonaligned: the New States in World Affairs*, edited by L. Martin, New York, 1962. See also, *Foreign Policy and the Developing Nations*, edited by Richard Butwell, Lexington, Kentucky, 1969.
6. P. Boyce, *Foreign Affairs for New States*, New York 1977, Chapters 1–3. The proliferation of multilateral organizations has been traced by J. David Singer and Michael Wallace in "Intergovernmental Organization in the Global System, 1815–1964," *International Organization*, Vol. 24, Spring 1970.
7. For the definitive account of the international politics of the Angolan liberation struggle see: John Marcum, *The Angolan Revolution*, Volume 2 (1962–1976), Cambridge, Mass., 1978.

threat of continued colonialism rarely became a matter of vital national security for developing countries, except for those states geographically close to wars of national liberation.

Controlling domestic foreign involvement, especially any hint of foreign interference, has always been a high priority among developing country foreign policy-makers. The most threatening interference, either from within the region or by any of the major powers, has occurred during domestic conflicts over policies of national integration. In countries where independence came only through wars of national liberation, and one or more factions may have received substantial foreign military and economic assistance, the victorious leader not only faced the challenge of consolidating domestic support but of pursuing a foreign policy that minimized the risk of foreign involvement with local dissidents. Other less threatening foreign dimensions of the struggles for national integration have been the various ethnic, religious, and racial transnational ties to groups that either controlled the governments of foreign powers or comprised important political constituencies in those countries. The personal pride, paranoia, or ideological vision of a particular ruler may also affect the degree of encouragement or discouragement toward foreigners, but, while idiosyncratic variables are typically more salient and even capricious in the foreign policy behavior of highly personalized authoritarian regimes, the much publicized actions by Idi Amin or Jean-Bédel Bokassa in Africa or Pol Pot in Southeast Asia are hardly typical.

Throughout Africa, and to a lesser extent in Asia, threats of secession and irredentist claims to redraw colonial frontiers have been and remain of critical concern to national leaders and their foreign policy establishments. The treatment of Moslems, Christians, ``overseas Chinese,'' migrant Hausas in West Africa, white minorities in East and Southern Africa — not to mention local communists, trade unionists, or intellectuals — has had important foreign policy considerations affecting relations with local, regional, and major powers. Among the tragic manifestations of these tensions are the 15 million refugees throughout much of the Third World.[8] Although usually treated by the Western press as humanitarian problems, most refugees reflect political disasters and, to the governments immediately concerned, they can be national security problems of high foreign policy significance.

Since World War II countless men, women, and children have perished as the direct or indirect casualties of interstate conflict, armed intervention, military coups, wars of succession, and insurrections in regions of the Third World. One scholar recently tabulated more than one hundred violent crises between and among developing countries during the period 1946–1977.[9] Yet despite chronic problems of instability that have strained the limited resources and tested the integrity of developing countries, the international impact of these local conflicts has been notably limited. Except for East Pakistan's successful revolt and transformation into Bangladesh — with the

---

8. Stephen Green, *Acts of Nature, Acts of Man,* New York, 1977.
9. Mark W. Zacher, *International Conflicts and Collective Security, 1946–77,* New York, 1979.

help of the Indian army, Soviet assistance, and the more than 1,000 miles separating East from West Pakistan — the territorial integrity of virtually all of the one hundred and twenty developing countries has remained unchanged. The rights of self-determination from colonial rule have not been extended to the descendants of historically independent nations that may now lie within former colonial territories. Not only have insurgencies or acts of local aggression failed to realign the former colonial frontiers, but thus far these local conflicts have not escalated into war between the major powers with important interests in the regions.

Although the record of peacefully resolving intraregional warfare in the Third World has not been good, it would not be correct to attribute the limited escalation simply to the mutual restraint of the United States and the Soviet Union and their joint desire to avoid nuclear confrontation. The availability of nuclear weapons has produced a terrifying interdependent relationship between the two superpowers that has been the dominant feature of world order during the past thirty years; but there also have been significant shifts in the scope and intensity of their competition for global influence that have been sensitive to the foreign policies of developing countries. The dilemma facing Third World elites has been, and continues to be, how to avoid becoming pawns in this competition while at the same time extracting sufficient political, military, and economic assistance to further domestic and regional objectives.[10]

Newly independent governments had five immediate foreign policy options for promoting a greater sense of national security: self-reliance, bilateral defense treaties or other special security arrangements with a major power, multilateral military alliances, reliance on the United Nations, or a regional collective security arrangement.

While no small state can ever be self-reliant, and developing countries face special difficulties in pursuing policies of economic self-reliance, many of them have avoided foreign military pacts, either bilateral or multilateral. To be successful these small states have usually benefited from the good fortune of being in a strategically unimportant geographical location, with a substantial degree of domestic cohesion and an absence of hostile neighbors. Policies of maintaining minimal foreign security ties, however, often have entailed self-restraint in the purchase of military equipment, the avoidance of certain forms of domestic repression, active diplomacy in support of regional norms that uphold the rights of sovereign equality, and the limitation of extra-regional military involvement in local conflicts.

Most developing countries have been reluctant to enter into bilateral defense treaties except in the face of overwhelming foreign and domestic threats, such as those confronting the divided states in Asia or the warring countries of the Middle East or northeast Africa. Otherwise, bilateral defense arrangements, which typically reflected a desire by nationalist leaders to expedite decolonization or to gain special political and economic advantages by identifying with one of the major powers early in the Cold War, have

---

10. R.J. Vincent, *Nonintervention and International Order,* Princeton, New Jersey, 1974, Chapter 9.

been abrogated. Not only did such arrangements prove to be a liability in pursuing closer political cooperation with other developing countries, but also they frequently exacerbated domestic political cleavages as well.

Among the other options for collective security, any hope that the United Nations would deal with threats of aggression quickly faded. The seeds of the UN's ineffectiveness were planted in the charter, but the real constraints grew out of the Cold War.[11] The United Nations has served important political and diplomatic functions in support of demands by developing countries for further decolonization and respect for their territorial integrity, and more recently, in legitimizing their call for a New International Economic Order. In the field of peacekeeping, however, the UN's limitations are well known, although it may be argued that the world body has helped to reduce the risk of conflict escalation.[12] At the regional level the foreign policies of developing countries have been more interdependent on issues of national security.

Efforts by developing countries to promote regional collective security have gone through several different phases in Asia, Africa, Latin America, and the Middle East. The initial post-World War II period, during which regional groups in the Third World were willing to opt for collective military alliances with the United States, was short-lived and was more a function of Washington's assessment of the Cold War than initiatives from the developing countries themselves. SEATO and CENTO never became effective as the smaller members concluded that the domestic and regional political liabilities, in addition to a fear of becoming pawns in the Cold War struggle, outweighed any possible benefits from such treaties.[13] India, Egypt, and Yugoslavia reinforced this trend as they led the formation of the nonaligned movement in order to open up greater opportunities to take advantage of the Soviet-American competition while avoiding too close an identity with either side.[14] Although the nonaligned movement has provided a useful diplomatic forum for expressing general concerns about the behavior of the superpowers, and, more recently, the inequities of world capitalism, it has had little relevance for dealing with local concerns.

From the perspective of the developing countries, regional collective security arrangements that are independent of all major powers would seem to hold the greatest promise, although the members of such organizations have been reluctant to surrender any of their sovereign prerogatives to a higher authority.

The Latin Americans were the first to seek a coordination of their foreign policies to enhance their collective security, beginning with the establishment of the International Union of American

---

11. Ruth B. Russell and Jeanette F. Muther, *A History of the U.N.'s Charter,* Washington, D.C., 1958, and Inis L. Claude, Jr., *Swords into Plowshares,* New York, 1964.
12. Larry L. Fabian, *Soldiers without Enemies,* Washington, D.C., 1971.
13. John Norton Moore, "The Role of Legal Arrangements in the Maintenance of World Order" in *The Future of the International Legal Order,* edited by C.E. Black and Richard Falk, Princeton, New Jersey, 1971.
14. Peter Willets, *The Nonaligned Movement,* London, 1978.

Republics in the 19th century, and these efforts have continued intermittently as a means of countering dominance by the United States. In 1945 the Latin Americans resisted the proposals to imbue the new UN Security Council with preemptive authority over regional organizations, and for a while it appeared that the intraregional authority might succeed in managing local conflicts while containing unwanted US interference in the southern hemisphere.[15] During the 1960s, however, the weakness of the Organization of American States (OAS) as a regional authority was dramatically shown by its incapability of dealing with the introduction of Soviet nuclear missiles in Cuba in 1962 and the 1965 unilateral American intervention into the Dominican Republic.

As the East–West split paralyzed the United Nations and the problems of regional conflict became a central foreign policy concern for many developing countries, the basic OAS approach began to appear more and more attractive even though the local security concerns in other regions were quite different. The three most notable regional organizations to emerge, the Arab League in 1945, the Organization of African Unity (OAU) in 1963, and the Association of Southeast Asian Nations (ASEAN) in 1967, have in common with the Organization of American States a preoccupation with intraregional problems.

Much of the cohesiveness of the OAU, the Arab League and ASEAN is derived from shared security concerns regarding the behavior of a regional power that does not belong to the organization: South Africa, Israel, and Vietnam respectively. All three organizations lack the capability to deal decisively with these issues, although they do provide forums to coordinate foreign policy. Less dramatically, however, these regional arrangements offer opportunities for consultation and reconciliation of differences, even though they lack formal peacekeeping capabilities. In reality the Arab League, the OAU and ASEAN may be more accurately described as instruments of national independence rather than of regional integration. Furthering the cause of national independence has entailed concerted diplomatic activities by the OAU and the Arab League to decolonize territories in their regions and to counter more radical efforts by Nkrumah in Africa and Nasser in the Middle East to promote regional unity.[16] The creation of alliances of states, rather than supranational authorities, has reflected the foreign policy priorities of the vast majority of developing countries which seek to minimize the external constraints on their domestic policies.[17] ASEAN, although ostensibly an economic grouping, has also served as an important forum for

---

15. Inis L. Claude, "The OAS, the U.N., and the United States," *International Conciliation,* 547, March 1962.
16. For the definitive study of Nkrumah's foreign policy see W. Scott Thompson, *Ghana's Foreign Policy, 1957–1966,* Princeton, New Jersey, 1969. On the transformation of the Pan-African movement into a regional alliance, see: I. Wallerstein, *Africa: The Politics of Unity,* New York, 1969. For an analysis of Nasser's role in the evolution of the Arab League see: Robert MacDonald, *The League of Arab States: A Study of the Dynamics of Regional Organization,* Princeton, New Jersey, 1965.
17. Lynn H. Miller, "Prospects for Order through Regional Security" in *Regional Politics and World Order,* edited by Richard Falk and Saul Mendlovitz, San Francisco, 1973.

discussing common domestic security problems and for coordinating intelligence and other services aimed at strengthening the independence of member governments.[18]

Judging the overall performance of regional security organizations is not easy. Supporters always can argue that the level of conflict in the respective regions would have been much worse had the organization not been in existence. Whether these organizations have been useful in reducing the risk of conflicts through prior consultation is very difficult to document, as few records of the actual deliberations exist and many of the understandings are reached directly between heads of state meeting alone. The record of the OAS, the OAU, and the Arab League in actually settling intraregional disputes has been generally poor.[19] Each, of course, has its special constraints: the presence of the US in the OAS; the heterogeneity and general frailty of the fifty-one members of the OAU; and the long history of intense local interstate conflict in the Middle East that reemerged following the withdrawal of colonial rule. ASEAN, with its comparatively smaller number of geographically dispersed states, has not been preoccupied with serious conflict among its members, although its capability for dealing with the Indochina wars has been very limited.

The modest efforts by regional organizations to peacefully resolve local conflicts do not necessarily reflect the foreign policy failures of the member governments. Some conflicts, such as wars of secession, may be viewed by a majority of states in the region as beyond compromise and, short of facilitating a peaceful surrender, the main task of the regional organization may be simply to help maintain international support for the incumbent government. Such a role probably will not be vital to the outcome of a conflict, but it could be highly significant.[20] This diplomatic activity no doubt also serves to discourage incipient secessionists or other insurgents who must calculate the reduced likelihood of substantial foreign assistance. Furthermore, a strong regional consensus may deter states close to the conflict to resist domestic or foreign pressure to allow their territories to become staging areas or otherwise abet the rebellion.

Other important consultations that occur within regional security organizations, but which are rarely publicized, include efforts to ensure that the foreign policies or domestic conditions of states at the regional or subregional level do not undermine the internal stability of other states. How to handle the millions of political refugees throughout Africa and Asia so as not to exacerbate interstate tension has become a preoccupation of governments within the region, even as they fail to accede to the humanitarian requests by private and intergovernmental relief agencies. Throughout the Third World issues relating to refugees, smuggling, radio broadcasts, or other matters affecting domestic tranquility are typically

---

18. Michael Leifer, "Conflict and Regional Order in Southeast Asia," International Institute of Strategic Studies, Adelphi Paper, London, forthcoming.
19. M. Zacher, *International Conflicts and Collective Security, 1946-77*, op. cit., and J.S. Nye, *Peace in Parts*, Boston, 1971, Chapter 5.
20. John J. Stremlau, *International Politics of the Nigerian Civil War*, Princeton, New Jersey, 1977.

dealt with through personal discussion among heads of state rather than being left to lower-ranking technocrats who represent these same governments at so many of the international and North-South economic discussions. The high foreign policy priority accorded regional security affairs may also reflect less tangible considerations such as cultural affinity, racial pride, or a sense of shared grievances against colonial exploitation.

Although some national leaders gain in stature with domestic constituencies by participating in regional summits and embracing the cause of regional nonaligned solidarity, this is not always the case. There have been enough instances when civilian or military heads of state have been deposed while off attending such meetings, or when huge investments in international conference centers for one-time meetings have become the focus of considerable domestic criticism, to question whether the symbolism of these meetings strengthens support for governments at home.[21]

Another elusive function of regional security organizations for developing country foreign policy-makers is the easing of latent tensions within the region by reinforcing minimal norms of acceptable or unacceptable foreign policy behavior. While all developing countries are weak, there are considerable disparities of power within regions. Regional powers such as Brazil, Indonesia, Iraq, or Nigeria have a relatively larger stake in the wider international community for which they frequently need the diplomatic and political support of their regional partners. These more powerful developing countries can incur substantial political costs if they press, or appear to press, too heavily on one of their smaller neighbors. At the same time, the formal egalitarianism of these organizations makes the relatively more powerful reluctant to agree to any supranational peace-keeping or other security functions which would constrain their freedom.

Finally, these organizations often claim high foreign policy attention from their members because they appear to have an influence on the policies of major outside powers, particularly with regard to decisions concerning whom to back and to what extent during periods of local conflict. The exact degree of restraint or assistance rendered by major powers—especially the US and the Soviet Union—that can be attributed to the guidelines established by a regional consensus in any one of these organizations is difficult to determine but, as will be noted in the final section, it is a subject that deserves greater attention by foreign policy analysts of both developed and developing countries.

Foreign Economic Policies of Developing Countries

Initial efforts by developing countries to insulate their political systems from foreign interference were complemented by economic policies

---

21. In Africa, where the annual summit rotates among the members, it has become diplomatic practice for the host government to build lavish conference quarters for the visiting leaders. Domestic turmoil in Uganda and Liberia may have been exacerbated by financial burdens of recent summits in those countries, and, in 1980, Sierre Leone spent almost $100 million, nearly 1/5 of the country's gross national product, for the four-day summit.

that through the 1960s stressed economic nationalism, import substitution, self-reliant economic development, and regional economic cooperation. These policies usually were politically popular domestically, and occasionally improved the short-term economic welfare of the ruling elites, but many were eventually discredited as unrealistic and too expensive. Constraints — foreign and domestic — typically overwhelmed the few opportunities to significantly transform small undiversified economies.[22]

The seizure of foreign investments and replacement of foreign managers and technicians with indigenous staff promised a quick redistribution of resources but carried high costs in terms of inefficiency and declining productivity, and jeopardized aid and investment deemed necessary to sustain growth.[23] While extreme economic nationalism might briefly serve as a rallying point to promote national unity, the subsequent frustration and dissatisfaction associated with high rates of unemployment and a scarcity of consumer goods prompted all but the most radical leaders to adopt more moderate policies. Even the larger and more favorably endowed developing countries lacked the local technicians and managerial expertise to run complex economic enterprises.[24] In a few cases there were even fears of antagonizing foreign powers with the capability to undertake covert subversion or give other forms of encouragement to powerful critics, including elements in a country's armed forces.

Import substitution strategies for economic development also frequently failed to meet expectations, and, in retrospect, it is difficult to understand the attractiveness of this approach for many of the smaller developing countries. Local markets often were too small and in many cases such investments merely shifted a country's dependence to imported capital goods without generating new sources of foreign exchange.

The rapid industrialization of the Soviet Union may have inspired some autarkic policies and for a while Moscow appeared to be a possible major source of funds to underwrite the large costs of programs to develop local heavy industry, but these hopes were largely unfulfilled.[25] Meanwhile there were a small number of developing countries that established dramatic export growth rates that affected the perceptions of ruling elites elsewhere in the Third World, especially as large amounts of private foreign investment began to flow to these countries.[26]

Augmenting economic nationalism and import substitution were numerous efforts to achieve greater sub-regional economic cooperation in many parts of the Third World. The process was somewhat analogous to the negotiations to estab-

---

22. Robert Rothstein, *Weak in the World of the Strong,* New York, 1977, Chapter 3.
23. *Economic Nationalism in Old and New States,* edited by Harry G. Johnson, Chicago, 1967.
24. Carolyn Stremlau, Indigenization of Management in Foreign Owned Firms in Nigeria, PhD Dissertation, Tufts University, Medford, Mass. 1974.
25. For a recent analysis of changing Soviet views on the development process see: Elizabeth Valkenier, "Development Issues in Recent Soviet Literature," *World Politics,* XXXII July 1980.
26. Joseph LaPalombara and Stephen Blank, *Multinational Corporations and Developing Countries,* New York, 1979, in addition to their article in this volume.

lish regional collective security arrangements. The formation of such arrangements were politically appealing, domestically and internationally, and for a while they were the focus of high government policy. Unlike the consultations and negotiations about mutual security concerns, where there was never any suggestion of a willingness to surrender sovereign prerogatives to some supranational organization, it was apparently assumed that specific economic arrangements could be settled through ministerial or sub-cabinet meetings and that mutually beneficial agreements would be forthcoming. Instead, after heads of state agreed to create such communities, their representatives typically brought to the "technical" discussions long lists of demands that were strongly endorsed by powerful interests back home and short lists of possible concessions.

Ironically, in many cases nationalism increased as a result of these efforts to promote economic unity.[27] Beyond the general commitment to further nonalignment and collective self-reliance through joint economic policies, there existed neither the immediate political incentives nor a degree of economic interdependence that would enable countries to negotiate short- or long-term mutual benefits across a range of issues, as was the case for the European Common Market. Nearly all attempts to establish substantial economic communities among developing countries at the regional and subregional level failed within a few years.[28]

The inability of developing countries to negotiate substantial agreements for regional and subregional economic communities has been overshadowed more recently by the broader consensus regarding structural inequities of the world economy. These demands began to coalesce with the formation of the Group of 77 developing countries at the First United Nations Conference on Trade and Development (UNCTAD) in 1964, developed into the platform for a New International Economic Order at the 1973 Summit of the Non-Aligned States in Algiers, and became the basis for the North–South dialogue at the Sixth Special Session of the United Nations in 1974. The record of these and subsequent negotiations is well known.

The industrialized countries have responded to the Third World's demands for acceptance of basic principles and the transfer of substantial resources by offers of incremental reform while stressing the political impracticability, the inequitable distribution of gains among developing countries, a host of technical difficulties, and the belief that to accept the Third World's demands would precipitate a severe economic slowdown in the North that would have a negative multiplier effect on the South.

Despite the lack of progress at the United Nations, and in the smaller Conference on Interna-

---

27. For examples of this see Charles Anderson, *Politics and Economic Change in Latin America,* Princeton, N.J., 1967 and Ali Mazrui, "Tanzania versus East Africa," *Journal of Commonwealth Political Studies,* Volume 3, November 1965, cited in Nye, *Peace in Parts, op. cit.,* p. 73.
28. Harold Jacobson and Dujan Sidjanski, "Regional Patterns of Economic Cooperation" in *Comparative Regional Systems,* edited by Warner Feld and Gavin Boyd, New York, 1980.

tional Economic Cooperation (CIEC) that ended in Paris in 1977, the North-South dialogue is certain to continue in the 1980s although, as Robert Rothstein notes in Chapter 8 of this volume, North-South issues rarely command the attention of national leaders or the senior echelons of foreign policy making in developing countries.

The reasons for the persistence of these demands, regardless of the North's reaction, no doubt reflect the enormity of developing country needs and a realization that in the long run only massive structural changes will be meaningful; to succeed, however, the most essential of these probably will have to occur within developing countries rather than internationally. NIEO demands, as Rothstein discovered in his analysis of UNCTAD, also reflect the dynamics of the bargaining process in which the movement's leaders, notably the representatives from advanced developing countries plus international civil servants, fear that a disaggregation of the demands would weaken the South's unity by bringing to light differential costs and gains in which the majority of the poorer countries would bear the heaviest burden.[29]

Even if a broad consensus can be sustained to support basic principles and general demands for a redistribution of global wealth, the essays in this volume suggest a growing willingness by developing countries to explore both the possibility of reform of the present system rather than its transformation and the prospects for new arrangements among developing countries themselves. To the extent that economic problems and their international dimensions become more highly politicized domestically and national leaders perceive opportunities to achieve material gains through closer international cooperation, then fresh efforts in this direction will be accorded high priority for developing country foreign policies.

Efforts to promote regional economic communities through free trade, common currencies, joint industrial programs, and common services were premature in the 1960s and attempts to revive them do not appear imminent. Exceptions to this trend may occur, however, when a relatively wealthy member of such a community is prepared to bear a disproportionate amount of the economic costs and does so without arousing political apprehension, as the Ivory Coast did for the francophone West African Entente in the early 1960s or Nigeria currently appears willing to do to promote the economic organization of West African states. There may also be new forms of nonregional multilateral South-South cooperation, such as that outlined by Bijan Mossavar-Rahmani in this volume, through a balance of political and economic interests.

Although the degree of South-South economic interdependence remains low and has not become a significant element in the foreign policies of most developing countries, recent changes in trading patterns that could affect long-range export-led growth strategies in several influential developing countries merit closer analysis. The percentage of world trade that flows among developing countries still amounts to only six percent but represents nearly a doubling of the

---

29. Robert Rothstein, *Global Bargaining, UNCTAD and the Quest for a New International Economic Order,* Princeton, New Jersey, 1979.

percentage of world trade since 1970; the annual increase in South-South trade was 36 percent (24 percent, excluding oil) between 1970 and 1978. Manufacturing exports of developing countries were the most dynamic element in this growth.[30]

Fuel is the only commodity imported by developing countries that comes almost entirely from other developing countries, and all other areas of developing country trade certainly will remain predominantly with OECD countries. In recent years barely 20 percent of developing country non-oil primary product exports and 30 percent of manufactured exports have gone to other developing countries. Moreover, the trade among developing countries is primarily concentrated within regions. Intraregional trade as a proportion of total South-South trade predominates in Latin America (79 percent) and Asia (70 percent), although it remains low in Africa (33 percent).[31] Intraregionally, South and Southeast Asia enjoy large trade surpluses from manufactured exports to Africa and West Asia, while Latin American sales of food to these regions yield a somewhat smaller surplus.

The strongest proponents of South-South trade, not surprisingly, have been the small number of newly industrializing countries seeking markets for manufactured capital goods that are generally not competitive in OECD markets. The narrow base of this most dynamic segment of South-South trade could arouse fears in poorer developing countries of a new form of dependence, and it is not yet clear whether the relatively richer exporting countries will be prepared to grant special market access or other incentives to facilitate further cooperation along South-South lines. Given current economic flows, which continue overwhelmingly along a North-South axis, it is doubtful that the trade among developing countries will become a major foreign policy issue in the 1980s. There may be, however, shared political and security concerns that will facilitate greater, if still modest, economic cooperation within the Third World.

Challenges of the Future

Several essays in this volume deal with international economic issues that will be of major importance to the national well-being of many countries in the Third World and which will influence the shape of their foreign policies. There are, however, at least three other interrelated problems that affect the security of developing countries and toward which the potential impact of their foreign policy decisions appears to be growing. Over the long run they could significantly affect the course of international politics. The three problems are: the scope and intensity of the US-Soviet rivalry; foreign intervention in regional conflicts; and external pressures that limit the freedom to control domestic affairs.

Unless there is a nuclear holocaust, revolution-

---

30. Trade among developing countries by main SITC groups by regions, Geneva-UNCTAD, TD/.B/C.7/21, Sept. 1978, pg. 5, cited by Robert Rothstein, *The Third World and U.S. Foreign Policy: Cooperation and Conflict in the 1980s*, Westview Press, 1981.
31. These statistics are drawn from trade among developing countries by main SITC groups and by regions and from an unclassified CIA study, *Preliminary Notes on Trade among LDCs,* December 1978, cited in Rothstein, ibid.

ary changes in the structure of international relations do not appear imminent and, despite the enormous disparities of political and economic power, relations will remain fundamentally based on mutual respect for the territorial integrity and sovereign equality of states.

The Soviet Union's lately acquired capability to project conventional force quickly into distant regions of the Third World, in an era of strategic parity with the United States, confronts developing countries with both opportunities and dangers. Third World governments can exploit or become the victims of the intensifying US-Soviet rivalry for world leadership in ways quite different from those that led them to form the nonaligned movement twenty years ago. While the relative decline of American power and the Soviet willingness to deploy conventional military forces present developing countries with the option of seeking military assistance from Moscow with somewhat less fear of reprisals from the United States, the Soviet conquest of nonaligned Afghanistan raises new concerns. In recent years, there have been a number of faint steps by developing countries that begin to suggest guidelines that could, in turn, affect the US-Soviet rivalry.

During the struggles to liberate Angola and Zimbabwe, African states acting in concert through the OAU and at the sub-regional level helped to legitimize Soviet-Cuban assistance to the movement for the Popular Liberation of Angola (MPLA), while discouraging the Soviet interference in Western, and later British-led, initiatives to effect a peaceful transition to majority rule in Zimbabwe. On the Horn of Africa, Soviet-Cuban military assistance to Ethiopia for the purposes of expelling Somali invaders was regarded by the overwhelming majority of African states as legitimate, and this judgment was conveyed effectively to the rest of the international community. Ethiopian-Soviet restraint in not pursuing those invaders into Somali territory was also significant, even though it is not clear whether this restraint reflected a respect for the majority of African opinion, a fear of an American response, or immediate military/logistical constraints. The outcome was, however, an important reaffirmation of the basic OAU principle of respect for territorial integrity, and it should increase the political costs of violating this norm in the future.[32]

The authority of the OAU will continue to be challenged from within and outside the region, as the European/African operations in the Shaba province of Zaire, the Tanzanian invasion of Uganda, the Libyan involvement in Chad, and the current divisions over the war in the Spanish Sahara all illustrate. If the members of the OAU can work more closely to coordinate their foreign policies on such issues, however, they may be able to insulate local conflicts from unwanted foreign interference and legitimize foreign involvement that they regard as justified. These judgments by the regional authority and any discernible respect accorded them by potential interventionists could, over time, become the basis for confidence-building among rival major

---

32. A forthcoming major study of conflict management in Africa, with case studies of the wars in the Horn of Africa and the Spanish Sahara, the Shaba invasions, and the struggle over Namibia will be: I. William Zartman, *Ripe for Resolution:Conflict and Intervention in Africa,* New Haven, Connecticut, 1981.

powers. After all, a major objective of developing country foreign policies in matters of regional security has always been to reduce the risk that the involvement of one major power will be viewed by another as irresponsible and unpredictable, because, as African diplomats often note with an aphorism, "when the elephants dance the ants get trampled."

Although developing countries lack the capability to deter a major power from intervening in a small state, they can act in concert to discourage such action, to increase the political costs once such an aggression has occurred, and perhaps to help facilitate a disengagement. In the aftermath of the Soviet invasion of Afghanistan, nearly all developing countries condemned this action. Whether such criticism, especially by the Islamic Summit, will influence Soviet actions is not clear, but the invasion has caused a deterioration of relations with other nonaligned countries, as noted in John Graham's account of the Havana Summit in this volume. Developing countries close to Afghanistan obviously have the most difficult foreign policy decisions with regard to how to deal with Afghan insurgents and whether to seek military support from powers outside the region. If these decisions can be supported by other nonaligned governments in the region, then legitimacy will be enhanced and the risk of rapid and uncontrolled escalation may be reduced.

The current freeze in US-Soviet relations imperils progress on strategic arms limitation and other issues of general concern to developing countries. If this freeze is to be broken, various face-saving measures will have to be accepted by both sides, and the Third World, particularly the countries of Northwest Asia, can play an important role in this process. The coordination by these countries on the criteria for granting recognition to the Karmal or a successor government in Afghanistan, for example, could affect Soviet decisions regarding the extent of their continued military presence and the amount of political participation that they and their clients in Kabul will tolerate.

Somewhat similar questions confront the nations of Southeast Asia in their relations with Vietnam and the Soviet Union over the invasion of Kampuchea. Although the five ASEAN countries were powerless to prevent the Vietnam invasion of Kampuchea, this action has pushed ASEAN nations into closer cooperation on security matters and led them to submerge their differing views on the role of China and the Soviet Union in Asia, at least temporarily. As they work in concert to try and insulate Thailand from the threat of further Vietnamese expansion, they face a number of diplomatic challenges in mobilizing support throughout the Third World for the continued isolation of the Vietnamese-backed regime in Phnom Penh.

In entirely different circumstances, there is recent evidence of a strengthened determination among the Latin American states to limit US political/military involvement in that region. The overwhelming vote by the Organization of American States in June 1979 against an American proposal to send a peace-keeping force into Nicaragua no doubt contributed to US restraint in not intervening to assist the beleaguered regime of Anastasio Somoza.[33]

---

33. Richard Fagen, "Dateline Nicaragua: End of the Affair," *Foreign Policy,* No. 36, Fall 1979.

The positions taken by developing countries on the situations in Kampuchea, Nicaragua, Iran, Uganda, Central African Empire, and Afghanistan were all influenced in part by their perceptions of the domestic policies and internal legitimacy of the regimes under attack; that such judgments are becoming more open and explicit is a significant change from previous diplomatic practice. Throughout the last thirty years, the most common characteristic of foreign policies of developing countries has been to defend the rights of other small states to carry out whatever domestic programs their rulers thought were in their own best interests. This universal approach is breaking down and will raise important and perplexing foreign policy questions for governments in the decade ahead.

The horrible injustices perpetuated by Pol Pot or Idi Amin make foreign intervention more tolerable and foreign assistance to Somoza or the Shah of Iran more difficult. These cases should be a warning to other leaders who might be tempted to pursue policies of extreme repression. In a further departure from past practice in African diplomacy, the OAU initially refused to receive the new Liberian Head of State, Master Sergeant Samuel Doe. The withholding of recognition and various forms of political and economic support to new governments that come to power by especially violent and reprehensible means could become a core element in regional and international politics in the years ahead. In Latin America, the Organization of American States has been grappling with the terms of reference for an Inter-American Commission on Human Rights that recently took the unprecedented action of exposing human rights abuses in Argentina, and the Organization of African Unity has shown a growing interest in the OAS experiment.

Another broad challenge confronting the foreign policies of developing countries is whether shared concerns of regional conflict and security can provide the fresh impetus for closer economic cooperation, as a means to enhance regional order. The key to any successful economic community, including the European Economic Community, has been the existence of a strong consensus regarding mutual security needs which has facilitated the acceptance of various asymmetries in the multilateral economic arrangements. It is doubtful that developing countries can proceed very far in building substantial economic communities in the coming decade, for reasons discussed earlier. However, the interaction of security and economic interests within Southeast Asia, the Caribbean, and parts of Africa could produce some important advances in this direction. Singapore, for example, appears willing to incur special economic costs for the enhanced security that its participation in ASEAN affords.[34] The recent decision by Venezuela and Mexico to provide oil at somewhat more favorable prices to the poor and highly unstable countries of the Caribbean region, or Nigeria's readiness to assume the principal financial burden of the economic community of West African states, may be further indications of a willingness by relatively

---

34. For a full explication of ASEAN's strengths and weaknesses see: Laurence D. Stifel, "ASEAN Cooperation and Economic Growth in Southeast Asia," *Asia Pacific Community,* No. 4, 1979.

more affluent developing countries to incur short-term costs for the sake of long-term regional order. In another context, it is doubtful that without the threat posed by South Africa, the neighboring developing countries — the so-called "Front-Line States" — would be so eager to establish joint economic arrangements.

Much has been written in recent years about the economic vulnerabilities of developing countries to uncontrollable outside forces. These dependencies are real and will require major and politically difficult domestic reforms, even if there is eventual progress in achieving a new international economic order. More immediately, however, developing countries do have limited but important foreign policy options for collective action to promote an international political order that is more responsive to their national interests. These opportunities would appear to be significant at the regional level.[35]

In the coming decade, relations among the world's major powers are likely to be sufficiently fluid to offer developing countries greater opportunities to promote adherence to general rules and procedures for moderating foreign interference and promoting closer political and economic cooperation. The scope and authority of regional organizations no doubt will continue to evolve slowly, and they probably will have to be based more on tacit than formal agreements. So much will depend, of course, on the willingness of governments to accord regional affairs high priority in the conduct of foreign policy and to allocate scarce diplomatic resources to regional affairs.[36] Although the general goal to promote good relations in the region traditionally has been given prominent attention in major foreign policy statements, the supporting analytic and policy planning capabilities within a developing country's foreign

---

35. Among the various proposals that have been raised over the years for strengthening regional organizations, and which may deserve reconsideration in light of changing international circumstances, are: standing arbitration, mediation, and conciliation procedures; regional peace-monitoring and peace-keeping capabilities, with or without mandatory cooling-off periods, buffer zones or other arrangements to give states within the region an alternative to requesting extra regional military assistance; procedures to monitor and draw attention to any significant changes in the quality and quantity of arms expenditures; human rights commissions; agreements to limit hostile propaganda across frontiers; more direct intergovernmental communication facilities; regional networks of mass communication; regular consultations on international security issues; agreements to limit nuclear proliferation; and restrictions on allowing foreign naval and air bases in the region.

36. Although foreign ministries of developing countries generally attract the best talent within the civil service, most remain small and understaffed relative to the rapidly expanding volume of international transactions. In addition to the large number of new embassies, the proliferation of intergovernmental negotiations on issues as diverse as tele-communications, deep-sea mining, disarmament, the role of women in development, and the New International Economic Order, plus a host of *ad hoc* regional and bilateral negotiations, has overburdened small foreign policy establishments. The frequent meetings with long and complicated agendas have overtaken policy formulation in many Third World capitals, with the result that instructions from home often fail to reach representatives in time to table positions; adequate reporting of these meetings also is a chronic problem for policymakers. Among other challenges in the 1980s will be the need to develop the analytic capabilities and negotiating procedures to facilitate cross-issue bargains.

ministry typically remain relatively weak for regional affairs.[37]

Over time, the closer coordination of foreign policies at the regional level should induce better perceptions of the strategic intentions of potential local adversaries and those major powers with important stakes in the region. The process should also serve to constrain potential interventionists and to reduce the risk of escalation once conflict has occurred. Ironically, progress toward improved collective security, closer regional economic cooperation, and greater social justice in the Third World may eventually result more from policies that reflect shared fears of growing instability and the risk of foreign intervention than from the long-held common aspirations for a new and more equitable international order.

---

37. To overcome the lack of expertise on countries and international relations within their respective regions, several universities and government institutes in Africa, Latin America, and Asia have recently established or are planning new programs of advanced training and research on regional security and economic affairs, for scholars and diplomats.

2. Developing States and the International Security System

EDWARD A. KOLODZIEJ
ROBERT HARKAVY

In contrast to the notions prevailing in some prominent quarters of international relations theory, there is increasing evidence that the growing interdependence of states (itself a much argued proposition) has been accompanied by greater, not less, reliance on military force or its threat in interstate and intrastate relations and that the developing states (LDCs) figure prominently in this trend.

This evolution is viewed here from two perspectives. After some introductory remarks pertinent to interdependence theory, the first part of the article presents data for 1968 and 1977 that support the view that the international security system is becoming more diffuse and decentralized with the spread of military force capabilities around the globe. Data are provided to indicate long-term trends in the incidence of various types of conflict. To these are added several measures, including arms expenditures, acquisitions, and production to indicate the scope, rate, and direction of the tendency of states, especially in the developing world, to rely on force or its threat as an arbiter of international conflict.

The second part of the article focuses more on the international security process, examining the evolving roles of the developing nations in a variety of crucial security domains or regimes, spanning arms transfers, economic warfare with a strategic dimension, terrorist and counter-terrorist activity, strategic basing access and arms control. Crucial here is the question of whether some key LDCs, heretofore thought of as essentially passive objects of major power policies in these areas, have now developed the capacity and the will to utilize actively a range of politico-military instruments for the extension of power and influence. To the extent this scenario is true, it might provide some diverse evidence of a trend toward diffusion and decentralization of the international security system.

Interdependence and Force

The increasing efforts of developing states to expand and improve their military forces and to rely on them in coping with domestic and foreign problems belies the optimism of many analysts of interdependence. They tend to equate the desirability of an international system that sees decreasing reliance on military force or its threat with the actual behavior of states concerned with their security.[1] The result is a confusing telescoping of normative and empirical analyses. They see the emergence of complex interdependence as actually supplanting traditional power politics. This view starkly contrasts with the insistent emphasis of students of Hans Morgenthau and

---

1. See Robert O. Keohane and Joseph S. Nye, *Power and Interdependence,* Boston, 1977, pp. 24–25.

others on the historical constancy of power politics as central, even primordial, in interstate relations. Within the postulated new system, military security does not consistently dominate the agenda of states; relationships other than military and quasi-military connect societies and governments; differences among states are increasingly resolved on a non-coercive basis since decision-makers share an interest in reducing the high costs, risks, and slim benefits associated with utilizing military power. Two prominent proponents of this view feel that these incentives, while stronger between developed states, can also be seen to be expanding among developing states in the economic and ecological areas now commonly referred to as global issues. Moreover, in contrast to traditional balance of power or geopolitical analyses,[2] many interdependence theorists argue that international regimes and outcomes in interstate conflicts are not "congruent with underlying patterns of state capabilities," if for no other reason than that international organizations — defined as multilevel linkages, norms and institutions among states — "will stand in the way."[3]

By way of summary, then, two primary sets of theses are heavily reflected in the writings of interdependence theorists. One posits the arrival, or at least imminence, of a new structure of international quasi-legal norms as translated through international organizations or regimes which are assumed to foreshadow a reduction of international aggression and intervention by force. The second closely related set heralds the transcendence of economics over traditional power politics, that is, over the Clausewitzian nexus of force and of diplomacy backed by force.[4]

These are not new themes. Before the First World War writers, such as Norman Angell, considered war to have become outmoded, even near impossible, both because of its increasing costs and because of what were then considered overriding economic (corporate, financial) linkages between states.[5] Lockean optimism and Wilsonian teleological visions about developing international legal norms which would inhibit violence also have some obvious, not-so-distant echoes in the Hague conferences at the turn of the century, the League of Nations Covenant, the Kellogg-Briand Treaty, and the like. Much of interdependence theory then would appear to be more of a reflection of the hopes of some Western scholars than a projection of disquieting trends based on empirically determined theory.[6]

---

2. See, e.g., Robert Gilpin's critique of the Nye and Keohane approach, "The Politics of Transnational Economic Relations," in *Transnational Relations and World Politics,* eds. Robert O. Keohane and Joseph S. Nye, Cambridge, 1972, pp. 48–69.
3. Keohane and Nye, *op. cit.,* p. 55.
4. In this vein, see Edward L. Morse, *Modernization and the Transformation of International Relations,* New York, 1976.
5. Norman Angell, *The Great Illusion,* London, 1909.
6. Only the post-Lockean-Wilsonian brands of interdependence theorists are addressed here. Another school, Marxist in orientation, identifies war and repression with capitalism and its allegedly inevitable tendency toward imperialism. See, for example, K. T. Fann and Donald C. Hodges, eds., *Readings in American Imperialism,* Boston 1971. The classic statement of the causal links between war, capitalism, and imperialism is, of course, V. I. Lenin, *Imperialism,* New York, 1939.

Beyond that, the posited logical nexus between growing interdependence and a declined inclination to use force might itself be questioned by a review of European history between 1870 and 1939. Germany and France had extensive levels of interdependence (in the contemporary sense of that term) prior to each of their three major conflicts, and the same was true for other European conflict pairings; for instance, Germany and Russia before 1914. Reversing the argument, it might be claimed that periods of relatively low levels of interdependence among South American states have coincided with lengthy periods of relative peace.

The interdependence theorists' visionary projection for international politics would appear to be ahead of its time for several reasons. First, developing states and their leaderships are in fact investing heavily in military hardware and are frequently relying on the use or threat of force to achieve their key internal and external objectives; these points will be at the center of the following discussion. It may be precisely *because* states are increasingly interdependent — that is, that their policy objectives depend partially but often crucially on the behavior of other states in greater or lesser measure — that some elites have turned increasingly to military instruments to advance their objectives and interests. Cooperative behavior may often be induced by essentially negative incentives. The ominously growing tensions over Persian Gulf oil, now sought both by the US and USSR, illustrate all too well the dangers inherent in interdependence.

Moreover, it should be remembered that the limits of security policy are by no means clear but vary from state to state. As Osgood reminds us, security goals are inherently subjective and go beyond obvious material elements like boundaries and resources:

> It is not only the subjective nature of security and its dependence on milieu goals that give the conception of national security its protean quality. It is also the broad and intangible character of the national self that is to be secured. The people of the nation personify the state and project upon it ideas of honor and prestige that become as much a part of their vicarious collective personality as are the nation's territory, allies, and vital interest.[7]

Developing states, no less than developed ones, cast their security policies in such pervasive terms. That they inevitably touch on every important facet of their existence should come as no surprise. Recently expressed Iranian pride at making the US "bend its knee" over the hostages, Argentinian and Brazilian desires for the *status* of nuclear powers, the utter inability of the United States government to persuade poor and — in some cases — unthreatened African and Latin American nations to forego purchases of sophisticated arms — all illustrate the subjective prestige dimensions of military power. Such considerations may be all the stronger in nations only recently removed from the perceived humiliations of colonialism, maybe even more so in fragmented and incohesive new nations where national security may become a surrogate for the absence of national unity.

The sanguine view of interdependence theo-

---

7. Robert E. Osgood, *Limited War Revisited,* Boulder, 1979, p. 103.

rists on international politics often distinguishes between security and other issue areas as if they were discrete concepts, or as if economic and ecological issues were resolved outside of the power context. Rather, the resolution of security issues — or the mutually perceived realities of military power balances — may often be a precondition for bargaining and compromise in other spheres among states.

The growth in the quantity and quality of military forces in the developing world and the diffusion of centers of global power suggest that decision makers seek at least to neutralize the advantages of militarily more powerful rivals. This may or may not involve the development of a clear doctrine for the employment of coercion to advance their states' policy goals. Increasingly, however, smaller states may have come to recognize the *deterrent* value of their military forces vis-à-vis even major powers. This has led some analysts to speak paradoxically of "the irrelevance of force," i.e., superpower force, based largely on the respective United States and Soviet experiences in Vietnam and Afghanistan, and providing an odd and distinct twist to the theses of interdependence theorists. Hence, according to Sanford Gottlieb:

> A 1977 Rand Corporation report for the Air Force notes: 'By the 1980s, force as a political instrument in international relations may have become seriously constrained by the availability of cheap precision-guided weapons and even of nuclear weapons to countries that in the past could not have afforded effective defenses against great powers.'
>
> Even if they cannot win military victories, the bush leaguers may now have enough clout to frustrate the objectives of the big leaguers. The use of force, for example, to assure a supply of oil would almost certainly be counterproductive. It would generate the kind of conflict that would prevent oil from flowing to North America, Europe and Japan.
>
> Under these circumstances, the superpowers must not only avoid a direct clash, but also ponder carefully the consequences of any further intervention in the third world, the arena of superpower competition.[8]

Finally, the greater relative significance of military force attributed by interdependence theorists to the relations of developing as contrasted with developed states (also to relations *between* the developed and developing, as perceived by Gottlieb and others) may also be too narrowly and prematurely conceived. In much the same way that one may question the distinctions between security and non-security issues, the division made between the security relations of developed and developing states, as two separate entities, can be exaggerated. The seemingly non-coercive strategies pursued by developed states in economic, ecological, and cultural areas — largely a function of the central nuclear balance of terror rather than growing interdependence — presuppose that these and other issues can be insulated from their relations with developing states. The Afghanistan crisis is only the latest in a series played out on the terrain of a developing state[9] but posing fundamental threats

---

8. Sanford Gottlieb, "SALT Treaty: What's at Stake?" *Dissent* (Fall 1978), p. 373.
9. A useful list of armed conflicts since World War II is found in Gaston Bouthoul and René Carré, *Le défi de la guerre: 1740–1974*, Paris, 1976, pp. 214–218.

to the stability of detente between the rival camps in the developed world.[10]

The long-term absence of direct military conflict between the Soviet and Western blocs in recent decades may in the past have been availed by the safety valve provided by competition between them in the developing countries, in all of its practical and symbolic aspects. That, too, is a hoary theme, recalling similar historical attributions to the role played first by overseas exploration and colonization, and then by the late 19th century climax of imperialism in sublimating what might have been more intense territorial rivalries within Europe.

Although the developed states, and especially the superpowers, possess an overwhelming amount of destructive capability, the developing states have been the primary terrain on which wars in the postwar period have beeen fought. While the nuclear balance partly explains the shift in big power competition to the developing world, it does not offer a fully satisfactory explanation for the high incidence of violence among LDCs. Many have grievances against each other that are distinguishable from the superpower conflict and many predate the modern period, as witness the Ethiopia-Somalia border dispute and the national rivalries in Indochina. The recent clash between Tanzania and Uganda evidenced new sources of interstate conflict, while the dispute over the western Sahara, involving Morocco, Algeria, Libya, Mauritania, and the Polisario, suggests the play of both old and new forces. Old antecedents of the conflict lie in traditional frictions between the Moroccan central authority and outlying tribes; a new element has been added by the Algerian and Libyan drives for dominance in North Africa and superpower interest in the phosphates of the region.

The India-Pakistan and Arab-Israel conflicts also have roots predating the Cold War, while the two Koreas problem has often but not always mirrored Cold War tensions. Recent years have seen the emergence of numerous additional flashpoints throughout the developing world: Omani and South Yemeni rivalry over Dhofar, territorial and captive ethnic problems between Iran and Iraq, Libya's borders with Tunisia and Chad, Zaire-Angolan rivalry in the Shaba province, East Timor, Baluchistan, Namibia, Vietnam's possible designs on Thailand, and many others. Even in long quiescent Latin America, there are increasing strains, not only evidenced by essentially internal problems in Nicaragua, El Salvador, and Guatemala, but also by the ominous buildup of superpower tensions in the Caribbean as Grenada seems added to the Soviet oribt. Peru has had border tensions with Chile and Ecuador; Argentina and Chile have a festering dispute over remote territories at the tip of Patagonia; and the former has revisionist designs on the British Falkland Islands.

Table 1 below presents one analyst's accounting of armed conflicts before and after 1947. What is striking is the increased number of such clashes, albeit considerably less lethal since 1947.

---

10. A recent and cogently argued defense of the view that the Euro-security system under American and Soviet leadership is basically stable, notwithstanding periodic Third World confrontations between the superpowers, is found in Anton DePorte, *Europe between the Superpowers,* New Haven, 1979.

TABLE 1*
Armed Conflicts: 1898–1947, 1948–1967

	1898–1947	1948–1967
Interstate wars	28	24
Insurgency type conflicts	19	31
Civil wars	8	9
Coups d'état, mutinies	0	18

*Source: Steven L. Spiegel, *Dominance and Diversity,* Boston: 1972, p. 12.

Of special interest is the increase in the number of internal conflicts and civil wars, illustrating the absence of order and security in the Third World. There is little wonder then why the regimes of developing states seek arms to defend themselves against internal rivals or external opponents, often allied with perceived adversaries at home.

This conflict-ridden setting prompts an examination of the role of force in the strategic policies of developing states. The discussion below necessarily stresses conflict over cooperative relations. This perspective is advised not only to prompt greater interest in the role of developing states in the international security system but also to provide at least a partial antidote to widely held assumptions about the perceived trend toward a decline in conflict resolution among states. Such views have more to recommend them as moral prescriptions than as a behavioral guide describing the actions of developing states. What is important to recognize is that the leaders of many of the developing countries appear to be acting on the assumption, by no means demonstrable, that military force is relevant to their problems and is a key tool of policy. If the developed states, and especially the superpowers, have gone through what might be termed as a post-Clausewitzian phase, which has spawned a rich literature in arms control theory and doctrine, the developing states still appear to be rooted in Clausewitzian thought and to be guiding their strategic policies accordingly.

Adopting a conflict mode of analysis does not suggest that the developing states have abandoned non-coercive means in pursuing their often competing goals. Developing states, no less than their developed counterparts, are able to sustain sets of conflict-cooperative relations simultaneously. This confusing but explicable circumstance recommends against exclusively adopting either a conflict or cooperative mode of analysis as a touchstone by which to describe the international system and the security subsystem. The discussion below should be incorporated into such a larger framework of analysis.

Some Indexes of Developing State Military Power

Several prominent indicators point toward increasing quantity and quality of arms in the possession of developing states and in their ability to use and service sophisticated equipment. Table 2 compares the military expenditures of developed and developing states between 1968 and 1977. It highlights several surprising trends. Much of the 14.8 percent growth in world military expenditures since 1968 is attributable to the developing states. During this period the military spending of developed states rose from $305 to $319 billion in constant 1976 dollars, an increase of 4.6 percent while expenditures among developing states jumped from $54 to $92 billion or 70.4 percent. If Oceania is considered primarily as

TABLE 2*

Military Expenditures, GNP, Per Capita Military Expenditures, Armed Forces, and Armed Forces per 1,000 of Population, Global and Regional Data, 1968 and 1977
(in billions)

	Military Expenditures (1976 constant $) 1968[1]	1977[1]	% Change	GNP (1976 constant $) 1968[1]	1976[1]	% Change	MILEX/GNP 1968	1977
I. Global								
World	358	411	14.8	4990	7240	45.1	7.2	5.7
Developed	305	319	4.6	4110	5700	38.7	7.4	5.6
Developing	54	92	70.4	877	1560	77.9	6.1	5.9
II. Regions								
North America	134	100	−25.4	1540	1970	28.0	8.7	5.1
NATO Europe	46	57	23.9	1110	1530	37.8	4.1	3.7
Warsaw Europe	118	155	31.4	920	1320	43.4	12.8	11.7
Africa	3	6	100.0	107	169	57.9	2.6	3.4
East Asia	34	48	44.1	592	1100	85.8	5.8	4.3
Latin America	4	6	50.0	212	361	70.3	1.8	1.5
Middle East	7	26	271.4	89	196	120.2	7.7	13.1
Oceania	3	3	—	83	114	37.3	3.5	2.5
South Asia	3	4	33.3	84	116	38.1	3.1	3.4

	Military Expenditures Per Capita 1968	1977	% Change	Armed Forces (in thousands) 1968	1977	% Change	Armed Forces per 1000 1968	1977	% Change
I. Global									
World	101	97	−4.0	24,300	26,300	8.2	6.83	6.19	−9.4
Developed	311	302	−2.9	11,900	10,600	−10.9	12.10	10.10	−16.5
Developing	21	29	38.1	12,500	15,600	24.8	4.83	4.91	1.7
II. Regions									
North America	604	414	−31.5	3,660	2,180	−40.4	16.50	9.07	−45.0
NATO Europe	152	176	15.8	3,150	2,800	−11.1	10.50	8.71	−17.0
Warsaw Europe	347	421	21.3	5,370	6,100	13.6	15.80	16.60	5.1
Africa	9	15	67.0	635	1,340	111.0	2.08	3.43	65.1
East Asia	28	32	14.2	6,680	7,850	17.5	5.37	5.20	−3.2
Latin America	14	16	14.2	1,060	1,440	35.8	3.98	4.27	7.3
Middle East	71	207	192.0	841	1,480	76.0	8.79	12.10	37.7
Oceania	164	137	−16.5	93	87	−6.5	5.24	4.20	−20.0
South Asia	4	5	25.0	1,970	2,180	10.7	2.86	2.59	−9.4

*Source: U.S. Arms Control and Disarmament Agency, *World Military Expenditures and Arms Transfers: 1968–1977*, Washington, D.C., 1979, pp. 27–31, 71–73.
1 Rounded to nearest billion

TABLE 3*
Military Expenditures, GNP, Per Capita Military Expenditures, Armed Forces, and Armed Forces per 1,000 of Population, Selected Regional States, 1968 and 1977

	Military Expenditures[1] (constant 1976 $)		% Change	GNP[2]		% Change	MILEX/GNP	
	1968	1977		1968	1977		1968	1977
I. Africa								
Nigeria	724	1348	86.2	12.3	31.9	159.3	5.9	4.2
South Africa	586	1764	201.0	22.6	32.3	42.9	2.6	5.5
Ethiopia	58	116	100.0	2.2	3.0	36.4	2.6	3.9
Somalia	17	29	70.5	.3	0.4	15.2	4.9	7.3
Morocco	168	419	149.0	5.7	9.3	63.2	3.0	4.5
II. East Asia[3]								
North Korea	948	2002	111.0	5.8	10.2	75.9	16.4	19.6
South Korea	443	1633	268.6	11.0	27.7	151.8	4.0	5.9
Thailand	238	583	145.0	9.3	17.2	84.9	2.6	3.4
Malaysia	200	474	137.0	6.3	11.4	81.0	3.2	4.2
Indonesia	639	1311	105.0	20.9	38.7	85.2	3.1	3.4
III. Middle East								
Iran	2119	7195	239.5	28.5	68.3	139.6	7.4	10.5
Iraq	953	1819	90.8	8.4	17.2	104.7	11.4	10.5
Egypt	563	1154	104.9	6.5	11.1	70.7	8.7	10.4
Syria	422	960	127.4	3.8	6.8	78.9	9.8	14.2
Saudi Arabia	1058	6912	553.0	16.7	44.0	163.0	6.4	15.7
Israel	976	2781	185.0	5.5	9.8	78.2	17.6	28.4
IV. Latin America								
Argentina	495	722	45.8	25.3	35.4	40.0	2.0	2.0
Brazil	1278	1536	20.2	65.7	148.7	126.0	1.9	1.0
Cuba	341	410	20.2	6.4	6.7[4]	4.7	5.3	6.2[4]
Peru	353	841	138.0	8.9	13.2	48.3	4.0	6.3
V. South Asia								
India	2035	2920	43.5	65.3	90.3	38.3	3.1	3.2
Pakistan	514	836	62.6	9.0	13.6	51.0	5.7	6.1

*Source: ACDA, *op. cit.,* pp. 32ff.
1 Rounded to nearest billion
2 In billions, rounded to nearest one-hundred milion
3 Data on North Vietnam not available
4 Data for 1975

Developing States

	Armed Forces (in thousands) 1968	1977	% Change	Armed Forces Per 1000 1968	1977	% Change	Military Expenditures Per Capita 1968	1977	% Change
I. Africa									
Nigeria	85	300	253	1.62	4.50	177.8	14	20	43
South Africa	55	67	22	2.58	2.50	−3.0	28	66	136
Ethiopia	45	225	400	1.82	7.23	300.0	2	4	100
Somalia	14	53	279	5.22	16.10	208.0	6	9	50
Morocco	70	85	21	4.90	4.57	−6.8	12	23	92
II. East Asia									
North Korea	410	520	27	30.60	29.55	−3.4	71	114	61
South Korea	620	600	−33	19.75	15.71	−20.5	14	43	207
Thailand	167	230	38	4.77	5.19	8.9	7	13	86
Malaysia	46	79	72	4.42	6.08	37.6	19	36	90
Indonesia	348	260	−25	2.97	1.84	−38.0	5	9	80
III. Middle East									
Iran	210	350	67	7.39	9.46	28.0	75	194	159
Iraq	90	140	56	10.18	11.67	14.6	108	152	41
Egypt	195	350	80	6.17	9.00	45.8	18	30	67
Syria	65	225	246	11.07	28.63	159.0	72	122	69
Saudi Arabia	60	60	—	10.24	7.89	−22.9	181	910	403
Israel	95	165	74	33.81	45.71	35.2	347	770	122
IV. Latin America									
Argentina	160	155	−33	6.93	5.92	−14.6	21	28	25
Brazil	340	450	32	3.73	3.81	2.1	14	13	−7
Cuba	110	200	82	13.29	20.83	56.7	41	44	7
Peru	75	125	67	5.86	7.62	30.0	28	51	82
V. South Asia									
India	1480	1270	−14	2.80	1.98	−29.3	4	5	25
Pakistan	357	588	65	6.21	7.79	25.4	9	11	22

a developed area, the developing states outstrip the percentage increase in developed state spending in every region. Most prominent is the Middle East which recorded increases of over 270 percent, followed by Africa (here including Arabophone North Africa) which doubled its military expenditures. In both instances the rate of military spending exceeded the growth in GNP. Meanwhile, North America experienced a decline of 25 percent. In three instances (Africa, Middle East, and South Asia), a higher percentage of a region's GNP was spent for military purposes in 1977 than in 1968. While the ratio of military spending to GNP fell for developed states by almost two percentage points (7.4 to 5.6 percent), the similar spending ratio for developing states held almost steady, falling only two-tenths of a percentage point from 6.1 to 5.9 percent while

GNP was increasing by almost 80 percent. These GNP-military spending ratios are confirmed as might be expected in per capita expenditure data. The developed states declined 2.9 percent on this scale, while the developing state percentage was a gain of 38 percent.

The trends suggested by these expenditure figures are mirrored in the growth of the armed forces of the developing states. All of the world's increase was attributable to the substantial expansion of developing states military forces. While the armed services of the developed countries were shrinking by almost 11 percent, those of the emerging world were being enlarged by over three million, expanding by 25 percent between 1968 and 1977. In this connection Africa has changed most over ten years. Armed forces are estimated to have increased from 635,000 to 1,340,000 or 111 percent. The Middle East follows with a 76 percent increase and then, surprisingly, Latin America — which has no outstanding military conflicts similar to those in Africa and the Middle East — registered a gain of almost 36 percent in personnel under arms.[11]

When the level of analysis focuses, as in Table 3, on individual country behavior the picture of expanding military spending in emerging states becomes sharper and more arresting. In every instance the states listed have allocated more real resources to military forces in 1977 than in 1968 measured in constant 1976 dollars. In 14 out of 22 instances, increases in spending have more than doubled. For South Korea and Iran these expenditures rose more than 200 percent over this period; Saudi Arabia exceeded all other states with an increase of 553 percent. In only one case (Brazil) did per capita expenditures decrease and then only by one dollar per person while overall expenditures were actually increasing by more than 20 percent.

A glance at armed forces levels provides additional evidence of the increase in military capabilities of developing state armies. Only four of the 22 states listed in Table 3, as a representative sample of regional powers, registered decreases in personnel under arms (South Korea, Argentina, India, Indonesia). On the other hand, overall military spending for these four states grew whether measured in total expenditures or in per capita outlays. This suggests that more funds were being spent on military equipment and on improving the quality and efficiency of these national armed forces, measured by newer and more sophisticated equipment.

Table 4 summarizes trends in the acquisition of increasingly sophisticated military hardware among developing states. Developing states have achieved considerable increases in firepower, range, and reliability over the entire spectrum of ground, sea, and air systems. Table 4 reinforces the image of an increasingly diffuse international security system, characterized by a rising number of centers of military force. For 1950 the Stock-

---

11. Accurate data about the strength of current national armed forces compared to their composition ten years ago are not readily available. That the trend is in the direction indicated by Table 3 is suggested by a comparison of the military capabilities of developing states listed in the annual publication of the International Institute of Strategic Studies. See *Military Balance* for *1965-66* and *1980-81,* passim.

TABLE 4*
Number of Third World Countries with Advanced Military Systems, 1950, 1960, 1970, 1977

	1950	1960	1970	1977
Supersonic Aircraft	—	1	28	47
Missiles	—	6	25	42
Armored Fighting Vehicles	1	38	72	83
Modern Warships	4	26	56	67

*Source: Stockholm International Peace Research Institute, *World Armaments and Disarmament: 1978,* New York, 1978, pp. 238-253.

TABLE 5*
Arms Imports by Five-Year Averages (in millions of constant 1976 dollars)

	Imports 1968-72	Imports 1973-77	% Change
I. Global			
World	9660.0	15280.0	58.2
Developed	2859.6	4083.6	42.8
Developing	6848.0	11166.0	63.1
II. Regions			
North America	322.2	312.4	−3.0
NATO Europe	1770.8	1280.2	−27.7
Warsaw Europe	1049.2	2383.4	127.2
Africa	356.2	1547.4	334.4
East Asia	3384.4	2496.2	−26.2
Latin America	331.4	753.0	127.2
Middle East	1671.4	5056.6	202.5
Oceania	135.4	125.4	−7.4
South Asia	419.2	514.8	22.8

*Source: ACDA, *op.cit.,* pp. 113-117

holm International Peace Research Institute indicates that no Third World state had supersonic aircraft or missiles, and only one possessed armored fighting vehicles, such as tanks or armored personnel carriers. By 1960, 38 countries had heavy armor in their inventories; 26 were manning warships; yet only one state (Taiwan) had supersonic aircraft. Ten years later the picture changes radically in an upward fashion in all these categories. Moreover, by 1977 almost 50 emerging states deployed supersonic aircraft, some as advanced as those found in the air forces of developed states. These included MiG 23s (North Korea, Syria, Iraq), Jaguars (Oman and Ecuador), Mirage 3s and 5s (17 states), and F-5s (16 states).[12] Over 80 developing states by then possessed heavy armor; 42 had various missile capabilities; and 67 disposed modern warships in their navies which have usually emphasized fast, light ships with impressive destructive capabilities.

The upward trends in the military expenditures and weapons acquisition data found in the preceding tables are reinforced by an examination of the arms imports of these states in Table 5. Using five-year averages for 1968-1972 and 1973-1977, the developing states clearly outdistanced the developed states in the amount and rate of growth of arms imports. Part of this trend, however, can be attributed to decreased arms trade *within* the NATO alliance and Western Europe's lessened dependence on the import of U.S. equipment. In 1968-1972, the developing states accounted for 70.1 percent of all transfers; in the next five-year period of 1973-1977, the percentage rose to 73.1 percent. Correspondingly, the rate of growth is also impressive since the base for developing state imports is greater to start with than for developed states. The former

---

12. SIPRI, *World Armaments and Disarmament: 1978,* New York, 1978, pp. 240-241.

increased their imports by nearly 43 percent; the latter jumped 63.1 percent.

The breakdown in Table 5 reveals that the greatest rate of increase in arms imports was in Africa, including states having among the lowest per capita incomes in the world. Over the last five years, imports into Africa leaped almost 350 percent over the previous five-year period. The Middle East is also a leader with an increase of slightly more than 200 percent. Paralleling the rate of increase in military power, Latin America is in third place in arms imports, followed by South and East Asia. Table 6 identifies arms imports by five-year averages for selected but key regional states. It presents a more detailed picture of the dynamics of arms imports at the local level.

These patterns appear significantly to be a function of the levels of regional conflict, as well as in some cases, a function of "petrodollar recycling." Moreover, the superpower competition fuels regional arms races since they are in most cases the principal suppliers of regional rivals. The Soviet Union is a major or principal supplier of Ethiopia, North Korea, Algeria, Syria, and Peru; the United States supports countries in Asia (South Korea) and the Middle East (Saudi Arabia and Israel).[13] Morocco, among others, is a partial exception to this pattern, receiving twice as many arms from France as from the U.S. to sustain its war in the western Sahara.[14]

More revealing perhaps than arms imports of the increasing reliance of developing states on military force is the growing number of them which produce indigenously or under license their own weapons, ranging over heavy armor, supersonic and subsonic aircraft, helicopters, missiles, and warships. Table 7 contrasts the number of

TABLE 6*
Arms Imports by Five-Year Averages for Selected States
(in millions of constant 1976 dollars)

	Imports 1968-72	Imports 1973-77	% Change
I. Africa			
Nigeria	23.8	38.2	60.1
South Africa	64.2	131.2	104.4
Ethiopia	17.8	103.0	478.7
Somalia	43.4	61.8	42.4
Morocco	15.2	95.4	527.6
II. East Asia			
North Korea	143.8	174.2	21.1
South Korea	474.2	218.4	539.4
Thailand	66.0	68.2	3.3
Malaysia	27.2	47.2	73.5
Indonesia	21.4	48.0	124.3
III. Middle East			
Iran	388.8	1444.6	271.6
Iraq	484.4	802.8	65.9
Egypt	507.0	395.2	22.1
Syria	151.4	827.6	446.7
Saudi Arabia	96.8	420.6	334.5
Israel	208.6	834.2	300.0
IV. Latin America			
Argentina	51.8	45.8	−11.6
Brazil	64.2	124.0	93.1
Cuba		Unavailable	
Peru	57.2	181.2	216.8
V. South Asia			
India	249.8	271.8	8.8
Pakistan	113.6	138.6	22.0

*Source: ACDA, *op. cit.,* pp. 118 ff.

---

13. China and the Soviet Union share almost equally as arms suppliers to North Korea, with the Chinese slightly ahead over the period 1968-1977, having sent $360 million in arms to Soviet transfers of $310 million. ACDA, *op. cit.,* pp. 156-158.
14. See Stephen J. Solarz, "Arms for Morocco?" *Foreign Affairs,* (Winter 1978/80), pp. 278-299.

TABLE 7:
Domestic Defence Production In Developing Countries 1965 and 1975

	Aircraft '65	Aircraft '75	Missiles '65	Missiles '75	Armoured fighting vehicles '65	Armoured fighting vehicles '75	Warships '65	Warships '75	Small arms '65	Small arms '75	Electronics '65	Electronics '75	Aircraft engines '65	Aircraft engines '75
China	x	x	x	x	x	x	x	x	x	x	x	x	x	x
India	x	x		x	x	x	x	x	x	x	x	x	x	x
Israel	x	x		x		x		x	x	x	x	x		x
S. Africa	x	x		x		x		x	x	x		x	x	x
Brazil	x	x		x		x	x	x	x	x		x	x	x
Argentina	x	x				x	x	x	x	x			x	x
Pakistan		x	x	x				x		x		x		
Chile		x					x	x	x	x				
Egypt	x[a]	x[b]	x[c]	x[d]					x	x				
Iran		x							(x)	x		x		
Indonesia	x	x						x		x				
N. Korea		x						x	x	x				
S. Korea		x						x		x				
Philippines		x						x		x				
Singapore								x		x		x		
Taiwan		x		x							x	x		
S. Vietnam							x		(x)					
N. Vietnam		x						x		x				
Colombia		x					x	x						
Dominican Republic							x	x	(x)	x				
Mexico							x	x	(x)	x				
Rhodesia					x					x				
Thailand		x										x		
Guyana								x						
Peru							x	x						
Saudi Arabia										x				
Gabon								x						
Bangladesh								x						
Burma							x	x						
Nepal										x				
Malaysia										x				

Source: International Institute for Strategic Studies, *Strategic Survey, 1976* (London, 1976), p. 22.
x = domestic defence production under way either as indigenous development or under licence.
(x) = no definite information available on whether production under way.
a Production of aircraft terminated in mid-1960s.
b Advanced plans to start aircraft production under licence within the framework of AMIO.
c Production of missiles terminated in 1965.
d Advanced plans to start missile production under licence within the framework of AMIO.

states manufacturing various categories of weapons in 1965 and 1975. The list has now grown to approximately 30 states.[15] The factors conditioning and prompting this growth are varied and complex, but most prominent among these is a desire to be increasingly independent of foreign suppliers and the pressures that they can exert over a nation's security interests. The views of Brazilian Air Force Minister Joelmir Campos de Araripe Macedo are typical of those found among Third World elites concerned with national security: "The time has come to free ourselves from the United States and the countries of Europe. It is a condition of security that each nation manufacture its own armaments."[16]

The weapons and spare parts now being produced are impressive, with Israel a pacesetter. Its small arms and electronic equipment are innovative and widely held in high regard. Its Elta 2001 radar is a marked improvement on the Cyrano system purchased from the French to guide its Mirage fleet, reportedly capable of tracking a target at low altitude against cluttered terrain. It also provides the Arava STOL military transport, Kfir supersonic fighter aircraft, Westwind reconnaissance aircraft, various kinds of missiles (Jericho, Rafael, Shafrir, Gabriel, Luz), the Sabra and Merkava battle tanks, and several fast patrol boats.[17]

Other prominent producers include Brazil, Argentina, Taiwan, South Korea, South Africa, and India. While a complete list of their indigenously produced weapons can be found elsewhere,[18] some examples may illustrate the growing dimensions of the initiative and enterprise involved.

The Argentinian and Brazilian aircraft industries manufacture several military aircraft. Argentina has developed the Pucara COIN combat and attack jet as well as trainers, helicopters, tanks, and small naval craft. Brazil produces the Bandeirante light transport, plus COIN, reconnaissance, and trainer aircraft. It has also developed the Cascavel and Urutu armored reconnaissance and personnel carriers. Complementing this output is growing work in submarines, patrol boats, electronics, and turbojet engines.

India deserves special notice. Hindustan Aircraft Limited (HAL) produces a wide variety of military aircraft, including the Kiran ground attack fighter and the Marut fighter-bomber, Pushpak trainer and Soviet MIG-21s on license. Under license it adapted the British Gnat fighter to Indian needs to the point where it played a leading role in the 1971 conflict with Pakistan. The recent Indian purchase of the French-British Jaguar is also noteworthy because the Indians will manufacture

---

15. There are several useful sources that sketch increasing Third World production gains. The bedrock is SIPRI's annual *World Armaments and Disarmament* that has a chart of indigenous and licensed Third World Production. The 1971 SIPRI publication, *The Arms Trade with the Third World,* New York, is also useful although now outdated. For a recent brief overview with citations to other works see Michael Moodie, "Defense Industries in the Third World: Problems and Promises," in *Arms Transfers in the Modern World,* ed. Stephanie O. Neuman and Robert. E. Harkavy, New York, 1979, pp. 294–312.
16. Quoted in Moodie, *op. cit.,* p. 298. See other, similar views of Third World elites reviewed in Moodie's article. For an Indian perspective that mirrors these sentiments, see K. Subrahmanyam, *Defense and Development* Calcutta, 1973 and Rajesh K. Agarwell, *Defense Production and Development,* New Delhi, 1978.
17. SIPRI, *Yearbook, 1978,* pp. 206–208.
18. *Ibid., passim.*

spare parts, some of which will be sold back to the U.K. It also constructs the Vijayanta tank, developed first by Britain's Vickers, armored personnel carriers, and various artillery pieces. By one count it has 30 ordinance plants and its Bharat Electronics is alleged to produce 70 different items for electronic warfare.[19] In greater or lesser measure much the same progress can be cited for the other states noted above and in Table 7.

Increasing indigenous arms production in the developing world has also led to a new and growing phenomenon: not only developed but now developing states are selling and transferring arms to other developing (and even developed) states. Developing states still account for only a small proportion of total world arms exports, 4.56 percent between 1968-1972 and even less at 3.8 percent between 1972-1977. At the same time the total of arms exports in 1976 constant dollars has doubled in a decade from $307 to $616 million. There is good reason to believe, moreover, that the Arms Control and Disarmament's (ACDA) figures substantially underestimate the real economic value of these sales. In the French case ACDA has, *on the average,* underestimated French transfers by more than a half billion dollars a year between 1966 and 1975.[20] The gap between ACDA and French official sources has grown since then to $1.5 billion in 1976 and $1.7 billion in 1977. The same discrepancies[21] can be noted for the United Kingdom.[22] There is at least one report that Israel in recent years exported over $400 million in military equipment to more than a dozen states, including West Germany.[23] According to other reports Brazil also expects to be doing $500 million in trade in the 1980s. Several Latin American countries, including Uruguay and Chile, and one African state, Togo, have agreed to purchase Bandeirante and Xavante aircraft. Libya and Qatar have also contracted for Cascavel reconnaissance vehicles. Meanwhile, India has shipped tanks to South Africa.

Pakistan already has the capability of servicing its Mirage fighters, and thanks to Chinese help has just opened a tank factory in a move designed to enlarge Pakistan's independence in arms acquisition.[24] The French have also used Pakistanis to train Arab pilots to fly Mirage aircraft.

Whether the expansion of Third World arms production has significantly increased the security independence of these states remains an open question.[25] A good case can be made that in many if not most cases it has not. Despite Israel's all-out

---

19. See Donald J. Goldstein, "Third World Arms Industries: Their Own Slings and Arrows," Unpublished paper delivered at the Annual Meeting of the American Political Science Association, Washington, D.C., September 1979.
20. See Edward A. Kolodziej, "Measuring French Arms Transfers: A Problem of Sources and Some Sources of Problems," *Journal of Conflict Resolution,* (June 1979), pp. 195-227.
21. Compare Edward A. Kolodziej, "France and the Arms Trade," *International Affairs,* (January 1980), and ACDA, *op. cit.,* p. 128.
22. Lawrence Freedman, "British Foreign Policy to 1985: IV: Britain and the Arms Trade," *International Affairs,* (July 1978), pp. 377-392.
23. Goldstein, *op. cit.*
24. Report of confidential sources, January 1980.
25. For recent analyses of LDCs' indigenous arms production capabilities, see Michael Moodie, "Defense Industries in The Third World: Problems and Promises," in S. Neuman and R. Harkavy, *Arms Transfers in the Modern World* (New York: Praeger, 1979), pp. 294-312; and Neuman, "Into the Crystal Ball: Indigenous Defense Production and the Future of the International

efforts, it remains crucially dependent on the US, not only for engines to power its home-designed tanks and aircraft, but more importantly, for an array of high performance aircraft, missiles, artillery, helicopters, and some naval craft.[26] Without such transfers, Israel's military forces would quickly be crippled, particularly given the military requirements of its highly sophisticated regional environment, and its need to balance off numerical inferiority with a qualitative edge. India, Taiwan, and South Korea are in comparable situations, and as is the case for Israel, there is no short-term prospect for their significant amelioration.[27] South Africa, now effectively laboring under a near-total embargo, has acquired a significant degree of weapons autarky only because its security environment presently allows that to be achieved largely without the home development of highly sophisticated systems.[28] While Brazil and Argentina likewise are nowhere near complete weapons autarky, in neither case is that yet an important security consideration.[29]

In some cases, moves toward weapons independence may have their political uses. Those countries easily availed of multiple sources of supply—India, Brazil, Argentina—may actually increase their leverage with major suppliers merely by moving toward indigenous production. Even in cases such as Israel's or Taiwan's, indigenous development may result in some extra leverage, if only because American corporate manufacturers may pressure a more forthcoming posture from their government lest a client become more independent and hence reduce its purchases from the larger power's companies, which will not be compensated for by royalty fees for component licenses.

Increasingly some developing states are becoming integral parts of a global arms production system and all the more so to the degree that their systems require foreign components, design assistance, and access to technological developments. There is a growing multilateralization of arms production that is a crucial part of the growing interdependence of states at the economic *and* security levels; indeed, one of the ironic consequences of the strategies of independence pursued by developing and developed states is the resulting intertwined dependencies that result from these strivings. There is no presumption, however, that this circumstance necessarily prompts cooperative behavior based on mutual interest. Much of what passes as cooperative

---

Arms Trade," paper delivered at the International Studies Association meeting, Los Angeles, March 19–22, 1980.
26. See, *inter alia*, "Israeli Arms Industry Has Grown Fivefold Since '73," *The New York Times*, January 15, 1977, p. 3; and Louis Kraar, "Israel's Own Military Industrial Complex," *Fortune*, March 13, 1978, pp. 2 ff.
27. On India's indigenous programs, see Raju Thomas, "India's Defense Policy: Strategic Compulsions and Domestic Economic Constraints," paper delivered at the conference on "Security Policies of Emerging States," Urbana, Illinois, May 16–18, 1980. For Taiwan, see "Nationalists Update Fighter Force," *Aviation Week and Space Technology*, May 29, 1978, pp. 14–16; and "Taiwan Center Designs Two Aircraft,"*ibid.,* pp. 14–16. For South Korea, see "Koreans Seek New Military Air Capability, *ibid.,* October 22, 1979, pp. 62–63.
28. See, among others, Robert S. Jaster, *South Africa's Narrowing Security Options* (London: International Institute for Strategic Studies, 1980), Adelphi Paper No. 159, pp. 12–17.
29. See Moodie, *op. cit.,* and "Brazil Emerges as a Supplier of Arms," *Los Angeles Times,* July 12, 1977, p. 10.

behavior conceals sharp bargaining and applied leverage, some tinged with implied coercion and threats, with arms production and sales as the instruments of manipulation. Israel bargains for co-production rights for the F-16 and F-18 fighters, simultaneously hinting at building its own aircraft, but ones which would require US engines and avionics.[30] The Jaguar contract between Britain and India may require the developed state to buy back spare parts of its own design. Egypt uses market leverage to prod licensing arrangements out of prospective Western European suppliers, as does South Korea in dealing back and forth between the US and Europe.

Still, the situations of the various major LDC's with respect to access to weapons varies greatly, and all remain critically dependent on the major powers. Some oil exporting states have the economic wherewithal and diplomatic clout to ensure almost open-ended acquisitions up to and even beyond absorption capacities, though with some occasional political limitations on the acquisition of the most advanced or destructive systems closely held by major powers. Some states tied to major powers (Cuba, Vietnam, and now Egypt) receive large amounts of military aid, a measure of their importance as allies, regional policemen and as additions to one side or the other of the scales of bipolar confrontation. Many are tied solely to one or the other great power (Cuba, Vietnam, Algeria to the USSR; Israel, Taiwan, South Korea, etc. to the US), while others receive arms from both major power blocs, often playing them off to leverage more and better arms. (The same behavior is evidenced concerning alternative American and European, or Soviet and Chinese sources.)

India receives most of its arms from the USSR, but relies also on Britain and France, while Pakistan is armed by the US, France and China.[31] Iraq, once a solid Soviet client, has now diversified into aircraft and other acquisitions from France, and Syria has done likewise at a less balanced level. Nigeria splits its acquisitions between East and West (mostly British arms in this case), while remaining primarily reliant on the USSR. Brazil and Argentina, once heavily reliant on the US, now receive the bulk of their weapons from West European sources.

Aside from the most advanced and closely held items, many of the LDCs are in a favorable leverage position for acquiring arms. The major powers seek influence, allies, strategic access, resources, and additions to their balance of payments in the bargain. Indeed, the customers are usually heavily wooed. The US, France and Britain vie for Saudi markets, the USSR and France for Libyan and Iraqi markets, and so forth.

In some cases, however, poor leverage results in difficulties in acquiring arms, and one can here speak of "reluctant" supplier relationships. For the most part, this applies to "pariah states" such as Israel, South Africa, and Taiwan, though some others—Pakistan in particular—have had similar problems.[32] Israel has become heavily reliant on

---

30. See "Israel Unveils Plans to Build New Fighter-Bomber," *Jerusalem Post Weekly,* March 2-8, 1980, p. 3.
31. For one recent review of global arms transfer patterns, see Michael Mihalka, "Supplier-Client Patterns in Arms Transfers: The Developing Countries, 1967-76," in Neuman and Harkavy, eds. *op. cit.,* pp. 49-76.
32. See R. Harkavy, "The Pariah State Syndrome," *Orbis,* Vol. 21, No. 3, Fall 1977, pp. 623-649.

the thin reed of US arms largesse, as has Taiwan because of Peking's leverage in discouraging other would-be suppliers. South Africa, now embargoed by all major powers—including, formally, France and Israel—is forced to rely on a combination of indigenous production, some licensed production based on earlier French technology transfers, and, very likely, a variety of clandestine governmental and private transactions, facilitated by Pretoria's gold hoard. Pakistan, long embargoed for major systems by the United States and the United Kingdom and forced to rely on obsolete Chinese military systems, now appears to have partially re-opened the US pipeline as a consequence of the Afghanistan crisis.

Numerous key LDCs, of course, loom large as potential future members of the nuclear club. Israel (with a perhaps already large arsenal of deployed weapons) and India are obviously beyond the threshold.[33] Pakistan, perhaps in collaboration with one or more Arab states on an "Islamic" bomb, may be within reach.[34] Taiwan, South Korea, South Africa, Iraq, Argentina, and Brazil lead the list of others commonly thought both to have the near-term capacity and aspiration for going nuclear.

The strategic meaning and utility of nuclear status, should it be achieved in any or many of the above cases, may be subject to great variation. Israel and South Africa (perhaps also Taiwan) are discussed in the context of last resort deterrence, should they be faced with national destruction by numerically superior enemies.[35] These countries, as well as South Korea and Pakistan, have played upon the fears of major powers (particularly the United States) that they will one day have to use nuclear weapons, in order to provide incentives for a continuing flow of conventional arms in cases where their leverage would otherwise be minimal. India's nuclear aspirations are usually considered partly based on prestige, and partly on the desire to acquire a deterrent vis-à-vis China's nuclear arsenal, though if Pakistan should move further toward a nuclear force-in-being, India will have an obvious, additional, important rationale. The Arabs seek nuclear weapons (Iraq, Libya, and perhaps a consortium involving others) to nullify Israel's nuclear deterrent while striving to attain conventional arms superiority.[36] Brazil's and Argentina's drives for nuclear status are usually ascribed almost solely to prestige considerations,

---

33. Among the numerous recent reviews of nascent LDC nuclear programs, see in particular John Kerry King, ed., *International Political Effects of the Spread of Nuclear Weapons* (Washington: U.S.G.P.O., 1979), a collection of essays from a colloquium sponsored by the CIA and DOD.
34. Recent Pakistani nuclear developments are analyzed in Onkar Marwah, "India and Pakistan: Nuclear Armed Rivals in South Asia," paper delivered at the World Peace Foundation Conference on Nonproliferation, Cambridge, Mass., May 1-2, 1980.
35. In Israel's case, see, *inter alia*, R. Harkavy, *Spectre of a Middle Eastern Holocaust* (Denver: University of Denver Press, 1977), Monograph Series in World Affairs; and S. Aronson, "Nuclearization of the Middle East," *The Jerusalem Quarterly*, No. 2, Winter 1977, pp. 27-44. For South Africa, see Jaster, *op. cit.*, pp. 44-48.
36. Regarding various Arab nuclear developments and associated potential rationales and doctrines, see in particular Paul Jabber, "A Nuclear Middle East: Infrastructure, Likely Military Postures, and Prospects for Strategic Stability," in M. Leitenberg and G. Sheffer, eds., *Great Power Intervention in the Middle East* (New York: Pergamon, 1979), pp. 72-97.

though Western analysts may perhaps underestimate the self-perceived security component involved. These might include, for instance, Argentina's fear of the population advantage of its northern neighbor, should it one day be translated into territorial aggression.[37]

In the future, the nuclear doctrines of several of these countries may come to be discussed in the terminology heretofore reserved for the Big Five (US, USSR, France, UK, Germany): first and second strike deterrence, mutual assured destruction (MAD), damage limitation, deterrence versus compellence, launch on warning, minimum and proportional deterrence, etc. Also, it is to be noted that some may, in the not-too-distant future, achieve some limited nuclear deterrent threats vis-à-vis the superpowers or China or Western Europe. Israel's nuclear force is already discussed in such terms in relationship to the USSR, and the latter may yet have to cope with several other small nuclear powers around its borders (Pakistan, Iran, Iraq, Turkey, South Korea, and others). Some commentators have pointed out that the seemingly strong and sincere interest by the USSR in non-proliferation is based not so much (as for the US) on "liberal" arms control ideals and norms, but on a pragmatic concern for a future that may see it, more than the US, within targeting range of several small nuclear powers.[38] That, however, is beyond the present scope of this paper, and its discussion would require elaborate analysis of potential LDC delivery technologies and Soviet defense systems in a variety of scenarios and circumstances (see, however, Jones in this volume).[39]

There are some initial signs that nuclear ties and diplomacy *within* the LDCs grouping have become an important and growing item for consideration. Pakistan's Arab connection has been noted, and its significance is often juxtaposed to the alleged nuclear cooperation between Israel and South Africa.[40] Taiwan and South Korea are often linked in this regard; likewise, India both with some Arab states and Argentina, and Iraq with Brazil. Saudi diplomacy aimed at detaching South Korea and Taiwan from Israel and Black Africa's seeming recent turn toward resumption of ties with Israel (hoping for the trade-off of Israel's loosening of its ties to South Africa) may also have some roots in a quietly but seriously recognized, crucial nuclear context.[41]

---

37. On Brazilian and Argentinian nuclear developments, see John Redick, "Non-Proliferation in Latin America," paper delivered at the World Peace Foundation Conference on Nonproliferation, Cambridge, Mass., May 1–2, 1980.

38. For a review of nuclear weapons doctrines potentially applicable to new nuclear powers, see Lewis A. Dunn and Herman Kahn, *Trends in Nuclear Proliferation, 1975–1995* (Croton-on-Hudson, N.Y.: Hudson Institute, 1975).

39. This point is elaborated upon in Geoffrey Kemp, "The New Strategic Map," *Survival,* March/April 1977, pp. 50–59.

40. See Lewis Dunn, "Proliferation Watch: Half Past India's Bang," *Foreign Policy,* No. 36, 1979, pp. 71–89, for a review of some of these nascent, limited connections.

41. Saudi efforts at breaking up a nascent "pariah bloc" are reported in "Taiwan Using Unofficial Diplomatic Ties to Avoid Becoming Outcast," *The New York Times,* September 9, 1977, p. 2; and "Israel Says It will Close Embassy in South Korea," *ibid.,* February 16, 1977, p. 7.

The potentially complementary nature of some of the intra-LDC nuclear ties are clear: Arab cash marries Pakistani technical expertise; Israeli weapons design and plutonium marries South African raw uranium, U-235 installations, and space for testing. There is a hint here of a nascent contest between a radical Third World nuclear axis and a pariah axis regarding nuclear developments, each striving to circumvent basically collusive and convergent superpower controls and designs, together militating again toward a more diffused global power structure. Israel, the Arabs, India and Pakistan, incidentally, may have come to prefer local nuclear balances plus attendant nuclear prestige to nuclear-free regional environments, for a variety of reasons, but with considerable convergence.

Developing States and the International Security Process: Domains and Instruments

We have indicated that many of the more important LDCs are increasingly capable of active, assertive and partially autonomous national security policies, characterized in many cases by more and more symmetrical influence or leverage relationships with the major powers. In part this results from their opportunity to work within an increasingly complex multipolar system, with its cross-cutting ideological and balance of power loci of conflict, in playing the major powers off against each other, hence achieving some degree of freedom of action. Many of the aspiring powers have also achieved an enhanced capacity to utilize a variety of political and economic instruments of security policy, and to be engaged in a variety of domains falling within the rubric of grand strategy, heretofore primarily reserved for the great powers. Partly this may result from increasing capabilities, but also partly from increasingly acquired experience in "playing the game" of global politics. These developments direct attention to what many of the larger LDC's are doing in some or all of the following areas, several of which are further discussed below:

- Sending of troops, "volunteers," or advisors abroad, for actual combat or for garrisoning intended to provide protection or deterrence for allies and friends;

- re-transferring of arms acquired from superpowers (with or without their blessing), or transferring of indigenously produced arms, to other states at peace or war, or to revolutionary factions;

- financing arms acquisitions for other states, at times on a large scale;

- promoting, abetting, financing terrorism — or, conducting counter-terrorist operations overseas;

- conducting long-range naval and/or aircraft military operations; also, fleet port visits or other symbolic displays of military power;

- influencing public opinion (by financial or other means) or suborning officials in other states;

- cooperating in bilateral or multilateral intelligence activities (with major powers and/or other LDCs), both regarding operations and information acquisition;

- denying rivals (and their superpower clients) strategic access through a variety of diplomatic instruments.

Volunteers and Advisors

There are numerous and increasing examples of the capability and willingness of LDC powers to send troops, volunteers, and training personnel abroad, in some cases at considerable distances from home. This geographically extended form of military diplomacy is sometimes utilized on behalf of a major power client (hence the term surrogate forces), but in other cases the LDC's interests and purposes may be central. In some cases, it may not be altogether clear just who is leading whom, or instigating whom to what purpose, as witness recent disagreements among analysts about the Soviet-Cuban connection in Africa.[42]

Whether or not characterized as a Soviet surrogate, Cuba's recent activities do provide the most telling example of global activities of this sort. It reportedly has 43,000 troops now engaged in some 14 African nations (the bulk in Ethiopia and Angola, others in Mozambique, Congo, Guinea, Guinea-Bissau, etc.) as well as in a few Arab states, like South Yemen and Libya.[43] Those forces have been effective, even decisive, in the Horn of Africa and Angola, where their relative military sophistication has overwhelmed more primitive foes. The Shaba invasion of 1978 and Cuban support for Dhofari insurgents in the South Yemen-Oman border region provide further illustrations of the increasingly ubiquitous Cuban role, which until recently had been quiescent even in Latin America. To the extent the Cubans can be perceived as acting somewhat under their own impetus and as animated by their own designs, we are witnessing a qualitatively different phenomenon than that evidenced earlier by British use of Gurkha and Fijian troops to combat colonial insurgencies, or France's use of Arab and African colonial troops against Germany. Here a small state is bent on influencing the shape of the international order through adroit use of its central leadership role among the Non-Aligned States and its still limited military capabilities. Its success to date is a commentary not only on its resourcefulness and risk-taking, but also on the divisions and weaknesses of its adversaries in the developed world.

Cuba's extended military reach is the most visible and significant among LDCs, but there are other recent examples, hinting at a burgeoning phenomenon. Moroccan troops (flown in by American, French and Belgian aircraft) were crucial in halting two invasions of Zaire's Shaba province from Angola; Zaire was also assisted by Egyptian advisors.[44] In the wake of the second Shaba incident an inter-African force of Moroccan and Senegalese troops, supplemented by units from Togo, Ivory Coast, the Cameroons, and Gabon, was formed to preserve order and bolster the Mobutu regime.

Pakistani fliers and training personnel have also been used to provide backbone for Arab forces in Jordan and Libya. North Korean fliers and Vietnamese manning surface-to-air missiles were involved on the Arab side in 1973, while Iranian forces fought in Oman against insurgents based in South Yemen. Libyan units tried to keep Idi Amin in power in Uganda when the latter was invaded by Tanzania, and were also engaged in the Chadian civil war in 1977–1978. Israeli advisors

---

42. See William LeoGrande, "Cuba's Policy in Africa: 1959–1980" (Berkeley: Institute for International Studies, 1980), forthcoming.
43. For a graphic portrayal, see "Countering the Communists," *Time*, June 5, 1978, pp. 26 ff.
44. See "U.S. Will Fly Moroccan Units to Help Zaire," *Washington Post*, June 3, 1978, p. 1.

were earlier active in Ethiopia. Recently, Taiwanese pilots were reported flying US F-5 aircraft in North Yemen under Saudi auspices, an effort contributing to Taiwan's search to escape from its current isolation.[45] North Koreans have abetted Cubans in the Ogaden, and fly MiGs in Madagascar. South Africans have in turn fought in Angola. While many of these activities fall under the heading of surrogate, they also bespeak of an extended strategic reach and, in some cases, of independent security strategies on the part of numerous nascent powers now moving toward regionally and extra-regionally oriented security diplomacy.

Hanoi's expansion in Southeast Asia suggests the difficulty of distinguishing between independent and "surrogate" behavior. Hanoi's military intervention in Laos and Cambodia, even before its takeover of South Vietnam, appears as much a product of traditional Vietnamese efforts to dominate the Indochinese peninsula as the result of prompting and assistance from the Soviet Union. The struggle for control of Southeast Asia can thus be viewed from at least three perspectives. Overlaying historical national animosities are ideological divisions between and within factions in Laos, Cambodia, and Vietnam. The superpower struggle and the Sino-Soviet split furnish additional and contradictory alignments within the region. Viewed from a global level, Hanoi may be seen to be a secondary power and in the service of the Soviet Union, its principal sponsor. On its own terrain, however, it has successfully challenged the United States and China and has installed favored regimes in Cambodia and Laos. It suits Moscow to support Hanoi, although it is by no means certain that it controls its every initiative or that Hanoi marches to Moscow's drum.

Arms Transfers Within LDCs

Numerous middle-range states, while still essentially dependent for the bulk of their own arms (particularly in the more sophisticated categories), have now become significant in their own right as arms suppliers, sometimes supplementing but also occasionally supplanting the roles of major powers. This can take various forms: where weapons are not otherwise available to a beleaguered dependent state; where big powers wish to maintain a low profile for fear of retribution or as a restrained posture for arms control purposes; or where a middle-range power is able to palm off obsolete equipment at a low price as it in turn is acquiring more advanced weaponry.

The transfer of arms sometimes is conducted with the permission (usually required by prior agreement) of a major supplier; sometimes it involves license-produced materiel. Controls of this sort are often loosely applied, or even deliberately evaded with the expectation of no more than a mild remonstrance, particularly where the original recipient has leverage over a major arms supplier. Small powers can often play a major role as arms suppliers during conflicts, even to the point of heavily influencing their outcomes.

During the Horn of Africa war of 1977, Ethiopia, though cut off from US arms and spare parts, was

---

45. William Safire, "Saleh in Our Alley," *The New York Times*, December 3, 1979, p. A25; and "Taiwan Using Unofficial Diplomatic Ties to Avoid Becoming an Outcast," *ibid.*, September 17, 1977, p. 2.

apparently sustained by re-supply of US-origin materiel from Yugoslavia, Israel, Libya, and perhaps Vietnam, in the latter case with the help of Soviet logistics. On the other side, Somalia, needing spares and replacements for its dwindling Soviet weapons inventories, apparently received Soviet-origin materiel from Egypt and Iraq (in the latter case in the face of Soviet remonstrances), and perhaps some US-origin weapons from Iran and Saudi Arabia.[46] Egypt has apparently also aided Morocco (once a Soviet arms recipient in the 1960s) with old Soviet weapons now obsolete in the Arab-Israeli context, but still useful for fighting in the less demanding arena of Spanish Sahara. Nigeria, oil-rich and equipped with Soviet and Western arms, apparently now at least aspires to a major role as provider of military aid to black forces in southern Africa. Pakistan, embargoed by the US after 1965 for most key systems, nevertheless apparently received American-made weapons from Iran and Turkey. Libya helped Egypt in 1973 with some French Mirages despite alleged prior French restrictions on such re-transfers. The recent Nicaraguan civil war also saw Argentina and Israel arm Somoza (at least until the latter was halted in this by Washington), while re-transferred arms went to the Sandanistas from Venezuela, Costa Rica, Panama, and various Arab radical states.[47] Both Israel and Jordan, meanwhile, have shipped obsolete armored equipment to South Africa which in turn may have assisted Israel with spare parts for its older French aircraft during or after the 1973 war.

The new actors in the arms trade virtually require extensive exports to achieve necessary production economies of scale; hence, to acquire a degree of independence for themselves they are likely increasingly to become aggressive arms salesmen. The efforts by some LDCs to achieve a modicum of arms independence through indigenous programs have been impelled by fears of their being made objects of arms control restraints or even embargoes in some circumstances. These efforts, however, allow them to become somewhat independent actors in some circumstances, viz., Israel in Central America, Brazil in the Middle East and in Chile. Some may even themselves become licensors of weapons production abroad, as witness the Israeli Arava STOL transports now to be built in Mexico. The future may also see increased off-shore production by major powers in Third World countries, perhaps particularly in Asia, consonant with trends in the behavior of multinational corporations which seek the advantage of lower labor costs abroad and the favor of middle-range powers with newly found wealth. If so, some LDCs will increasingly acquire enhanced roles as arms suppliers.

---

46. For some information on arms transfers during the Horn war, see, *inter alia,* D. Laitin, "Somali Territorial Claims in International Perspective," *Africa Today,* Vol. 23, No. 2, April/June 1976, pp. 29–38; "Conflict in the African Horn," *Current History,* December 1977, pp. 199–204, 205; and "Ethiopia: The Cuban Connection," *Newsweek,* June 6, 1977, p. 51–52.
47. "Somoza's Fall Intrigues Latin America," *Washington Post,* July 23, 1979, p. A 15; "PLO, Israel Compete for Latin Allies," *Washington Post,* August 20, 1979, p. A 18; and "Direction of New Nicaragua Unclear," *Washington Post,* July 24, 1979, p. A10.

Third Party Finance

This is a rather recent and unique phenomenon, almost entirely a reflection of the OPEC petrodollar surplus accumulated since 1973. States such as Saudi Arabia or Libya, producing no arms themselves, nor initiating significant re-transfers, nevertheless play a major role in the arms trade as financiers of others acquisitions. The significance of the financing is sometimes overshadowed by the influence exerted on a major supplier, like the US or France, to supply arms even where its political interests or arms control aspirations might otherwise dictate restraint. This can produce serious policy dilemmas for a major power.

In recent years Saudi Arabia has financed directly or indirectly billions of dollars of US weapons to Morocco, Pakistan, Tunisia, Egypt (before Camp David), Jordan, Sudan, and North Yemen.[48] In some of these cases, US and Saudi policy aims were convergent, and the former was relieved of what otherwise might have been burdensome requests for military grant aid. Saudi pressure played an enabling role in American policy reversals in Somalia and Morocco. In the latter case Washington would have run serious risks in its relations with Algeria, a major oil and gas supplier, in supplying over $200 million in military arms to Morocco.[49] The Saudis have also financed Syrian and PLO arms acquisitions from the Soviet Union. US dollars thus feed arms to Israel and, indirectly, its adversaries in the Middle East, with Saudi Arabia playing the role of middleman in the latter instance. In less publicized ways Iraq, Kuwait and Libya have also played similar roles. Libya, for example, finances most of the Soviet arms used by the Polisario guerrillas.[50]

Strategic Access: Bases, Facilities, Overflights

For long, the developing nations have been objects of the major powers' competition for overseas military access, involving a variety of facilities: permanent foward air and naval bases, air staging points, locales for naval refueling and port visits, and numerous technical facilities related to communications, intelligence, antisubmarine warfare, navigation, satellite observation and data relays, and so forth.[51] Whereas earlier in the postwar period many such facilities were availed the West by lingering colonial holdings and by the US formal security alliance system, they have of late increasingly had to be bargained for through military and economic aid.[52] The

---

48. See in particular Adeed Dawisha, *Saudi Arabia's Search for Security* (London: IISS, 1980), Adelphi Paper No. 158, esp. pp. 17-31.
49. On the Moroccan case, see "U.S. Allows Single Arms Sale to Morocco," *Washington Post,* February 10, 1979, p. A 17; and "Carter Aides Split on Issue of Arms Sales to Morocco," *The New York Times,* October 19, 1979, p. A 7.
50. See "Sahara War: U.S. Rallies Behind Morocco," *The New York Times,* February 18, 1980, p. A 3.
51. Among recent general coverages of big powers' competition for basing access are Alvin J. Cottrell and Thomas H. Moorer, *U.S. Overseas Bases: Problems of Projecting American Military Power Abroad* (Washington, D.C.: Georgetown Center for Strategic and International Studies, 1977), Washington Paper No. 47; and *United States Foreign Policy Objectives and Overseas Military Installations,* prepared for the U.S. Senate Foreign Relations Committee by the Congressional Research Service (Washington, D.C.: 1979).
52. For analysis of this trend, see R. Harkavy, "The New Geopolitics: Arms Transfers and the Major Powers' Competition for Overseas Bases," in Neuman and Harkavy, eds., *op. cit.,* pp. 131-151.

Soviets have recently greatly expanded their global network of facilities by a judicious use of arms transfers, almost always where close prior ideologically based ties have been established. Recent US diplomacy geared to acquiring access in Egypt, Oman, Somalia and Kenya has also well illustrated what is involved.[53] Hence, some LDCs have been able to increase their own military power in exchange for providing access to major arms suppliers, and the overall impact is a further shift of power toward the developing world.

In the past, many LDCs provided access to major power clients in the context of alliances or where an obvious convergence of political aims existed; indeed, major powers installations and garrisons were often welcomed, as they provided a trip-wire implying a commitment to protection of the smaller country and hence a deterrent to others aggression. In many cases, such factors still are important (note Israel's efforts to obtain an American presence and Cuba's apparent satisfaction with a Soviet presence), but in others, either divergent security aims or fears about the internal repercussions from compromised sovereignty are overriding, as witness Saudi reluctance to host a permanent US military presence, and Oman's quiet handling of its provision of bases to the US.

Two recent trends, however, indicate a more active and geographically more ambitious involvement by some LDCs regarding basing diplomacy. First, some have begun to seek their *own* points of strategic access, in some cases outside their own immediate regions, and not always as surrogates. Then, many LDCs have become heavily engaged in the diplomacy of denying access elsewhere to regional antagonists and their big power allies, often involving nations far afield along possible staging routes for arms and military forces, hence, with a potentially crucial impact on regional conflict outcomes or on the chances for effective big power intervention.

Cuba, for instance, in transporting men and materiel to Angloa, apparently utilized staging access in, among other places, Barbados, Guyana, Cape Verde, and Sierra Leone. Israel made use of Kenyan airfields and airspace *en route* home from the Entebbe raid; Pakistan, in receiving re-transferred arms from Indonesia in one earlier conflict, was apparently availed of staging access in Sri Lanka. Vietnamese as well as Soviet influence may have been crucial to obtaining staging points for the Soviet arms airlift from Central Asia across South Asia during the Vietnam-China conflict.

Concerning base denial, since the 1973 war Arab oil powers have mounted an all-out diplomatic effort to block future potential US arms re-supply of Israel if another war should erupt, an effort which has been targeted at Spain, Portugal (the Azores), Italy, the UK (Diego Garcia), the Philippines, and others. There have been reports of large cash inducements to Portugal. Meanwhile, in the recent war in the African Horn, Somalia's relationships with several Middle Eastern states apparently forced the USSR, in re-supplying arms to Ethiopia, to conduct unauthorized flights over Pakistan, and perhaps Iran, Egypt and Sudan

---

53. See "U.S. Sending Experts to Seek Persian Gulf Military Sites," *The New York Times,* January 11, 1980, p. A 8; "Oman to Be Supply Link for U.S. Fleet," *ibid.,* January 28, 1980, p. A 6; and "Snags Arise in Talks on Access to Bases," *ibid.,* March 30, 1980, p. A8.

as well.[54] Iraq recently has been reported trying to block US development of air and naval facilities in Oman, Somalia and Kenya with threats, cash and oil diplomacy; also, it has been reported working on Djibouti, Madagascar and the Seychelles to reduce their commitments to French and British naval presences.[55]

Some nations, professing the desire for neutrality (but perhaps also aiming at regional hegemony in a big power military vacuum) have worked for removal of big power facilities from whole regions. Hence, India (but also Tanzania, Mauritius, and others) has loudly advocated Indian Ocean demilitarization, while simultaneously tilting toward the USSR in its politico-military orientation despite the latter's clear reluctance to see its forces removed from the region. Both Iraq and Iran have claimed the desire to have both Eastern and Western military presences kept out of the Persian Gulf.

Terrorism and Counter-Terrorism

Some LDCs finance and otherwise abet a variety of terrorist movements as part of their overall security strategies. This can involve activities within target countries where revolutions are desired, and also more open-ended, global activities where the diplomatic personnel and citizens of an adversary state have become targets. Variously, this can involve the provision of arms, diplomatic cover through the issuing of false passports, transport aboard national airlines, seconding of embassy intelligence agents as participants in operations, provision of training camps, and, of course, money.[56] Libya, Algeria, Iraq, North Korea, Cuba, and South Yemen have all engaged in these activities; the first named is normally held accountable for assisting not only the PLO, but, among others, the Sandanistas, Basque guerrillas, the Polisario, Philippine Muslim insurgents, the IRA, and terrorists in Turkey, Iran, Syria, and Oman. Algeria was long the headquarters for a variety of terrorist groups, and it has been held responsible for some untoward occurrences in Spain's Canary Islands. North Korea and Somalia have apparently been the locales of major terrorist training camps, as have Tanzania and Mozambique for Zimbabwe guerrillas.

Israel, meanwhile, has long combatted the global terrorist effort against its own citizens and overseas supporters with an equally global anti-terrorist effort, involving counter-intelligence, organizational penetration, and some assassinations. A small country, like Israel, has extended its global reach for clandestine operations to pay its foes in kind and to serve as a deterrent to possibly more extensive terrorism by them.

Arms Control, Disarmament, and Peacekeeping

As the 1978 UN Special Session on Disarmament (SSOD) suggests, LDCs have displayed increasing interest in playing a role in global arms

---

54. See "Airlift to Ethiopia," *Newsweek,* January 23, 1978, pp. 35–36.
55. See "Iraq's Challenge," *The New York Times,* February 8, 1980, p. A 31.
56. For one recent *tour d'horizon* of global terrorism, see the symposium edition of the *Journal of International Affairs,* "International Terrorism," Vol. 32, No. 1, Spring/Summer, 1979.

control negotiations.[57.] As a group the LDCs have forcefully advocated limitations on the vertical proliferation of big powers as a price for serious attention to their own horizontal weapons proliferations. Progress in nuclear or conventional nonproliferation is alleged to hinge, therefore, on limitation agreements among the developed states, especially the US and USSR, on such matters as SALT, a comprehensive test ban treaty, and conventional arms talks.

Of course, most LDCs must judge arms control, as applied to themselves, in the light of their own security interests. American advocacy of regional recipient arms restraint is usually greeted with annoyance or silence, not only because of its alleged paternalism, but because it also threatens to freeze the present North-South military asymmetries. Some nations fear, at any rate, being disadvantaged by universally or regionally applied restraints, such as what was at least envisaged at Ayacucho. Israel worries about a big power agreement on Middle Eastern weapons shipments, lest it inevitably be disadvantaged in the bargain, even aside from verification matters. Meanwhile, in the UN and elsewhere, radical Third World nations push for superpower action against the Israeli and South African nuclear programs, lest they balance what might otherwise become disadvantageous conventional military positions vis-à-vis more numerous foes.

As a group, the LDCs have successfully prodded the major powers into hiving off some areas of the world (including its underseas and outer space dimensions) from their arms control competition, where they alone now have the technological wherewithal to operate. The Outer Space, Seabed, and Antarctica arms control arrangements were consummated in part under LDC pressures and in turn have been related to attempts at overall internationalization of these domains (i.e., Law of the Sea and space communication negotiations). And recently, the larger powers have been pressured toward international control of underseas mineral resources in exchange for the LDCs not insisting upon further extension of national sovereignty over coastal waters which, of course, would restrict the naval movements of the major powers. This is an example of how LDCs have used their majority voting bloc in international organizations to pursue common security interests (or to bargain them for economic gains).

For some LDCs tensions have arisen over arms control possibilities, between adherence to general Third World preferences and those of big power mentors. India supports Indian Ocean demilitarization though it might remove a potentially assisting Soviet naval presence (along with the American one). Some nations rhetorically advocate regional nuclear free zones, though

---

57. See "U.N. Special Session on Disarmament," U.S. Department of State Bulletin Reprint (Washington, D.C.: U.S. Government Printing Office, August 1978); and William Epstein, "U.N. Special Session on Disarmament: How Much Progress? *Survival,* Vol. 20, No. 6 (November/December 1978): 248-254.

58. For further discussion of some of these linkages, see R. Harkavy, "Harmonizing Policies across Arms Control Domains: Dilemmas and Contradictions," in R. Harkavy and E. Kolodziej, *American Security Policy and Policy-Making* (Lexington, Mass.: D. C. Heath, 1980), pp. 129-147.

such arrangements would probably also require termination of big power nuclear presences or the transit of nuclear-armed submarines, which might be needed to provide nuclear umbrellas for some of them. While some LDCs have advocated a nuclear no first-use pledge by the larger powers, South Korea (along with much of Western Europe) fears that such a commitment would reduce the credibility of America's protective security pact.

In the nuclear arena LDCs have used the promise written into the Non-Proliferation Treaty whereby they would be assured of transfers of peaceful nuclear technology once on board the treaty and hence under safeguards. This has forced the extant nuclear powers to transfer peaceful nuclear technology even though the long-range impact of those transfers may inevitably militate toward an expanded number of nuclear weapons states, either because the transferred and safeguarded technology may be copied and reproduced indigenously (perhaps clandestinely), or because in some instances the Non-Proliferation Treaty may be abrogated only after large-scale transfers. In other words, under the umbrella of an arms control arrangement, the larger states may be forced to comply with what may potentially result in a crucial shift in power between North and South.

Some developing states have made important contributions to UN peacekeeping and observer efforts in Greece, Cyprus, Korea, the Middle East (Sinai, Gaza, Lebanon, Golan Heights), and the Congo. They are useful often *because* they are small and can not be easily accused, as are the great powers, of harboring hegemonial aspirations, though the recent experience in Lebanon indicates some of them may also not be altogether disinterested. Sometimes they can create a useful buffer between antagonists to buy time for peace efforts and to preclude or restrain superpower entry.

Conclusion

This survey of the strategic military policies and behavior of developing states has several implications for students of strategic policy and international relations. First, in greater or lesser measure these new states are today devoting more resources to the quantitative and qualitative development of their military systems than they were a decade or so ago. This change can be measured by military expenditures, men under arms, weapons production and imports and development of nuclear programs. On the whole the developing states are also strengthening their military capabilities at relatively faster rates than developed states when viewed across these measures. Certainly every state is not allocating the same amount of resources nor developing comparable military capabilities. Nor is the trend upward in all cases. Declines can also be detected. But the overall picture is one of a growing diffusion of military power around the world. The factors prompting and supporting this expansion are varied and complex. Their identification and analysis go beyond the scope of this review and would require a case by case study of state behavior to link actions and policies at the micro-level to the macro-phenomena sketched in part one.

Second, the developing states are using or threatening to use military force on an unprecedented scale to advance their interests and objectives, however defined. The geographic reach of these states parallels the breadth and sophistication of the coercive and non-coercive means used to press their claims. Like the great powers before them, they are intervening with regularity in the internal affairs of other states, including support for terrorism or for rival factions to regimes in power. They act as important conduits for the financing and re-transfer of arms or as arms suppliers directly. They also have asserted themselves with increased force in regional and global arms control, disarmament, and peacekeeping.

The larger implications of this review as they bear on regional and international security are, paradoxically, both certain and unclear. They are certain in the sense that we can no longer speak of the global security system as exclusively bipolar. A host of new actors, deploying real military power, often substantial economic means and tangible diplomatic influence, are now participants whose behavior is an integral part of the world security order, imperfect and partial as it is. The Eurocentric system has ended and superpower bipolarity has eroded as LDCs and some developed states, like France, insist on playing enhanced roles in regional and international security. The developing states can no longer be treated simply as clients or proxies of larger powers. This perspective, if it were ever true, has increasingly less relevance to the significant and enlarging security functions which these states now discharge. They are often as capable of manipulating other states as they are susceptible to being influenced from abroad. The behavior of militarily more powerful states, like the United States or the Soviet Union or France, is subject to more influence and control by these ostensibly weaker powers than is currently appreciated. It is misleading and even potentially mischievous to view them exclusively or primarily as objects of big power security or arms control policies.

What is less certain, however, are the potential consequences of a more diffuse global security system. Although each individual actor may be seen to be acting in a way to maximize his security interests, the system as a whole has less direction and fewer points of control. Initiative lies progressively in the hands of a larger number of players, possessing enhanced military capabilities and acting under variable conditions of freedom and restraint. Never before have so many states been so interdependent for their security and yet so bereft of means and mechanisms to harmonize their actions if for no other reason than to minimize the mutual harm and damage that they can inflict. Doubts about the stability of the system increase since we know little about the factors influencing the military strategic behavior of the developing states or how to influence them to control or manage armed conflict, to lower mutual threats or fears and to encourage trust and the resolution of conflict. The very dimensions of the global security system and the dynamics of interstate and intrastate security relations pose a new problem for students and practitioners alike. We need to revise our strategic maps by integrating the strategic policies and behavior of developing and developed states within a common framework of analysis. As the discussion above suggests, work on this task is long overdue, and the present effort can be said to have merely scratched the surface.

3. OPEC and NOPEC: Oil in South-South Relations

BIJAN MOSSAVAR-RAHMANI

Introduction

Oil pricing policies of the Organization of the Petroleum Exporting Countries (OPEC), Western efforts notwithstanding, have yet to be seriously challenged by other developing countries.[1] In fact, the non-OPEC developing countries (NOPEC), though widely presumed to have been hardest hit by the 1973-74 and 1978-79 oil price increases, have managed to maintain a united front with the OPEC countries, particularly in negotiations with the industrial world on the restructuring of the international economic order.

This essay explores the reasons for this apparently contradictory behaviour. While at least some NOPEC countries were seriously affected by the 1973-74 and 1978-79 oil price increases, for the majority the energy problem as characterized by shortages in electricity, firewood (the principal source of fuel consumed in the domestic sectors of these countries), and capital, long preceded the formation of OPEC. These countries have therefore publicly — and accurately — noted that their depressed economic performance stems not only from higher world oil prices, but also from the general worsening of NOPEC terms of trade caused by the steady increase in costs of imported industrial goods at a time of fluctuating and sometimes dropping prices for raw materials on which these countries depend for the bulk of their foreign exchange earnings. Increased protectionism on the part of the industrial countries and disappointing aid by the members of the Development Assistance Committee (DAC) of the Organization for Economic Cooperation and Development (OECD) have also contributed to the economic difficulties of many NOPEC countries.[2] The NOPEC countries believe that only through diplomatic solidarity and economic cooperation with the OPEC countries can they strengthen their overall bargaining position in any new round of negotiations over North-South economic issues.

The OPEC countries, in turn, have both consciously and unconsciously encouraged and reinforced this posture by building up an intricate web of economic and political relationships with

---

1. This article was made possible by a Visiting Research Fellowship at the Rockefeller Foundation, New York. The author is also indebted to C. Anthony Pryor with whom he jointly completed an earlier study of oil and the balance of payments of developing countries. Needless to say, the author alone is responsible for the contents of this article.
2. It should also be noted that economic activity in developing countries is responsive to many influences of domestic origin, including those stemming from weather conditions, natural disasters, and political disruptions of economic life as well. India's output, for example, which rose by five percent in 1978, declined by almost three percent in 1979 as adverse weather conditions affected agricultural production and supply shortages hampered industrial activity.

their NOPEC neighbors—a network of food and other imports, guest workers' remittances, favourably priced oil and/or assurances of oil supplies during shortages, plus substantial cash and other aid.

But this loose OPEC-NOPEC relationship could be severely strained in the 1980s and 1990s, if oil supplies become even more scarce and if oil prices continue to climb in response to tighter markets or new signs of political instability in the volatile oil producing regions. The lower income oil importing NOPEC countries would be the first to be closed out of the market in any scramble for scarce, high cost oil.[3]

For many NOPEC countries, the policy instruments, both domestic and foreign, available to prevent such a situation are extremely limited. This is particularly true for those countries whose prospects for export earnings are dim, who have high external indebtedness, who are technologically dependent on the outside, and whose domestic oil and energy resources are untapped or show little potential for development. A large number of NOPEC countries fall into this category. They will remain hostage to developments in the world energy market largely beyond their control.

While there are no early or easy solutions available to these countries, their formidable dilemma can be at least somewhat alleviated through an OPEC-NOPEC "settlement" involving balance of payments support, assistance in tapping indigenous oil and gas resources, and security of supplies, among others. OPEC can be prodded (gently for fear of evoking a backlash) to enter into such a cooperative relationship, not only out of altruism, but out of enlightened self-interest; for the oil producers, keenly aware of the risks of greater international isolation, remain dependent for support on the rest of the developing world for their oil price policies and other diplomatic initiatives.

Avoiding an OPEC-NOPEC Split: 1974–80

Before exploring how such a relationship might be shaped, it is important to examine in greater detail why an OPEC-NOPEC split did not occur in the 1970s. First, the NOPEC countries were not uniformly affected by the oil price increases of the past decade. The developing countries, it should be recalled, vary tremendously, not only in size, language, religion, and culture, but in resource endowment, level of economic development, oil import requirements, and ability to finance oil imports where necessary. As a result, the NOPEC countries are singular in their relative positions *vis-a-vis* the world oil market, and this heterogeneity has, in part, been a major factor behind their unwillingness and perhaps inability to form a common front against OPEC. Some NOPEC countries have indeed suffered important balance of payments difficulties resulting directly or indirectly from sudden oil price increases. Others have been hit less hard or have succeeded in weathering the price increases surprisingly well. Still

---

3. Some NOPEC countries re-export a portion of their oil imports either in the form of crude or refined products. The terms oil importing and oil exporting countries as used throughout this article refer to *net* oil importing and *net* oil exporting countries, respectively.

others have actually benefitted—in some instances handsomely—from the oil price hikes.

For example, in 1973, just prior to the first major oil price increases, only eight NOPEC countries (Oman, Brunei, Trinidad and Tobago, Angola, Syria, Tunisia, Congo, and Bolivia) were net exporters of oil, with total exports of 738,000 barrels a day (b/d), valued at $1.35 billion a year.[4] But as the price of oil increased, these and other NOPEC countries started to tap oil reserves that had previously been noncommercial and inaccessible at the lower prices. By 1978, the ranks of the oil exporting NOPEC countries had swelled to 15 (with the addition of Egypt, Mexico, Malaysia, Peru, Bahrain, Zaire, and Burma); the NOPEC countries were exporting 1.74 million b/d, valued at about eight billion dollars. The number of NOPEC oil exporting countries and the volume and value of their exports are all expected to steadily increase in the coming years. One interesting side effect of this development has been the growth of a common interest between the NOPEC oil exporting nations and the members of the Organization of the Petroleum Exporting Countries in maintaining high—and rising—oil prices; some nations, in fact, have sought to join the Organization itself.

The situation with respect to the remaining 85 or so NOPEC oil importing countries is of course quite different. But it is again important to further differentiate between these countries in order to classify them according to their relative positions. These oil importing NOPEC countries can be grouped into two general categories: the largest oil importing countries (defined as importing more than 100,000 b/d each), and all the rest. In 1978, only nine NOPEC countries had oil imports exceeding 100,000 b/d—Brazil, South Korea, Turkey, Taiwan, India, the Philippines, Thailand, Cuba, and Singapore in descending order of imports. (See Table 1.) Yet significantly, at 3.17 million b/d, the imports of these nine countries in 1978 represented over one-half of the total 5.83 million *gross* oil imports of all oil importing NOPEC countries.[5] Brazil alone accounted for about one-sixth of the total. If the nine largest importers are excluded, the oil imports of the remaining NOPEC countries amounted to a modest 2.66 million b/d in 1978, equivalent to only 4.2 percent of total world production that year. Five countries (Pakistan, Morocco, Jamaica, Panama, and Chile) imported 50,000 to 100,000 b/d each, 13 others imported between 25,000 to 50,000 b/d each, 20 countries imported between 10,000 to 25,000 b/d each, and the remaining 33 countries imported less than 10,000 b/d each.

The nine largest NOPEC oil importing countries, all but two of whom—India and Cuba—are middle and high income industrializing developing countries, have been able to continue importing large volumes of oil; in fact, the combined oil imports of this group rose from 2.40 million b/d to 3.17 million b/d between 1973 and 1978. (India

---

4. Based on the year-end f.o.b. price for Saudi Arabian marker crude.
5. The 1978 *net* oil imports of all NOPEC countries was 4.09 million b/d, adjusted for some 1.74 million b/d in exports by the 15 NOPEC exporters. The share of the nine largest importers of *net* NOPEC imports is a staggering 77 percent.

TABLE 1
Net Oil Imports of NOPEC Countries in 1978 and 1973
(in 1,000 b/d)

Country	1978	1973	Country	1978	1973
Oman	−287.1	−283.5	Barbados	7.3	5.5
Brunei	−245.5	−213.8	Somalia	6.4	2.3
Egypt	−259.0	27.2	Mauritius	6.9	2.4
Mexico	−300.0	93.4	Yemen, Arab Rep.	8.2	3.9
Trinidad and Tobago	−199.9	−113.8	Cameroon, Rep. of	9.1	7.4
Angola	−121.8	−142.6	Ethiopia	10.1	15.7
Syrian Arab Rep.	−73.2	−78.5	Malta	9.8	9.4
Tunisia	−58.9	−51.0	Guyana	10.0	9.6
Malaysia	−64.1	12.6	Liberia	10.3	12.1
Peru	−42.6	41.8	Surinam	11.0	12.6
Bahrain	−40.0	10.1	Mongolia	10.2	6.4
Congo	−38.2	−30.9	Senegal	11.3	8.8
Zaire	−4.2	18.2	Mozambique	12.2	11.5
Bolivia	−8.0	−32.1	Honduras	11.7	10.7
Burma	−0.9	4.7	Papua New Guinea	12.2	9.0
Guinea-Bissau	0.3	0.6	Paraguay	11.6	6.6
Western Samoa	0.3	0.3	Tanzania, Rep. of	14.1	20.9
Comoros	0.5	0.2	Rhodesia	13.7	11.2
Burundi	0.7	0.4	Zambia	16.3	18.9
Gambia	0.7	0.4	Cyprus	16.5	16.9
Central African Emp.	1.1	1.2	El Salvador	15.6	12.9
Rwanda	1.1	0.5	Yemen, Dem. Rep.	18.5	10.2
Upper Volta	1.4	1.3	Costa Rica	18.4	12.7
Nepal	1.5	1.7	Nicaragua	19.5	12.3
Chad	1.4	1.0	Vietnam	20.9	46.8
Benin	1.7	2.5	Ghana	22.2	15.9
Belize	1.6	1.0	Guatemala	26.0	23.8
Laos	1.9	3.3	Korea, Dem. Rep.	26.2	16.0
Cape Verde	2.9	5.5	Jordan	28.1	13.7
Mali	2.5	1.7	Dominican Rep.	33.6	23.0
Mauritania	2.6	1.9	Sri Lanka	34.0	23.5
Niger	2.7	2.0	Lebanon	38.5	50.4
Malawi	3.1	2.3	Ivory Coast	33.3	22.3
Togo	3.1	2.2	Colombia	28.7	−54.5
Haiti	3.2	2.6	Argentina	25.1	78.3
Sierra Leone	4.0	6.5	Uruguay	40.3	36.4
Guadeloupe	4.2	2.8	Bangladesh	36.1	13.8
Afghanistan	4.8	8.4	Kenya	45.9	49.0
Guinea	5.9	5.1	Cuba	168.4	139.5

TABLE 1 (Continued)

Country	1978	1973	Country	1978	1973
Uganda	6.4	8.3	Thailand	194.1	162.1
Madagascar	6.9	13.8	Philippines	236.4	182.0
Fiji	7.0	7.1	India	318.1	338.6
Panama	51.3	61.6	Taiwan	313.8	184.1
Sudan	42.2	17.8	Turkey	338.0	172.4
Chile	64.3	71.7	Korea, Rep. of	482.2	297.7
Jamaica	60.3	34.8	Brazil	943.0	687.9
Morocco	78.9	57.5			
Pakistan	83.1	57.6			
Singapore	178.9	235.1			
TOTAL net imports				4,094.2	3,655.1

Source: Organization of the Petroleum Exporting Countries, *OPEC Review*, Vol. III, No. 3, Vienna, 1979.

and Cuba should be viewed as special cases, the former because it is a major producer and exporter of manufacturing goods and the latter because it is a recipient of massive Soviet aid).

The relatively high incomes of most of these countries have given them greater flexibility in the adjustment of their external transactions than is available to most NOPEC countries. The majority of these countries rank among the highest in terms of per capita gross domestic product (GDP), and their relative wealth, rapid growth, and stability have given them preferential credit treatment in international financial markets, where they have tended to enjoy — and use when necessary — greater access to external financing than has been available to most NOPEC countries.

The remaining 77 low income oil importing NOPEC countries present an extreme contrast with their more affluent neighbors in many important respects. Their average per capita GDP is only a fraction of that of the top nine oil importers. These countries are typified by low rates of national savings, domestic investment, and overall economic performance. According to the International Monetary Fund, even during the five years preceding the first major oil price increases (1967-72), the annual growth in real purchasing power of export earnings of these countries was less than one-half that of all oil importing NOPEC countries, and no improvement in their real purchasing power was to be expected over the short term.

While nine countries account for over half of all oil imported into all NOPEC countries, it would be false to conclude from this that oil import costs are of little importance in the total imports and external balances of the rest. The fact is that the dominant share of these few countries in that aggregate is primarily a reflection of their sheer economic size and only secondarily a reflection of high demand for oil by their economies. The oil imports of other NOPEC countries, while representing a minor fraction of the total, are just as important to those countries as are the much larger imports of the predominant importers — and even more so for those unable to pay.

The concerns of the other 77 lower income oil importing NOPEC countries have therefore been more legitimate and more credible as far as OPEC has been concerned. But even this latter group is far from homogeneous, and as such, cannot speak with one voice. Argentina, for example, was an importer of oil in 1978 but has been itself a major producer whose output is expected to increase significantly to bring its oil supply and demand largely into balance before too long. Others within this latter group are also increasing domestic production and are expected to become either largely self-sufficient or even join the ranks of the oil exporters.

Furthermore, the ability of these countries to finance oil imports, either through stepped-up exports or through additional receipts of aid or even through commercial borrowing has also differed widely. For example, Zambia and Cyprus imported nearly equivalent quantities of oil in the year 1978. Yet Zambia's accumulated external debt at the end of 1978 was 1.7 billion dollars to Cyprus's 245 billion dollars. Elsewhere, India and Taiwan also had similar net oil imports, whereas India's external debt at the end of 1978 stood at nearly 16 billion dollars to Taiwan's 3.5 billion dollars.

Again, however, these differences should not mask the plight of countries most seriously affected by higher world oil prices. In recognition of the special needs of such countries, OPEC embarked on an ambitious bilateral and multilateral aid program in 1974 to redress — at least in part — some of the balance of payments and more general development difficulties faced by these countries, both on humanitarian grounds and in order to blunt repeated attempts by the industrial countries and the higher income NOPEC countries to rally developing world support against OPEC pricing policies. The strategy has worked well. The high levels of aid to date, and the promises of much more to come, have been instrumental in preventing an OPEC-NOPEC split.

Many NOPEC recipients have settled for just such promises of quick cash, soft loans, and other balance of payments assistance to help them finance their current account deficits rather than press the oil exporters to stabilize oil prices.

By any standards, the OPEC countries have been extremely generous in their assistance to the NOPEC countries over the last five years. Between 1975 and 1980, for example, OPEC's Official Development Assistance (ODA) consisting of disbursements of grants and loans at concessional terms totalled between five to six billion dollars a year, according to statistics compiled by the Organization for Economic Development (OECD). But even these figures (which are shown in Table 2) probably underestimate actual OPEC giving, as OECD readily admits that their data are incomplete since not all OPEC countries necessarily report total bilateral flows. Moreover, OECD statistics do not include flow of non-concessional funds from OPEC to NOPEC which reportedly amount to as much as the concessional flows each year.[6]

In recent years, OPEC aid has represented an

---

6. Total OPEC disbursements of concessional aid dropped back in 1978 to $3.7 billion from $5.9 billion a year earlier, although this drop reflected, for the most

TABLE 2
Total Official Flow of Resources to NOPEC Countries and Territories by Region from OPEC Countries and Arab/OPEC Multilateral Institutions
1975 to 1978
($ million net disbursements)

	1975	1976	1977	1978[a]
I. Europe				
OPEC Countries	$ 98.0	$ 255.6	$ 40.2	$ 232.5
Arab/OPEC Institutions	—	2.0	3.7	—
Sub-total	98.0	257.6	43.9	232.5
II. Africa				
OPEC Countries	3,700.0	2,052.8	1,582.4	1,118.2
Arab/OPEC Institutions	191.0	460.9	1,128.1	890.1
Sub-total	3,891.1	2,513.7	2,710.5	2,008.3
III. America				
OPEC Countries	207.7	221.8	367.1	130.9
Arab/OPEC Institutions	—	—	7.5	8.2
Sub-total	207.7	221.8	374.6	139.1
IV. Asia				
OPEC Countries	2,177.5	3,001.6	1,897.4	1,472.1
Arab/OPEC Institutions	16.0	39.5	105.7	111.5
Sub-total	2,193.5	3,041.1	2,003.1	1,583.6
V. Unspecified				
OPEC Countries	261.1	615.2	890.2	590.5
Arab/OPEC Institutions	8.0	50.1	258.6	461.0
Sub-total	269.1	665.3	1,148.8	1,051.5
VI. TOTAL	$6,659.5	$6,699.5	$6,282.4	$5,015.5

Source: Adapted from Organization for Economic Cooperation and Development, *Development Cooperation,* OECD, Paris, November 1979.
[a] preliminary

part, decreased flows to Egypt from other Arab donors following the signing of the Camp David accords. OPEC concessional aid rebounded in 1979 and in 1980 as the oil exporters move to partially alleviate the balance of payments difficulties created for some NOPEC countries by the most recent oil price increases.

average of over two percent of the donors' combined GNP, while assistance from the OECD countries in DAC has totalled only about 0.3 percent of their GNP. Four such countries (Sweden, Norway, the Netherlands, and Denmark) have had high and rising ODA to GNP ratios, but the average ratio for all OECD countries in the

1970s was held down by the disappointing records of the three largest industrial countries, the United States, Japan, and West Germany. While most of the OECD countries had earlier endorsed an aid target of 0.7 percent of their GNP, these countries have in practice only provided one-half of this amount. Moreover, only one-half of their total ODA is earmarked for the poorest countries. Thus in practice, the actual concessional flows to the neediest NOPEC countries is only one-quarter of what the OECD countries themselves have collectively targeted.

The OPEC countries now provide an estimated one-quarter of all aid to the developing world. The OPEC countries hold the top six ranks among all donors as regards the proportion of aid to GNP. Two of them, Saudi Arabia and Kuwait, rank among the six largest bilateral donors in absolute terms.

While until 1974 OPEC aid was largely concentrated in Arab countries, it now reaches all parts of the world. This trend toward greater geographical diversification is shown by the rapid growth in the number of non-Arab recipients in recent years to about 65 in 1978. According to OECD statistics, of the total 1978 official flow of resources to all NOPEC countries from OPEC countries and Arab/OPEC multilateral aid institutions, nearly 40 percent went to non-Arab nations.

These flows have been channelled in a variety of ways: bilaterally through such state institutions as the Saudi, Kuwaiti and Abu Dhabi Funds, through such regional organizations as the Arab Fund for Economic and Social Development and the Islamic Bank, through the Vienna-based OPEC Special Fund, and finally, through such international institutions as the United Nations, the World Bank, and the International Monetary Fund.[7]

While OPEC has not sought to tie its aid to the recipients' oil import bills, the total 1978 official flow of resources to the oil importing NOPEC countries with a per capita GNP of less than $400 (excluding India) from the OPEC countries and Arab/OPEC multilateral institutions amounted to close to one-half of the value of the recipients' combined oil imports.

A number of NOPEC countries have benefitted in other ways from increased OPEC revenues. The ambitious development programs of the Persian Gulf OPEC countries, for example, have required a substantial inflow of guest workers, not only from neighboring NOPEC countries but from countries as distant as South Korea and the Philippines. In 1977, NOPEC countries provided the Persian Gulf region with a labor force of between 2.5-3 million who transmitted some $5.5 billion to their home countries, according to one estimate. NOPEC countries have also been beneficiaries of billions of dollars a year in increased trade with the OPEC countries.

Finally, another important factor that has

---

7. Some of this aid has consisted of outright grants, particularly in emergency situations requiring quick balance of payments support, as well as of "soft" loans. In 1978, the ODA component of total bilateral commitments by OPEC countries was 76.1 percent, consisting of both grants (73.3 percent of the total) and ODA loans (26.7 percent of the total). Moreover, the grant element of ODA loans was 49.9 percent, and of total ODA, 86.6 percent, according to OECD statistics.

prevented an OPEC-NOPEC split is that both sets of countries share a common denominator in their underdevelopment, have similar aspirations, and face many of the same development tasks.

The NOPEC countries view OPEC as the single most successful attempt by a group of developing countries to reverse sharp and often disadvantageous fluctuations in export prices of raw commodities. Not surprisingly, many aspire to and have publicly called for the creation of similar price-fixing associations for their own exports; they would appear awkward indeed if they were to criticize the only existing model of such an association. Moreover, many NOPEC countries are nervous and uneasy about attempts at placing a ceiling on or in any way limiting what they see as a sovereign right by exporters of raw commodities to set their own prices.

OPEC has publicly championed the right of these countries to organize their own commodity price associations and has in fact been the prime force behind the establishment of the so-called Common Fund for buffer stocks aimed at stabilization of commodity prices. It was OPEC insistence that any discussions of oil prices and security of oil supplies be held in the context of global development issues that persuaded the industrial countries to participate in the Conference on International Economic Cooperation in Paris in the mid-1970s; indeed, OPEC's role in setting oil prices remains the only important leverage available to the developing countries for the purpose of engaging the industrial ones in negotiations over broader North-South issues. The NOPEC countries have therefore become, in a special sense, political constituents of OPEC.

The split in OPEC-NOPEC ranks that had once again been expected in some circles after the more than doubling of oil prices following the Iranian Revolution has therefore not taken place. Several oil importing NOPEC countries did call for a special meeting to discuss oil prices at the United Nations Conference on Trade and Development held in Manila in June 1979, but were not able to generate sufficient support for such a move among the group as a whole. The OPEC representatives argued that the NOPEC countries should concentrate instead on organizing to win higher prices for their own commodities, and promised support at the 1981 round of North-South talks for which preparatory meetings are now underway.

The issue of oil prices was again briefly raised at the September 1979 meeting of the heads of state of Non-Aligned Movement, but the final *communiqué*

> emphasized that the international energy issue should be discussed in the context of global negotiations within the United Nations with the participation of all countries and in relation with such other issues as the problems of development of developing countries, financial and monetary reforms, world trade and raw materials, all of which have an important bearing on the establishment of the New International Economic Order.

Both the OPEC and NOPEC countries have thus worked hard to avoid a drawn-out public confrontation on oil prices. Even in the unlikely event that the oil importing NOPEC countries could unite on this issue despite their own vast differences, they would probably fail to bring sufficient pressure to bear on OPEC to change its overall pricing policies. Instead, these countries would simply provoke OPEC retaliation in the form of a cutback in actual and promised aid, a reduction in lucrative trade, and perhaps even expulsion of large numbers of NOPEC guest workers from the oil producing countries. In recognition of this, the NOPEC countries have understandably resorted to quiet bilateral diplomacy to gain direct OPEC cash aid. And OPEC, by and large, has obliged them.

Prospects Facing NOPEC Countries
It will take a more imaginative and systematic aid package to enable many of these oil importing NOPEC countries to survive the increasingly difficult period of scarce and high cost oil ahead.

In 1979, OPEC's total crude oil production stood at about 31 million b/d, just over 28 million b/d of which were exported. OPEC proven reserves of crude oil have been estimated at about 450 billion barrels, sufficient to meet about 40 years of demand at existing levels. Of course, this proven reserves figure will be adjusted upward as new information about reserves is obtained through additional exploratory activity. Higher oil prices will also finance improved engineering research and practices, permit greater average well depth, increase total number of producing wells drilled, and generally enhance the quantities of commercially accessible oil in the wells. Even with additional discoveries, however, the physical capacity of the OPEC countries to actually increase daily average production levels is limited by a number of technical and important economic and political constraints. Among these are the desire to conserve oil and thereby stretch out oil wealth for use by future generations, the limited economic absorptive capacity of oil revenues at home, and the lack of reasonable investment opportunities for surplus funds abroad.

OPEC's physical production capacity in the mid-1980s is expected to be no more than 37-38 million b/d (on a sustainable basis) which, if adjusted for rapidly growing domestic requirements, translates to a physical ceiling on exports of about 32-33 million b/d, or no more than about 10-15 percent above 1979 levels. Moreover, it is not at all certain that the OPEC countries will be prepared to export even that much oil.

Given the limited incentive on the part of the OPEC countries to export additional quantities of oil on the one hand, and increasing world demand on the other, pressure will continue to build for even higher oil prices. Supply interruptions resulting from military action, political conflict, or from internal upheavals in the major oil exporting countries can lead to further price "shocks." And higher prices — and the subsequent higher revenues accruing in the OPEC countries as a result — will further reduce the incentive to export, leading to a vicious price circle. The prospect of $50 or even $70 a barrel oil by the middle of the decade is no longer a remote one.

Yet in the coming years, economic growth in the NOPEC countries will be accompanied by a more energy-intensive period, as demand shifts away from non-commercial to commercial fuels, with increasing mechanization of agriculture, migration to the cities, growth in the transport and industrial sectors, and increased electrification in rural and urban areas.

Studies are underway to determine how government policy in these countries can affect the ratio of energy use to economic growth through expanded conservation programs and the adoption of less energy-dependent development schemes. If these efforts succeed, the NOPEC countries can start out by building economic structures that are energy efficient *vis-a-vis* the industrial countries.

Even with greater efficiency, total energy demand will continue to increase at a rapid pace in the NOPEC countries, nearly doubling within the next ten years and increasing an estimated three-fold by 1990.

Some NOPEC countries will move to satisfy part of this growing demand by stepping up development of indigenous coal and hydropower potential. Others might rely on greater use of traditional energy resources such as firewood and animal wastes, which, together, still supply 50-90 percent of total energy demand in NOPEC countries. An important potential exists for maintaining and even increasing the efficiency and contribution of such fuels. Moreover, there are other energy systems available today that can make an important contribution to rural energy supply. These systems include biomass plants and solar devices for heating, cooling, water pumping, and even electric power generation.

Despite such options, however, the NOPEC countries cannot easily disengage themselves from the continued, and even growing demand for oil, at least in their modern sectors. Given its convenience and versatility, and until recently, relatively low cost, oil has come to play an important role not only in basic support of industrialization within these countries, but as an important fuel in the transport sector and even in household use. Any discussion of reduced dependence on oil must focus on the sectors in which oil is presently consumed. Do they allow for reasonable substitution with domestically available fuels? What is the lead time necessary for the development of these domestic fuels and will there be sufficient capital available with which to do so?

While it may be technically possible to substitute one type of fuel for another, the economic or even social implications of such substitutions are not often known. There are indications that certain sectors of the NOPEC countries' economies have reacted surprisingly rapidly to energy price increases because of the relative simplicity of their economies. Kenya is one particularly useful example, where higher electricity rates have resulted in significant conservation in the industrial sector. However, in relation to liquid fuels, the transportation sector represents the severest constraint to rapid substitution. In many countries, transportation accounts for a large percentage of all consumed oil. In addition, the structure of transportation is more directly related to productive enterprises, i.e. freight, than it is in the industrial countries. This linkage between oil and the transport of freight suggests that any curtailment of oil use directly affects economic activity, thereby exacting a toll which many NOPEC countries would be unprepared to pay.

Decisions about curtailment of oil consumption or imports based on balance of payments and other considerations can have significant — and perhaps again unacceptable — consequences in other sectors of the economy as well. In many rural areas, for example, liquid fuels, though consumed in relatively small quantities, play a critical role in the transport of agricultural products from village to market towns and for electric power generation for irrigation and other uses. While it is certainly possible to substitute for these uses over time through the more efficient deployment of solar facilities or through the production of liquid fuels from biomass, reaction by governments to a short-term balance of payments problem, for example, could drastically affect the rural sector's ability to ultimately respond to change.

Where will the much needed oil and liquid fuels come from? Some NOPEC countries, as noted earlier, are currently self-sufficient in oil and even export relatively large quantities. According to one estimate, oil production in these NOPEC countries will grow at close to 20 percent a year until 1985, only seven percent of which will be consumed domestically.[8] These countries appear to be making full use of the export earnings accruing from higher oil prices to support rates of economic growth much higher than those of other NOPEC countries. They are also continuing to borrow large sums from external sources to supplement import purchasing power and further support such growth; the borrowing capacity of these countries has been enhanced by the actual and prospective strength of their oil export earnings.

The odds on discovering major new oil deposits in the nine largest oil importing NOPEC countries as a group and thereby achieving self-sufficiency do not appear very high, although India and Brazil responded to the 1973–74 oil price increases by accelerating domestic oil exploration and development and were producing about 250,000 b/d and 200,000 b/d respectively in 1978. With additional development of new fields and application of enhanced recovery, these two countries' oil output is expected to grow by over 50 percent each by 1985. All nine countries have also initiated or accelerated programs to develop other domestic sources of energy as well; with few exceptions, these countries have non-oil energy resources that could be tapped further.

In addition to certain supply options, many of these countries could significantly restrain further growth in oil imports by slowing down the present push into energy-intensive industries such as steel and petrochemicals and by pursuing, instead, alternative economic development strategies. Brazil, the single largest importer of oil in this group, for example, reportedly plans to add more steel-making capacity than all the industrial countries combined between now and 1985. Two other large oil importers, Taiwan and South Korea, are also rapidly building up their steel and petrochemical capacities, thereby continuing — and even increasing — their dependence on imported oil. These countries are well aware of the trade-offs between development of such industries and the high costs, both economic and political, and are presumably willing and able to meet those costs.

The nine largest net oil importing NOPEC countries are generally expected to be in a good position to continue to maintain the growth in their oil imports through a combination of

---

8. Bryan Cooper (ed.) *OPEC Oil Report, Petroleum Economist,* London, November 1979, p. 69.

commercial borrowing and stepped-up exports. During 1979, this greater flexibility enabled these countries to maintain a high rate of import growth; they are expected to increase imports in real terms again in 1980. Moreover, many of them have begun to forge a new set of relationships with various oil exporting countries in trade, investment, and technology cooperation aimed at acquiring preferential oil supply treatment.

It is difficult to be equally optimistic about the prospects facing many lower-income oil importing NOPEC countries. Commercial lending will be especially tight for such NOPEC countries, and substantial new official compensatory financing will have to be forthcoming if they are to continue to be in a position to finance their oil and other non-oil import requirements.

The outstanding public and publicly guaranteed long-term debt of the NOPEC countries as a group at the end of 1978 was close to $212 billion in nominal terms, or nearly three times the amount outstanding at the end of 1973.[9] It should be noted, of course, that much of the increase shown by these figures is a reflection of the high rate of price inflation during the 1970s and of substantial real growth in the domestic economies and foreign trade of the NOPEC countries during this period. Moreover, the distribution of this debt is highly uneven, with the greatest share borne by the major exporters of manufacturers and the oil exporting NOPEC countries that have traditionally relied heavily on external financing to accelerate their development. (See Table 3.)

Nevertheless, the debt burden of the lower income NOPEC countries is large — and will continue to grow at a rapid rate as these countries

TABLE 3
NOPEC Countries', Public and Publicly-Guaranteed Long-Term External Debt in 1978 and 1973
($ billion)

	End of 1978	1973
I. Major Exporters of Manufacturers[a]	82.4	34.6
II. Net Oil Exporters[b]	53.4	12.8
III. Low Income Countries[c]	28.0	10.8
IV. Other Oil Importing NOPEC Countries	47.7	17.8
V. TOTAL	211.5	76.0

Source: Adapted from International Monetary Fund, *World Economic Outlook — Situation of the Non-Oil Developing Countries,* Washington, D.C., March 1980. (Confidential)

a Comprise Hong Kong, Taiwan, South Korea, Singapore, India, Israel, Brazil, Argentina, Greece, Portugal, South Africa, and Yugoslavia.
b Comprise Bahrain, Bolivia, Congo, Ecuador, Egypt, Gabon, Malaysia, Mexico, Peru, Syria, Trinidad and Tobago, and Tunisia.
c Comprise 38 countries whose per capita GDP, as estimated by the World Bank, did not exceed the equivalent of U.S. $300 in 1977.

continue to borrow to meet growing current account deficits. Significantly, a feature of this projected increase in net borrowing, apart from its sheer magnitude, will be a probable shift in the composition of new external debt. Long-term NOPEC debt to private creditors has risen faster than that to official lenders, and it is estimated to

---

9. The International Monetary Fund has estimated that this total outstanding debt will grow to $278 billion at the end of 1980.

have approached one-half of the total outstanding debt at the end of 1979. At the end of 1973, the corresponding proportion had been just over one-third, with the component held by private creditors divided about equally between financial institutions and other private lenders. By the end of 1979, however, 80 percent of the privately held debt was in the hands of financial institutions, reflecting the increasingly prominent role of international commercial banks in lending to the NOPEC countries during the past decade. The role of the banks is expected to remain prominent in the 1980s but not — in view of the banks' growing concern about exposure risk in many NOPEC countries — to show another disproportionate rise, particularly with respect to the lower-income oil importing NOPEC countries. Without access to sufficient financing, these countries will be unable to satisfy all their needs for imported oil even if there is to be enough oil to go around through the 1980s — which now seems highly unlikely.

Yet lower-income oil importing NOPEC countries have substantial potential for increased indigenous fossil fuel production. Although as a group the NOPEC countries contain more than one-third of the world's potentially proliferous oil regions, they remain basically unexplored compared to the industrial countries in general, and to the United States in particular.

One indication of the intensity of exploratory activity is drilling density as measured by the number of wells drilled per thousand square miles of prospective oil-bearing areas. In 1976, the drilling density in all NOPEC countries was seven (five in the oil importing NOPEC countries) as compared to a drilling density of 290 in the industrial countries (and a staggering 780 in the United States) and to 109 worldwide. (See Table 4.)

A recent study prepared for the World Bank identified 70 NOPEC countries with a potential for oil and gas production, of which only 22 already produce oil and gas or are about to do so. Of the remainder, 38 countries have prospects of making significant discoveries, but in only seven has exploration been adequate, and in another seven, moderate.

Perhaps the single most important reason for this historical neglect of the potential of the NOPEC countries has been the availability of supplies of low-cost oil from the Middle East which, until recently, prevented diversion of

TABLE 4
Oil Exploration Drilling Density in 1976

	Prospective Petroleum Area (million square miles)	Drilling Density (no. of wells per thousand square miles)
I. World[a]	30.5	109
II. Industrial Countries (of which U.S.)	9.0 (3.1)	290 (780)
III. OPEC Countries[b]	4	20
IV. NOPEC Countries (of which net oil importing)	12.9 (8.6)	7 (5)

Source: Bernardo Grossling, cited in World Bank, *Energy Options and Policy Issues in Developing Countries*, World Bank, Washington, D.C., 1979.

a Excluding centrally planned economies.
b The relatively low density in OPEC countries is due, in part, to the very favourable geological conditions, i.e. large individual fields, which do not apply elsewhere.

resources for investment in high cost areas. This prevented both the international oil companies and many local governments themselves from making the necessary exploration investments. Rapidly increasing world oil prices since 1973 have of course changed the relative economics of indigenous energy sources everywhere, and today, many oil and gas reserves that were previously uneconomic because of small size, the expense of primary or enhanced recovery, or even high transport costs have become commercially viable.

Many lower-income oil importing NOPEC countries lack the financial means as well as the managerial and technical skills required for an effective exploration and development program. And the international oil companies, for their part, are still not willing to risk their own venture capital in many of these countries which they view as either offering unattractive contract terms or as too unstable politically.

These countries would thus benefit from a combination of direct financial aid in exploration and development of indigenous oil and gas resources in the form of grants and long-term, low-interest loans, some form of outside "guarantees" for investments made by private concerns, and even assistance in creating government institutions (presently lacking) to deal effectively with the international oil companies. OPEC can provide much of this support.

Future OPEC Support
OPEC has already demonstrated its willingness to give generous — though not unlimited — cash assistance to the NOPEC countries, both for reasons of altruism and enlightened self-interest. What is now needed is a more systematic approach to aid-giving on the part of the OPEC countries which takes into account both the short- and long-term as well as the cash and non-cash requirements of the lower-income oil importing NOPEC countries. For example, a comprehensive package can be fashioned combining: at least partial compensation for future oil price increases for the neediest NOPEC countries; support for oil and gas exploration and development within these countries; and finally, guarantees of secure, relatively low-cost supplies of liquid fuels, notably liquified petroleum gases (LPG). Such a package need not become financially prohibitive or burdensome for OPEC.

Indeed, OPEC itself is currently looking for ways and means of channelling additional assistance to the NOPEC countries. OPEC's important Ministerial Committee on Long-Term Strategy devoted a significant portion of its two-year study to the future course of OPEC relations with the rest of the developing world. The final report of this committee makes the following recommendations, among others:[10]

1. The OPEC Special Fund should be transformed into a development agency with a "substantially" increased initial authorized capital

---

10. Adapted from OPEC, "Report of the Group of Experts Submitted to and Approved by the Fourth Meeting of the Ministerial Committee on Long-Term Strategy," London, February 22, 1980. (Confidential)

(Algeria and Venezuela have proposed a capital of $20 billion). The agency would undertake to: finance developing countries' balance of payments deficits; finance, under favorable terms, economic development projects recognized by the recipients as priority projects, including the development of their domestic renewable and non-renewable sources of energy; finance projects intended to reinforce integration between developing countries in order to promote their collective self-reliance; finance projects intended to upgrade the value of raw materials produced by developing countries; underwrite export credit between developing countries, particularly in the area of energy supply; finance commercial operations by developing countries; and underwrite loans floated by developing countries on world financial markets. It was also recommended that the new agency give priority to the least developed and to the most seriously affected countries, and promote the procurement of goods and services available in the OPEC countries themselves as part of its loan policy. (This recommendation has already been adopted, and the agency's capital has been increased by $1.6 billion to a total of $4 billion.)

2. The oil importing NOPEC countries should be given assurances about the security of their oil supplies — at official prices — as a matter of priority over supplies to industrial countries, and OPEC should work out a specific mechanism to ensure that this policy is implemented.

3. OPEC should assist the oil importing NOPEC countries in meeting the increased costs of their oil imports through a series of loans and grants. For this purpose, these countries should be grouped into three categories according to their income, level of economic development, and the size of their oil imports.

— The least developed countries with an annual per capita income below $300 and oil imports in the range of 10,000 b/d, should be given grants or interest-free long-term loans to cover the future increases in the price of their imported oil. This group includes 33 countries whose combined net imports in 1979 are estimated to have been 124,000 b/d.

— Countries whose annual per capita income is more than $300 but less than $1,000 and whose individual net imports of oil are more than 10,000 b/d, should be given favourable long-term loans, the terms of which would include a grant element of 25–50 percent to cover all future increases in the price of oil up to 100,000 b/d worth of oil imports. There are currently some 42 countries in this category whose combined net imports in 1979 were estimated at two million b/d.

— Countries whose per capita income is more than $1,000 or whose imports exceed 100,000 b/d should be given medium-term loans on a commercial basis to cover part or all of the increases in the price of their imported oil. The combined net imports of these countries were estimated at 2.3 million b/d in 1979.

Such a grant/loan plan is clearly workable on a one-time basis, although the cumulative assistance required over a several-year period of steady oil price hikes could become prohibitive if the OPEC countries continue to match every increase in the nominal price of oil above the original base-year price. One possible solution to this problem might be for OPEC to match not the nominal oil price increase with grants and loans, but rather to match the real price increase after adjusting for inflation and currency fluctuations. If the Long-Term Strategy Committee's recommendation for an annual increase in the real price of oil of as much as three percent is adopted, such a commitment to the oil importing NOPEC countries could be carried out with little difficulty.

In 1981, for example, the total amount of grants, long-term loans, and commercial loans extended under the OPEC scheme outlined would be under $1.7 billion, or less than one-third the average annual level of concessional flows from the OPEC to the NOPEC countries during the past five years. Broken down by individual components, this assistance becomes even more manageable: about $850 million or 50 percent of the total would be in the form of commercial loans, according to the OPEC formula; about $765 million or 47 percent would be in long-term loans (of which 25–50 percent of quantities below 100,000 b/d would be a grant element, equivalent to $190 million to $380 million) and only about $46 million or 2.75 percent of the total assistance would be in the form of outright or direct grants.

The World Bank estimates the total investment requirements for oil and gas exploration, development and production of all NOPEC countries between 1976–85 at about seven billion dollars a year on average, of which the requirements of the oil importing NOPEC countries account for close to four billion dollars. If OPEC were to provide fully one-half of the total projected requirements for oil and gas exploration and development in the latter countries over the next five years, using some variation of the earlier formula, its commitments in loans and grants (loans to the higher-income NOPEC countries, grants to the poorest) on an annual basis would be another two billion dollars or so.

Finally, for those lower-income oil importing NOPEC countries with limited promise for development of indigenous oil and gas who are most likely to be squeezed out in any future scramble for scarce, high-cost oil, OPEC should consider sales of LPG on a concessional basis.[11]

LPG is a mixture principally of butane and propane found dissolved in crude oil or in associated and non-associated natural gas. It is recoverable in an oil refinery or in special separation facilities. It has a high calorific content, is a clean-burning premium fuel, and has applications in chemical processing as well. Historically, LPG has been produced as a by-product in the oil industry, and its markets have been limited. The international oil companies made no effort to expand its markets or its international trade since LPG was too costly to produce, store, transport, terminal, and distribute in an era of cheap and plentiful oil. LPG produced with associated gas was usually flared along with it. Today, close to one-half of all natural gas produced in the OPEC countries is still flared and wasted along with substantial amounts of LPG, which, if gathered and utilized, could go a long way toward meeting incremental energy demand in the smaller NOPEC countries.

---

11. See Bijan Mossavar-Rahmani, "OPEC and the Indian Ocean in the 1980s," *OPEC Review,* Vol. III, No. 3, Vienna, 1979.

LPG is especially appropriate for the latter countries because it does not require a large and costly infrastructure, and because it can be readily substituted for refined oil products in a very wide range of uses, including transport, with only minimal alterations to existing equipment and hence little extra cost.

Although the OPEC countries and several industrial countries, notably Japan and the United States, are all now looking more seriously to LPG to meet their fuel needs, its availability has grown at a rapid pace, as an increasing number of separation and processing facilities continue to come on stream, particularly in the Persian Gulf region. Availability will be especially great in Kuwait and Saudi Arabia. In the latter country, for example, expansion of the Ras Tanura Refinery and completion of the massive associated natural gas gathering system could double total Saudi output to some 15 million tons a year by the mid-1980s, or about one-and-a-half times the total world trade in LPG in 1978.

If the OPEC countries went as far as to sell their entire exportable volumes of LPG to the NOPEC countries at one-half the present market price, the total discounts would be no more than several hundred million dollars a year.

Conclusion

Thus the total size of this three-pronged package would be about four billion dollars in 1981 (less than one-half the expected OPEC assistance in 1982), rising to about $11 billion by 1985, reflecting compensation for a three percent rise in the real price of oil each year. Such sums are easily within OPEC's financial reach (the OPEC countries total oil revenues in 1981 may top $300 billion), and if disbursed, will probably provide the only meaningful source of assistance to the NOPEC countries for the express purpose of alleviating the gradual transition away from low-cost imported oil. Thus, while there is some concern particularly in the higher-income NOPEC countries about the economic costs of such increased interdependence or even about the likelihood of increased political conditions set by the OPEC countries related to their own interests on such issues as Palestinian rights, most NOPEC countries have few other alternatives at least in the short-to-medium term.

The NOPEC countries as a group have already ruled out the possibility of breaking up their common front with OPEC and siding instead with the industrial countries on the issue of oil prices. Even if the NOPEC countries could unite on this point and be prepared to forego substantial volumes of OPEC assistance — both of which are highly unlikely — an alliance with the industrial countries would hardly assure them of plentiful, low-cost oil in the decade or two ahead. Indeed, it is against the industrial countries that the NOPEC countries will have to compete for increasingly limited oil supplies and on unequal terms. Finally, the NOPEC countries for the most part realize that the main problem facing them is not oil but underdevelopment resulting from what they view as fundamental imbalances in North-South relations, and that the OPEC "oil weapon" is the single most important source of leverage they have available to correct those imbalances. Nonetheless, an expanded aid package will help assure that rather than becoming divisive, oil remains an economic and political bond between OPEC and NOPEC.

4. Atomic Diplomacy in Developing Countries

RODNEY W. JONES

The spread of nuclear science and technology has been underway for about forty years. Although the rate of diffusion has been lower than was once expected, and the distribution has remained uneven with the heaviest concentrations in the industrialized world, several less developed countries (LDCs) have nevertheless made considerable headway with nuclear programs. Not surprisingly, nuclear issues have become an increasingly important part of the foreign policy calculations of the more technologically advanced LDCs, affecting energy, economic and security relationships with their neighbors and with industrialized countries. Such issues are also a significant strand in broader processes of collective North-South bargaining over the world's distribution of wealth and political power.

A growing literature has monitored important aspects of these developments, though the paramount concern has tended to be that of security and arms control from the perspective of the industrialized world.[1] Studies of nuclear weapons proliferation have dominated this literature, focusing mainly on problems in three areas: (1) the systemic consequences of proliferation, i.e., the dangers to international security and world order; (2) the motivations or incentive structures of decisions to acquire or develop nuclear weapons capabilities; and (3) the policy instruments, strategies and institutions which may prevent or control proliferation.[2] Another body of literature authored from the perspective of the LDCs offers a counter to the conventional nonproliferation studies by arguing that LDCs with nuclear programs are interested for the most part in the use of technology for energy and economic development rather than for military purposes, i.e., essentially for domestic rather than foreign policy needs.

Both of these perspectives lose sight of the

---

1. See William B. Bader, *The United States and the Spread of Nuclear Weapons*, New York, 1968; Leonard Beaton, *Must Arms Spread*, Middlesex, England, 1966; and William Epstein, *The Last Chance: Nuclear Proliferation and Arms Control*, New York, 1976.
2. Ted Greenwood, Harold A. Feiveson and Theodore B. Taylor, *Nuclear Proliferation: Motivations, Capabilities, and Strategies for Control*, New York, 1977; Albert Wohlstetter, *et al.*, *Swords from Plowshares: The Military Potential of Civilian Nuclear Energy*, Chicago, 1979; Richard Rosecrance (ed.) *The Future of the International Strategic System*, San Francisco, 1972; and George Quester, *The Politics of Nuclear Proliferation*, Baltimore, 1973.
3. Indian authors have been prolific and readily accessible proponents of this point of view, partly because of use of the English language. See, for example, the contributions in Onkar Marwah and Ann Schulz (eds.) *Nuclear Proliferation and the Near Nuclear Countries*, Cambridge, Mass., 1975, and Robert M. Lawrence and Joel Larus (eds.) *Nuclear Proliferation Phase II*, Lawrence, Kansas, 1974, as well as the impressive compendium of official Indian statements and bibliography in J. P. Jain, *Nuclear India*, New Delhi (two volumes), 1974. The economic interests of LDCs in nuclear energy are comprehensively reported in the *Yearbooks* and other publications of the Stockholm International Peace Research Institute (SIPRI), and in the *IAEA Bulletin* and specialized publications of the International Atomic Energy Agency in Vienna.

broader foreign policy uses of the nuclear capabilities which LDCs are in the process of developing.[4] Whether those capabilities are applied exclusively to peaceful purposes or in practice also embrace a military dimension (even if the latter is camouflaged or denied) they become factors in the foreign policy calculations and the potential influence of the state concerned.

Only a few LDCs so far have invested heavily enough in nuclear technology for it to be a major factor in their foreign relations, and those countries differ markedly in other attributes of size, level of industrialization, domestic political values, regional security perceptions, and international ties. (See Appendix: Attributes of Nuclear-Potential LDCs). Several of these nuclear-capable LDCs are unusually important, however, either because they are recognized as regional powers or because they are immersed in escalation-prone conflicts with neighbors. Thus we may expect through comparison to discover certain parallels as well as unique features in the foreign policies of nuclear-capable LDCs. Moreover, the parallels may by increasingly significant in the future as a result not only of nuclear technology diffusion in developing areas but because states learn from the precedents others set and therefore may amplify the parallels.

This essay focuses on the diplomatic utility of nuclear capabilities for the more prominent LDCs, exploring how influence is derived by them from nuclear assets and exercised in bilateral and multilateral relationships to improve national standing, perceived security, access to desired resources and development potential. It proceeds from the hypothesis that LDCs often perceive weapons-relevant nuclear capabilities to be peculiarly rich and flexible sources of influence inasmuch as possession of those capabilities generates uncertainties and potential security risks. Neighboring states, the nuclear weapons powers and their major alliance partners find the uncertainties uncomfortable and are predisposed to pay a price to resolve or ameliorate them. In short, anxieties about proliferation become instrumental for nuclear-capable LDCs, within certain limits.

INTRINSIC APPEALS OF NUCLEAR TECHNOLOGY FOR DEVELOPING COUNTRIES

Much of the appeal of nuclear technology to LDCs undoubtedly stems from its peaceful domestic economic applications. Most important among these, of course, has been the harnessing of nuclear energy in reactors to generate electricity economically and on a large scale for industrial and urban consumption. Nuclear science also plays an important, direct role in medicine and agricultural research. Moreover, technology spin-offs from nuclear research or engineering experience with the development of a nuclear power industry—in the form of new scientific and engineering skills, or capabilities in metallurgy and electronics— does stimulate diversification of allied industries, manufacturing processes, man-

---

4. Three recent exceptions are Ernest W. Lefever, *Nuclear Arms in the Third World: U.S. Policy Dilemma,* Washington, D.C., The Brookings Institution, 1979; Stephen P. Cohen and Richard L. Park, *India: Emergent Power?* New York, 1978; and Ashok Kapur, *India's Nuclear Option: Atomic Diplomacy and Decision Making,* New York, 1976.

power supply, economic output and development in a variety of sectors. Nuclear technology seems to offer the potential for LDCs to leap-frog economic development obstacles, accelerate the process of overcoming widespread illiteracy and poverty, and generally free themselves from their "less developed" conditions.

Atoms for Peace: A Perspective

This notion that nuclear science and technology could play a strategic role in the modernization and industrial development of LDCs was promoted, perhaps even overrated, by a few industrialized countries and, after 1957, by the International Atomic Energy Agency (IAEA), in efforts to direct nuclear development wherever possible into constructive channels.[5] It was vigorously propagated by the US following President Eisenhower's Atoms for Peace program announcement in 1953.

Atoms for Peace was the result of a policy review which concluded that holding technical nuclear information in total secrecy would not prevent nuclear weapons proliferation — the principles of ordinary atomic bomb design were by then widely known in scientific circles — but would impede the peaceful exploitation of nuclear energy. The major premise of the Atoms for Peace approach was that the US could supply civilian nuclear technology — in which it then held a commanding lead — on concessional terms for development purposes, in exchange for "peaceful use" assurances and safeguards for undertakings by the recipients. Proliferation would be discouraged both by the recipients voluntarily honoring legal undertakings and by the technical sanctions — the ability to cut off nuclear exports and assistance — implicit in bilateral agreements for peaceful nuclear cooperation. The nonproliferation effectiveness of this approach in areas left unprotected by superpower security commitments relied to a considerable extent on a recipient's continued dependence on future US commercial nuclear supplies, a condition which some recipients sought to evade or diminish over time, and eventually to undermine. US technological assistance itself, under Atoms for Peace, would contribute inevitably to the nuclear self-reliance of recipients in the long term.

To compensate for the inherent limitations of the Atoms for Peace approach, the US also sought to strengthen nonproliferation arrangements through multilateral cooperation and international institutions. These included the IAEA safeguards system and the Nuclear Non-Proliferation Treaty (NPT) of 1968. The ultimate aim of these efforts was to induct qualified countries into nuclear energy production, and to engage their nuclear power programs in an interdependent system of nuclear cooperation such that participants might be faced with the risk of losing reliable nuclear-generated electricity supply if they chose to

---

5. J. E. Hodgetts, *Administering the Atom for Peace*, New York, 1964; George Quester, *Nuclear Diplomacy: The First Twenty-Five Years*, Cambridge, Mass., 1973; Arnold Kramish, *The Peaceful Atom in Foreign Policy*, New York, 1963; Bertrand Goldschmidt and Myron Kratzer, *Peaceful Nuclear Relations: A Study of the Creation and the Erosion of Confidence* (for the International Consultative Group on Nuclear Energy), New York and London: The Rockefeller Foundation/Royal Institute of International Affairs, 1978.

initiate nuclear weapons production. The intention was to hold the economic stakes in peaceful uses of nuclear energy hostage against the temptations to produce weapons. Though intriguing in concept, the task of making this choice inescapable for non-weapon states has proved infeasible in some cases.

General Foreign Policy Goals

If the internal goals of establishing nuclear research and power programs in LDCs were largely framed in terms of economic modernization and development, they typically had some rationale in external objectives. Most LDCs interested in nuclear technology seemed to believe it would be a means of enhancing their power and prestige. Some have been faced wih intermediate military security dilemmas that nuclear capabilities theoretically could help to resolve, while others viewed such capabilities as a hedge against remote or contingent security threats. Finally, a few LDCs saw commercial opportunities in nuclear technology — the prospect of competing in foreign markets, earning hard currency and coping with trade or payments imbalances.

Such broad categories become more meaningful, of course, when they are specified in terms of the problems and perceptions of particular countries, but it is important to understand also how even these general categories often overlap in the context of nuclear policy. As a means to international power and prestige, peaceful and military applications of nuclear technology are both relevant, but can be so in different ways. An LDC which emphasizes civilian nuclear energy may enhance its power and prestige, for instance, by expanding industrial production, improving domestic living standards, engaging in international trade and cultivating a cooperative reputation and interdependent or allied relationships in world affairs. Its power and prestige in this respect will be largely a function of its domestic and external economic success. Though not exactly an LDC, postwar Japan illustrates this pattern, and it is probably the approach to which Mexico aspires. Alternatively, an LDC can seek to augment its military power and prestige directly by the acquisition of nuclear weapons or weapons capabilities. In the latter case, however, the category of power and status and that of security objectives may become virtually indistinguishable. China and India both appear to exemplify this goal-convergence pattern.[6]

---

6. For a recent report on the Chinese civilian program, see John R. Lamarsh, "China's Nuclear Power Program," *The Bulletin of the Atomic Scientists,* Vol. 36, No. 5, May 1980, pp. 28-31. See also Banning Garrett, "China Policy and the Strategic Triangle," in Kenneth A. Oye, *et al., Eagle Entangled: U.S. Foreign Policy in a Complex World,* New York, 1979, pp. 228-263; Morton Halperin, *China and the Bomb,* New York, 1965; Ralph Clough, *et al., The United States, China, and Arms Control,* Washington, D.C., The Brookings Institution, 1975; and Jonathan D. Pollack, "China as a Nuclear Power" in William H. Overholt (ed.) *Asia's Nuclear Future,* Boulder, Colorado, 1977. Similarly, for India, see H.N. Sethna, "India's Atomic Energy Programme — Past and Future," *IAEA Bulletin,* Vol. 21, No. 5, October 1979, pp. 2-8; Rodney W. Jones, *Nuclear Proliferation in South Asia? Dangers and Options for U.S. Policy* (under contract for the Foreign Affairs and National Defense Division, Congressional Research Service, Library of Congress), Washington, D.C. (forthcoming); and Ashok Kapur, *India's Nuclear Option, op. cit.*

Other possible forms of goal convergence involve linkages between foreign commercial nuclear activity and security on one hand, and between commercial activity and power and prestige on the other. An LDC which becomes sufficiently proficient in nuclear research or power plant construction could cooperate, for example, with oil-producing LDCs, exchanging nuclear technology for fossil fuel, thereby enhancing its economic and energy security. Alternatively, it could use revenues from foreign nuclear sales to purchase conventional military equipment to improve its military security. Power and prestige benefits would also flow to an LDC which develops the capacity to act as a commercial nuclear supplier because that role would presuppose that it had become largely self-sufficient in nuclear technology and correspondingly invulnerable to nuclear embargo. As cases in point, two LDCs — Argentina and India — have already made modest commercial nuclear sales, while Mexico, South Africa, South Korea and even Pakistan may eventually pursue such a course.

It is not necessary for a state to become self-sufficient in nuclear technology, or even to develop a civilian nuclear energy program, to acquire a nuclear weapons capability. Such a capability can be developed directly, and at comparatively small expense, by constructing so-called "dedicated facilties" for military purposes. China did this earlier and both Israel and Pakistan are presumed to have done so. On the other hand, the more self-sufficient a state becomes in nuclear technology for peaceful purposes, the more likely it is to concurrently acquire the means of constructing weapons even when this is not its actual intention. Such capabilities, of course, may still be constrained by resource deficiencies, safeguards or other obligations imposed by nuclear cooperation. To understand how LDC nuclear programs shape foreign policy, it is crucial to know about the features of dependence or interdependence in their nuclear relationships with other countries. This also entails a minimum of background technical discussion.

Nuclear Materials, Technology and Cooperation

Atomic weapons get their enormous explosive power from the instantaneous fission of certain nuclear materials. Not all nuclear materials are "fissile", i.e., have the necessary physical properties for explosive chain reaction. The most common form of uranium (U-238), for example, is not fissile. Atomic weapons normally are made from either of two fissile materials — the 235 isotope of uranium (U-235) or the 239 isotope of plutonium (Pu-239). Obtaining either fissile material in sufficiently pure form for explosive purposes requires special technology.

Fissile U-235 coexists with U-238 in natural uranium, but the U-235 isotope represents less than one percent of the material. To make weapons-grade material, the U-235 proportion has to be boosted to about 90 percent through a process known as "enrichment". Enrichment facilities traditionally have been extremely difficult and costly to construct, and their operation has depended on the consumption of large quantities of electricity. Until very recently, only the nuclear weapons powers had uranium enrichment facilities. Two mulitnational consortia based in Europe,

EURODIF and COREDIF, have been established to provide enrichment services; most of the participants in each are non-weapons states. Among LDCs, Brazil, Pakistan and South Africa are seeking to purchase or develop their own enrichment facilities.

Plutonium, the other weapons material, is not naturally available. It is produced in nuclear reactors by the partial conversion through irradiation of U-238, which constitutes the bulk of conventional nuclear fuel. Since plutonium and uranium are different elements they can, unlike isotopes of the same element, be separated from each other by a relatively simple chemical process. Facilities in which the irradiated (spent) fuel is treated to recover separately plutonium and residual uranium are known as reprocessing plants. Such plants require radiation shielding and remote-handling equipment, but represent rather small investments compared to enrichment technology. Recovery of plutonium from irradiated fuel has been regarded as the likely path to a weapons capability for most LDCs. India and Argentina have acquired reprocessing plants, Israel is presumed to have done so, Brazil is currently purchasing the technology, and South Korea, Taiwan, Pakistan, Iraq and Iran have made efforts to do so.

Acquisition of significant quantities of weapons-grade fissile material is the most crucial step in making nuclear weapons, and controls over that step are the focus of technical efforts to prevent proliferation. One of the prinicpal reasons for the difficulty in establishing preclusive controls over fissile material is that fissile material is a necessary ingredient in reactor fuel. Controlled fission of U-235 in a reactor core releases the energy needed to generate electric power. Pu-239 can be used for the same purpose, and it traditionally had been assumed that plutonium would be so used to conserve uranium as the latter becomes scarce. Thus, the material used for bombs is integral to a civilian nuclear energy system.[7] Countries which seek to maximize their independence in nuclear energy often argue, therefore, that national enrichment or reprocessing facilities are indispensable to their civilian programs.

Achieving complete nuclear independence is nevertheless a difficult undertaking even for many industrialized countries, and for various reason it has not been economically advantageous for

---

7. Until fairly recently, it was widely assumed that Pu-239 from the spent fuel of power reactors, when operated normally for electricity generation, could not be used for nuclear explosives. Economic burn-up of power reactor fuel results in the accumulation in the spent fuel of plutonium isotopes other than Pu-239, and the other isotopes interfere with the efficient fission detonation of separated plutonium. Recognition has spread, however, that while such spent fuel is not an attractive source of fissile material for nuclear weapons, it can be used for that purpose. This recognition of the possibility of ``latent proliferation'' (i.e., possible diversion from civilian nuclear energy facilities to nuclear weapons production) has been a major cause for recent revisions of U.S. nonproliferation policy. See Spurgeon M. Keeny, et al., *Nuclear Power Issues and Choices: Report of the Nuclear Energy Policy Study Group* (also known as the *Ford-Mitre Report*), Cambridge, Mass., 1977; Michael A. Guhin, *Nuclear Paradox: Security Risks of the Peaceful Atom*, Washington, D.C., American Enterprise Institute, 1976; and Gene I. Rochlin, *Plutonium, Power and Politics: International Arrangements for the Disposition of Spent Nuclear Fuel*, Berkeley and Los Angeles, 1979.

most countries to strive for that goal. Instead, it has been more efficient to purchase nuclear equipment and services from a small number of industrialized countries — the major suppliers.

For more than two decades, the US was the supplier of choice because of its qualitative technological leadership and nuclear manufacturing capacity. This leadership depended essentially on two key elements, power reactor technology and uranium enrichment services. The most cost-effective power reactors were originally developed and marketed by US companies. These were light water reactors (LWRs) which required slightly enriched (about three percent U-235) uranium fuel and, therefore, depended on uranium enrichment services. Until the mid-1970s, the US also maintained a virtual monopoly over low-enriched (LEU) fuel services, i.e. exportable quantities of LEU. By combining the sale of LWRs and assuring LEU fuel supplies, the US achieved temporary predominance in the international nuclear field. By virtue of this position, the US was able to persuade many recipients to accept safeguards and other assurances of peaceful use as conditions of continued cooperation.[8]

Even when the US supplier role was paramount, however, it was never exclusive, and US predominance has eroded as other suppliers have entered the market. Canada, an early alternate supplier, marketed reactors of a different design which were also favored by some recipients because they seemed more conducive to nuclear energy independence. These were heavy water moderated reactors (HWRs) which operated on natural uranium fuel and thus bypassed enrichment services and corresponding US fuel supply influence. For technical reasons, HWRs produce weapons-grade plutonium more readily than LWRs. HWRs have been favored in particular among LDCs by India, Pakistan and Argentina, and the material for India's 1974 explosion was derived from a Canadian-supplied HWR reasearch reactor. While HWRs bypass the need for enrichment services, their independent operation requires possession of heavy water production facilities. As is usually the case with spent fuel reprocessing facilities, LDCs have also needed foreign assistance in constructing heavy water plants. India quite early, and Argentina recently, however, have successfully contracted for such assistance, greatly enhancing their prospective nuclear program self-sufficiency.

Competition among nuclear suppliers became pronounced in the 1970s, making it easier for LDCs to purchase technology on less restrictive terms. Ironically, the new suppliers — particularly in Western Europe — were offering in some cases US-licensed technology, particularly LWRS, in competition with the US companies from which the licenses originated. But the critical erosion in the once commanding US export position was due to the development of surplus uranium-enrichment capacity both in the Soviet Union and Western Europe. This undermined the US monopoly of LEU exports and correspondingly reduced its influence in the realm of international nuclear cooperation.[9] It has been an important foreign

---

8. Goldschmidt and Kratzer, *op. cit.*
9. Thomas L. Neff and Henry D. Jacoby, "Nonproliferation Strategy in a Changing Nuclear Fuel Market," *Foreign Affairs*, Summer 1979, pp. 1123-1143.

policy concern of the more advanced nuclear LDCs to encourage the continuing diversification of nuclear suppliers so as to minimize dependence, or political vulnerability to unilateral pressures from the US or any other nuclear supplier, based on technological inequality.

DEVELOPING COUNTRY PERSPECTIVES ON INTERNATIONAL CHALLENGES

The Dependency Syndrome

The dependency syndrome is a political expression of the late-industrializing regions of the world, a frame of mind colored by the nationalist struggle by former colonies and protectorates for independence from imperial powers. Most LDC governing elites today share beliefs that their national aspirations for industrialization, economic growth and political modernization are impeded by structural factors in the international political and economic systems. These factors are supposedly rooted in a highly inegalitarian world distribution of power and wealth which violates the norms of international law and univeral conceptions of justice. Moreover, those structural factors have a self-perpetuating character; they follow the iron law of "he who has, gets." Typically, the more powerful industrialized states protect or expand their interests at the expense of the weak.

As it became evident after decolonization that formal sovereignty was no panacea for the problems of development, the new LDC elites often fastened on economic factors in their relations with former colonial powers, or in the international trading system, as the chief obstacles to consolidating the substance of independence. The factors perpetuating dependency persisted beneath the surface, making formal independence a seemingly hollow accomplishment. Real independence and national power would come, they believed, only after economic sovereignty was achieved. Since the impediments were structural, politics and power were needed for their demolition. Political approaches had a domestic side, usually some mixture of nationalization of foreign assets, and public ownership, planning and investment of national resources. But political remedies also had to incorporate elements of foreign policy, especially defenses against retaliation from foreign corporations and their states of origin for acts of nationalization, and measures to promote access to capital, technology and resources, high prices for commodity and primary good exports, and eventually access to foreign markets for manufactured goods produced by the LDC in question.

While there is no doubt that profound economic and political dependencies have not only characterized relations between industrialized countries and LDCs but will continue to do so for some time, there have also been important international political and structural factors which in effect provide LDCs with assets and opportunities for gradually overcoming economic weaknesses. Taking advantage of these assets and opportunities, however, can necessitate assiduous attention to foreign policy. Influence is seldom a one-way street, even in blatantly dependent relationships, because of the constancy of national competition in world politics over security, political and economic stakes, and because the industrialized countries are at odds with each other in many different ways.

The primary postwar cleavage, of course, is East-West — between the Soviet Union and its allies on one hand and the NATO, OECD countries and some LDCs on the other. Within the Western family, however, there are also various forms of vigorous political and economic competition with the US by the new economic superpowers (West Germany and Japan), the former colonial and secondary nuclear powers (the UK and France), the European Community, and other individually important states or groups of states. Even within the Soviet European bloc, significant divergencies exist and may eventually become more pronounced. Industrialized region differences are reflected in the maintenance or development of distinctively preferential relationships with major LDCs or developing regions, and such competition provides fertile ground for LDCs to play an important role in setting the price for the cooperation or exchange they are in a postion to withhold. The flourishing of the "power diffusion" literature, though its focus is essentially on the decline in relative power of the US, is itself an indicator of the inexorability of the trend toward decentralizaiton of political power and related economic capabilities.

As a substantive matter, nuclear technology has been a relatively minor consideration for most LDCs in coming to grips with their economic dependency problems, but it has nonetheless attained a disproportionate dependency-related symbolic importance.[10] For a small minority of LDCs, nuclear technology has represented an important investment and within them an indispensable focus of livelihood and professional opportunity for the associated technical elite, usually composed of public servants who are associated with or outspoken on national planning issues. Naturally, technocrats have a stake in justifying their activity and in ensuring that it flourishes, and they become adept at linking their domain with the feelings aroused by dependency issues in domestic politics and foreign policy. A second reason is that nuclear technology is "high technology" and the latter is intuitively associated with those industrial and scientific capabilities which by their very nature can eliminate dependency, or at least transform it into more tolerable relationships of interdependence. Finally, of course, there lurks along with the presumption that all forms of dependency are rooted in power structure another presumption that possession of nuclear weapons fundamentally conditions the power structure among nations. The symbolic issues have been particularly important to the larger LDCs which (like France) have declined to join the NPT — especially India, Argentina, Brazil

---

10. See George Quester, "INFCE and the Less Developed Countries," in Rodney W. Jones, *Next Steps After INFCE: U.S. International Nuclear and Nonproliferation Policy* (A Report for the U.S. Department of Energy, by the Georgetown University Center for Strategic and International Studies), Washington, D.C., March 1980, pp. 201-250; Munir Ahmad Khan, *Nuclear Energy and International Cooperation: A Third World Perception of the Erosion of Confidence* (for the International Consultative Group on Nuclear Energy), New York and London: The Rockefeller Foundation/Royal Institute of International Affairs, 1979; Peter Clausen, "Nuclear Conference Yields Potential New Consensus," *Arms Control Today*, Vol, 9, No. 6, June 1979, pp. 1-4.

and Yugoslavia—and also to some that have joined.

Repercussions of the Oil Crisis

OPEC's sudden transformation of the international petroleum system in 1973-74 had a number of important consequences for LDC foreign policy calculations and, in the case of several, for the nuclear factor in their foreign relations. It gave enormous impetus of course to the collective use of LDC power in international economic relations, a point we take up in the next section. More important for our purposes here was the dual effect of the skyrocketing prices of oil and the political embargo on supplies to certain countries or perceptions around the world of future energy prices and security of access to this energy resource. Energy security suddenly entered the national security lexicon.[11]

Prior to the 1973-74 oil crisis, the cost of nuclear power generating technology—despite supplier subsidies and competition for sales—had kept electricity generated by conventional power plants at a decided price advantage over nuclear power in most parts of the world. With the four-fold rise of oil prices over a few months and the possibility—since borne out—that oil prices would continue to spiral upwards—it was thought at first that nuclear generation of electricity would attain a major price differential in its favor. In addition, because of the extraordinary resource-consuming efficiency of nuclear power, nuclear resource embargoes were unlikely to be as effective as those of oil, or at least would permit diversification among a wider variety of suppliers. In some oil-poor countries, India for example, nuclear fuels also existed in substantial if not abundant quantities. As it turned out, however, no dramatic price differential in favor of nuclear power materialized, but the perception of needs to reinsure or diversify energy supply remained.

Since nuclear technology prices also rose—and nuclear alternatives continued in any event to have the drawback of long lead times for installation—there was no headlong rush by oil-poor LDCs into nuclear power purchases. Instead, ironically, there was a surge in nuclear development and new interest by oil-exporting countries, which also had new revenues to put into such expensive technology. Iran, for example, soon unveiled grandiose plans for the installation of a dozen or more huge power reactors. A highly questionable investment in light of Iran's abundant gas reserves, it was drastically curtailed in 1979 following the Islamic revolution. Others including Libya, Saudi Arabia and Iraq were less conspicuous or more cautious in exploring nuclear technology. Interest blossomed however even in Venezuela, another major OPEC member. Though nuclear energy planning in Mexico predates recent disclosures of much larger national oil reserves, Mexico continues to place considerable emphasis on nuclear power development. In addition, augmented oil producer revenues in the Middle East may have given birth to a new pattern—the financing of nuclear technology acquisition by politically favored oil-poor LDCs, e.g., for Pakistan's uranium enrichment program.

---

11. David Deese, "Energy: Economics, Politics and Security," *International Security,* Winter 1979/80, pp. 140 ff.

The North-South Dialogue Context

Nuclear technology has not been in the mainstream of the North-South dialogue on international economic relations, partly because the divisive nuclear issues by consensus have had more to do with arms control than economics, and functional issues have been compartmentalized in separate international agencies and conference fora. The mainstream North-South economic issues have been dealt with since 1964 by the Group of 77 and UN Commision on Trade and Development (UNCTAD) and the political issues by the Non-Aligned Movement (NAM) for an even longer period beginning with the 1955 Bandung Conference. Nuclear issues germane to LDCs have normally been embodied in the IAEA (or its predecessor), the United Nations Committees on Disarmament, and the NPT negotiation and review conferences.

LDC interest in the use of collective pressure to achieve economic objectives gained enormous momentum with OPEC support and demonstration of resource cartel power, and resulted in the systematic reformulation of demands for a New International Economic Order (NIEO). Only one section of thoese demands—pertaining to "technology transfer"—directly covered nuclear technology; NIEO was more concerned with restructuring trade, international financial institutions, foreign assistance, and the behavior of multinational corporations.

Recent offshoots from the North-South dialogue mainstream, however, suggest that nuclear technology issues may become somewhat more central to LDC concerns and collective organization. Iran hosted an international conference on nuclear energy at Persepolis in April 1977, following the 1975 NPT Review Conference. A major grievance expressed at Persepolis was LDC disenchantment with industrialized country interpretations of the NPT, in particular Article IV.[12] More recently, Yugoslavia, India, Argentina, and Indonesia are reported to have formed an LDC coordinating group on nuclear technology, while Yugoslavia proposed a United Nations conference on nuclear energy to follow the 1980 NPT Review Conference and to provide an alternative forum for LDC complaints about discrimination in nuclear technology transfer. Unlike the NPT conference forum, the UN conference will lend itself to participation by those more vocal, nuclear-capable LDCs which have refused to join the NPT. But the date set for the UN conference, scheduled for 1983, will put some distance between it and the NPT Review Conference.

International Security and Arms Control

Managing international security in the nuclear era, paradoxically, unites as well as divides the major powers. Driven by a mixture of insecurity and self-assertion, the superpowers augment and diversify nuclear armaments in a process that some label "vertical proliferation," yet acknowledge a common security imperative of avoiding nuclear warfare. Thus they adopt postures of strategic deterrence and, to assure stability in mutual deterrence, negotiated arms control. The

---

12. Article IV of the NPT includes the undertaking among treaty members to disseminate nuclear information and technology for peaceful purposes.

resulting nuclear stalemate provides a nuclear security umbrella over superpower allies on either side of the European divide, and selectively elsewhere, in respective superpower spheres of influence. Inhibitions on nuclear warfare are paralleled by mutual superpower interests in crisis management, to avert direct collisions between their military forces and, above all, to prevent escalation to the nuclear level. The very self-consciousness of superpower nuclear restraint, of course, highlights the persistence of deep military and political competition conducted in developing regions by means of the enlistment of allies, securing of geopolitical access, far-flung deployment of naval forces, unilateral military intervention, arms transfers and use of proxy military or paramilitary forces.

From the standpoint of LDCs, great power competition and security managment represent mixed blessings. Most appreciate the nuclear stalemate not only because it implies avoidance of a nuclear holocaust but because it also constrains unbridled aggression by the great powers against developing regions. Some LDCs now benefit from or eventually hope to get protection from the extension of superpower nuclear umbrellas outside Europe. On the other hand, many LDCs find their own interests adversely affected by the way the superpower nuclear stalemate influences the propensity for superpower involvement in developing regions. Weaker LDCs which fear the regional domination of a more powerful neighboring LDC may look hopefully or in vain to one or another great industrial power as a protector, while the corresponding regional power may resent overtures by its weaker neighbor in search of foreign protection. Witnessing the moderating of superpower competition or tendencies toward condominium that accompany detente, many LDCs also resent the resulting diminished competition with economic and financial assistance for their favor. In some cases, LDCs may even be tempted to manipulate local tensions to stimulate or revive desultory great power rivalry, so as to improve their own bargaining positions on economic or regional issues.

Such crosscutting interests make for varied LDC responses to global and regional arms control efforts. Most LDCs take nuclear arms control proposals seriously, not necessarily as conflict-resolving panaceas but rather as limited tools useful for security managment and as means of diplomatic counterpressure on the great powers. The utility of arms control restraints are assessed by LDCs in terms of how they affect the principal strategic balance, regional security relationships, and the interconnections between global and regional security conditions. They are assessed, too, in terms of their consequences for political and economic relationships at both levels. LDCs, however, measure arms control arrangements, much as developed countries do, in terms of how their own specific interests are advanced or undermined in these intersecting issue areas.

The global nuclear nonproliferation regime that was built around IAEA safeguards and the NPT in the 1960s attracted broad though by no means universal LDC participation and support.[13] In the

---

13. See William Epstein, *The Last Chance, op. cit.,* and Enid Schoettle, *Postures for Non-Proliferation: Arms Limitation and Security Policies to Minimize Nuclear Proliferation,* Stockholm International Peace Research Institute, New York, 1979.

course of NPT negotiations, a number of important bargains were struck, reflecting LDC interests in principles of equality, balanced obligation, or equity. Formally, of course, the NPT is an unequal treaty in that it recognizes the existence of nuclear weapon states (WS) but seeks to freeze their number at five, including China (the only LDC so defined). Other parties to the treaty, the non-nuclear weapon state (NNWS), undertake to relinquish a sovereign option, that of developing nuclear weapons, and to accept fullscope IAEA safeguards that verify their compliance. WS are not required to accept IAEA safeguards on their domestic facilities, though the US, UK and even France have voluntarily offered to place their civilian facilities under IAEA safeguards. Nonproliferation by definition perpetuates the WS-NNWS distinction, and it is in that sense that the NPT is necessarily unequal. The bargains struck, therefore, could not balance obligations equally, i.e., make them legally identical for both sets of states, but could go a long way toward making them equivalent in import and therefore equitable in practical terms.

In exchange for the NNWS undertaking not to acquire nuclear weapons, the NPT imposes obligations on the weapon states to engage in negotiations to cease their own nuclear arms acquisition (so-called "vertical proliferation") and to reduce or eventually eliminate their nuclear arms stockpiles. Thus there is a mandate in the NPT for arms control measures such as those associated with strategic arms limitation (SALT), mutual and balanced force reductions by NATO and the Warsaw Pack (MBFR), bans or limits on the testing of nuclear weapons, and the current negotiations on a comprehensive nuclear test ban (CTB).

A second important NPT obligation is the undertaking to disseminate or facilitate the exchange of nuclear information, cooperation and technology among all treaty members for peaceful purposes. NNWS which have accepted the nonproliferation restrictions naturally believe they should be treated as reliable recipients of peaceful nuclear assistance. This obligation to disseminate peaceful nuclear information and technology is shared by all NPT parties, not just by weapon states, but its material impact was greatest on the weapon states. Their interest in freezing the geographical spread of weapons might otherwise be expected to inhibit their willingness to offer such cooperation, and they have been among the relatively few states which possessed technology worth disseminating.

Both treaty obligations were important to developed NNWS as well as to LDCs, on energy cooperation as well as arms control grounds. They were not, therefore, explicitly North-South issues. Industrial countries without nuclear weapons such as Japan, West Germany, Italy, Belgium, Sweden and Switzerland were just as interested in strategic arms limitation and flourishing nuclear energy cooperation as the most vocal LDCs, but there were undoubtedly some differences in perceptions. LDCs were concerned that the industrialized European countries and Japan would be favored by the Western weapon states through nuclear cooperation, with a similar pattern on the Soviet and East European side, as a result of alliance relationships as well as because of higher absorptive capacity for advanced technology. In short, the nuclear-capable LDCs feared *de facto* discrimination. This perception figured centrally in the justifications several nuclear-capable LDCs, including India, Brazil and Argentina, issued to explain why they ultimately decided not to subscribe to the NPT even on a conditional basis.

Shortly after the NPT came into the force in 1970, the international oil crisis of 1973 and India's nuclear explosion of 1974 placed nuclear cooperation in a new perspective. The Indian explosion showed how "civilian" nuclear facilities could be used for explosive or military purposes.[14] Fear of oil shortages looked as though it might lead a variety of countries to impulsively acquire nuclear technology, including what came to be known as sensitive facilities — the plants incorporating enrichment and reprocessing technologies for the production or recovery of fissile material. South Korea, Taiwan and Pakistan sought reprocessing technology from France, and West Germany concluded a huge contract with Brazil in 1975 for the sale of reactors with enrichment and reprocessing facilities for a full fuel cycle. These developments reflected the growth of commercial competition among nuclear suppliers. They led both to nuclear export policy reviews and to informal, initially secret, coordination among the suppliers, meeting in London, to reduce the proliferation risks of their competition for nuclear sales.

What emerged was the Nuclear Suppliers Group (NSG), which developed lists of sensitive technology and export guidelines. Its members, all developed countries, agreed to take account of the guidelines as conditions of sale in their export policies. The result was neither quite a nuclear cartel of advanced countries nor an embargo of nuclear technology to LDCs, but something which to LDCs had the appearances of both.[15] In practical terms, NSG export restraints fell most heavily on LDCs.

Although LDCs broadly may feel they have reasons to resent the NSG's barriers to nuclear technology transfer, the irony is that the barriers most acutely affect those LDCs which are nuclear have-nots, and least affect the nuclear-capable LDCs, where sensitive technology acquisition is in several cases a *fait accompli*. Moreover, this distinction between nuclear have-nots and nuclear-capable LDCs partly coincides with propensity to join or reject the NPT respectively. As a result, NSG restraints on nuclear dissemination theoretically affect LDCs which are NPT members more adversely than those which are not. This point is naturally contentious among NPT members since it challenges the nondiscrimination principle as it applies to members. On the other hand, it does not discriminate against NPT non-members *per se*, and thus provides no incentive to recalcitrants to join the treaty.

Indeed, the emergence of the NSG tended to confirm the suspicions of most NPT holdouts in developing areas that the nonproliferation regime based upon that treaty would be employed by the developed countries as another means of

---

14. John Maddox, "Prospects for Nuclear Proliferation," *Adelphi Papers* No. 113, London: International Institute for Strategic Studies, 1975.
15. Steven J. Baker, "Commercial Nuclear Power and Nuclear Proliferation", Cornell University Peace Studies Program, Ithaca: Cornell University, May 1975, and his "Nuclear Proliferation: Monopoly or Cartel?," *Foreign Policy*, Summer 1976, pp. 202–220.

perpetuating economic and technological dependencies among the LDCs. In such cases, LDC foreign policies have frequently included among their strategies efforts to evade, reform or even overthrow the NPT nonproliferation regime. The last approach, overthrowing the regime, has only rarely been pursued, however, since most LDCs value nonproliferation restraints on others even when they seek in individual cases to except themselves or develop a nuclear weapons option. Consequently, while LDC disenchantment with the limited results of strategic arms control negotiations and irritation with supplier restrictions on nuclear transfers was forcefully expressed in the 1975 NPT Review Conference, the validity of the treaty was ultimately upheld without defections. Pressure for reform of the NPT regime may be sharper in August 1980, at the second NPT Review Conference, however, because of accumulating LDC resentment that the obligations of the weapon states and advanced nuclear states are not being met or, as evidenced by the NSG, are actually being violated. The currently dismal outlook for SALT II completion and resumption of SALT III and MBFR negotiations may strengthen these negative perceptions of the NPT bargain.

An important early example of LDC initiative in reforming or supplementing the NPT regime on a regional basis is the Treaty of Tlatelolco, which was concluded as NPT negotiations reached their final state in the late 1960s.[16] It is the foundation for a nuclear weapons free zone (NFZ) in the Latin American region. Most Latin American countries (22 in number) are full members of the Tlatelolco arrangement, but four are not, including Argentina, Brazil, Chile, and Cuba. None of the four are NPT members either. Brazil originally was an enthusiastic sponsor of Tlatelolco and has both signed and ratified the treaty, but with the proviso that it would come into force for Brazil only when all other expected members have become full members. Chile's position is similar to Brazil's. Argentina was lukewarm from the outset, signed but did not ratify the treaty in 1967, and only in 1977 announced its intent to ratify — a step that has yet to be completed. If Argentina does ratify and Cuba joins, and if certain protocols are completed by foreign states with interests in the region, Tlatelolco would come into full force.

As a regional LDC initiative in which the obligations under the treaty are formally equal, Tlatelolco may be a more palatable arrangement for some of its members than the NPT. The relative success of Tlatelolco has not, however, been duplicated in the Middle East, Indian Ocean region, South Asia or other regions proposed as NFZs. It may well be that the relative insulation of Latin America from great power geopolitical rivalry, in contrast to these other troubled regions, was a necessary condition for Tlatelolco. Moreover, a crucial impetus for the Tlatelolco initiative was the 1962 Cuban missile crisis, precisely because it threatened to entrench US-Soviet strategic nuclear competition in the hemisphere. Protocols signed by all the recognized nuclear weapons states, by which they undertake not to

---

16. See John R. Redick, "Latin America: Policy Options Following INFCE," in Jones, *Next Steps After INFCE, op. cit.*, pp. 271–340; Alfonso Garcia Robles, *The Latin American Nuclear-Weapon Free Zone*, The Stanley Foundation, Occasional Paper No. 19, May 1979.

introduce nuclear weapons into the region nor threaten states in the region with the use of nuclear weapons, are essential underpinnings of the Tlatelolco arrangement. The composite effect of the protocols is a substitute in the region for the concept of direct nuclear guarantees of protection that some LDCs sought without success from the superpowers as a condition for joining the NPT.

Conventional arms control presents a challenge of different character to LDCs.[17] While most LDCs have supported nuclear arms control and nonproliferation sufficiently to allow the evolution of a regime resting on the IAEA, NPT and Tlatelolco, they are typically opposed to great power or regional schemes designed to systematically control the flow of conventional armaments to developing countries. Conventional arms, of course, are not so stigmatized as nuclear arms, and (as Kolodziej and Harkavy discuss in this volume) are vigorously pursued by LDCs, normally for authentic security reasons, albeit often at some economic sacrifice. Yet the country suppliers of sophisticated conventional arms are largely identical with the commercial suppliers of advanced nuclear technology, are few, and are concentrated in the industrialized world. Thus LDCs perceive a structural dependency in conventional arms transactions that impinges on vital security interests and that conceivably can be manipulated in tandem with nuclear and economic cooperation to impose undesired political conditions.

Fortunately from the LDC standpoint, the major suppliers have never achieved sufficient agreement on the desirability or mechanisms of controlling conventional arms transfer to establish anything resembling the institutions of the nonproliferation regime. Strenuous US-Soviet competition for geopolitical influence blocked Western efforts to achieve arms transfer restrictions in specific regions, such as the Middle East, where the Soviet-Czech arms deal with Egypt in 1955 punctured multilateral restraint. Competition by Western European countries for arms sales has also become increasingly intense, particularly since the 1973 oil price escalation and mounting pressure on industrial economies to expand exports to pay for energy. President Carter's hopeful unilateral and multilateral arms transfer restraint initiatives foundered on a combination of such pressures which were greatly intensified by joint Soviet and Cuban military intervention in the Horn of Africa in late 1977 and the recent events in Iran and Afghanistan.

Nonetheless, conventional arms transfers to LDCs have not been unbridled, partly because most LDCs (the new oil-rich excepted) have not had the wherewithal to purchase large quantities of sophisticated arms on cash-and-carry terms. Since credit or concessionary terms from the suppliers have usually been necessary, the suppliers have either had the opportunity or have been forced to make choices in the recipients they supply. Under these conditions, suppliers have applied policy judgement which vary over

---

17. For a recent review of related issues, see Michael Moodie, *Sovereignty, Security, and Arms,* The Washington Papers, No. 67 (Center for Strategic and International Studies, Georgetown University), Beverly Hills, California, 1979.

time but normally reflect a mixture of unilateral restraint and selectivity as well as commercial competition. Hence, for strategic or political reasons, some LDCs have been favored and others have not, resulting in untidy and changing but nonetheless discernible patterns of arms transfer restrictions.

LDCs that have been deprived or disadvantaged by conventional arms transfer restrictions naturally seek to lift or overcome them. Since there is no central regime of restrictions, it is difficult to assault them frontally. Moreover, as is true among nuclear-capable LDCs on nonproliferation issues, some LDCs desire arms restraint on their neighbors even while they seek to evade it on themselves. Hence, LDC policies designed to cope with arms transfer restrictions are sometimes subtle and complex. It should occasion no surprise, therefore, to find nuclear-capable LDCs which tacitly link nuclear development policies with their interests in conventional arms acquisition in some circumstances.

NUCLEAR ASSETS AND FOREIGN POLICY STRATEGIES OF DEVELOPING COUNTRIES

In virtually all those LDCs where nuclear assets are sufficient to impinge on foreign policy, nuclear policies tend to be developed by a narrow circle of technical specialists, under relatively secret conditions and typically with little informed legislative or public debate. Within limits, there are still variations among them in openness of nuclear decisionmaking and also in how central nuclear issues are to foreign policy. NPT members are the most open as a rule, but there are significant exceptions such as Iraq and Libya. More pluralistic, industrially advanced LDCs such as India, Yugoslavia, Brazil, Argentina and Mexico permit or even take pride in some public discussion and ostensibly maintain open relationships of international nuclear cooperation. Countries faced with urgent security problems or elements of international ostracism, such as Israel, South Africa, Taiwan, and even Pakistan, have generally placed tight restrictions on nuclear issues. Cuba and Vietnam have shut off their societies even more fundamentally from international scrutiny. Occasionally, when domestic politicization of nuclear issues occurs — as was the case in India following China's first nuclear explosion in 1964 or in Pakistan in recent years — those issues naturally become more prominent in foreign policy as well.

Issue Linkage Opportunities

As the nuclear capabilities and associated personnel of LDCs expand, or as policy requirements dictate, interest grows in how nuclear factors can be applied to foreign policy purposes. Apart from direct military defense applications — to which we will return below — the foreign policy utility of nuclear capabilities usually depends on whether they can be linked to other policy goals and activities. This leads LDC policymakers to explore issue linkage opportunities in what amounts to a learning process. Exploring such linkages can be open and explicit, or indirect and unstated. Issue linkages involving nuclear capabilities tend to be primarily implicit for the more secretive or internationally isolated LDCs, most explicit for a few militant LDCs which seek to exercise leadership in Third World movements, and normally a variable mixture adjusted to circumstances for the remainder.

Nuclear issue linkage strategies are likely to be most profitable to LDCs which occupy a strategic location, are rich in a scarce strategic resources, have extensive ties with a major power, or are engaged in diverse networks of international cooperation. The key to foreign policy linkages for LDCs meeting one or more of these conditions is to make what they actually do, might do, or could refrain from doing with their nuclear programs, conditional, i.e., linked to desired responses from major powers, local neighbors or the international community on other matters. The settings in which issue linkages are established can be bilateral, multilateral, or some combination of both, and the gains LDCs seek by linking such issues can be psychic or material, open-ended or specific.

The Struggle for Autonomy

All states share a political imperative of striving for increased autonomy. Among LDCs, the quest fundamentally depends on setting in motion and successfully managing the processes of political, military, and economic modernization. As is true among developed countries, the level of autonomy that can be expected in a world where trends favor increased interdependence will depend in part on the original size, resources and social cohesion of the LDC in question. Policies of self-conscious isolationism may in certain cases — such as that of China under the leadership of Mao Ze-dong or Vietnam currently — maximize political autonomy for a time, albeit at the expense of other aims. But over the long term the preferred form of autonomy for most LDCs is likely to be the capacity to balance the domestic impact of the outside world with the exercise of compensatory external influence, by drawing up internal strength from active participation in international trade, finance, politics, diplomacy, and institutions.

Gaining external credibility and influence in bilateral relationships with particular states can be facilitated by participation in international institutions and organizations (see Rothstein in this volume). These centralize a great deal of diplomatic deliberation, functional activity, and intelligence information, and provide avenues of potential access to the centers of national decisionmaking. Access to the United Nations family of organizations can be particularly important to small developed states and most LDCs as a means of concentrating their limited numbers of professional diplomatic and technical representatives in locations where their counterparts from other nations congregate, information is rapidly disseminated and negotiations can be conducted constantly or initiated on short notice.

A pecking order of relative status, influence and reputational qualities naturally develops in international institutional fora as the composite effect of the interplay of many factors. A state's resourcefulness and expertise on technical issues, including those of a science and technology, can be one such factor. LDC nuclear expertise can affect international decisionmaking not only in the nuclear energy and safeguards forum of the IAEA but in a broad range of development and resource allocation issues. It can intersect with the whole spectrum of industrial and energy issues, mineral exploration, international communications, food production, medicine, and transportation. It can influence outcomes of debates over international allocation of development finance, multilateral energy cooperation, regulation of trade, management of ocean or seabed resources, distribution of communications frequencies and slots in geostationary orbits. Nuclear-capable LDCs are better equipped to challenge the technical arguments and policy positions of developed states on equal terms, and to organize coalitions of less expert LDCs on matters of common interest in international negotiating fora. These same advantages can be brought to bear within Third World diplomatic forums ranging from the Group of 77 and NAM to the Organization of African states and the Alliance of South East Asian Nations.

Realizing autonomy goals may be facilitated by influence in international institutions, but the decisive payoffs often materialize in bilateral transactions. Manipulation of nuclear policies can improve an LDC's opportunities to manage interdependent relationships at its end, even though its recipient status may imply asymmetry in those relationships. Four techniques of structuring nuclear cooperation have been used with some success by the large nuclear-capable LDCs to improve their autonomy and bilateral bargaining positions with major powers. One is the deliberate cultivation of diverse ties of nuclear cooperation by purchasing research facilities, power reactors, fuel, fuel services and fuel cycle facilities from several suppliers instead of a single supplier, even when this approach is less economically efficient than standardizing domestic nuclear technology around supplies from a single source normally would be. A second is to invest in sensitive technology and other nuclear options despite the fact that related services can be purchased at much lower cost. The third is to become a seller of nuclear technology and services to other LDCs, even in a modest way. And, fourth, there are signs of incipient LDC peaceful nuclear cooperation on regional lines.

Only the larger or richer nuclear-capable countries have been able to pursue such strategies, but the process is gathering momentum. India was an early leader in the diversification and sensitive technology approaches, purchasing research and power reactors separately from the U.S. and Canada (while negotiating with France and Britain), obtaining heavy water supplies from the US, Canada and most recently the Soviet Union, purchasing heavy water production technology from Germany and France, and cooperating with France on fast-breeder reactor research.[18] Both India and Argentina began reprocessing facilities very early. Mexico and Brazil based their initial nuclear investments on US technology, but Brazil agreed to commit huge investments at the next stage to West Germany when the latter agreed in 1975 to include sensitive technology in a package deal, and Mexico in the last two years has system-

---

18. Ashok Kapur, *India's Nuclear Option, op. cit.,* is revealing on this point. See also Roberta Wohlstetter, *The Buddha Smiles: Absent-Minded Peaceful Aid and the Indian Bomb* (prepared for Energy Research and Development Administration), Los Angeles, April 30, 1977.

atically explored new nuclear cooperation opportunities with Canada, France, Germany, Sweden, Italy and Japan.[19] Supplier diversification and sensitive technology acquisition strategies have also been employed by Iran, South Korea, and South Africa. The LDC strategy of breaking the advanced nuclear supplier monopoly by bidding for nuclear supply contracts has been led by Argentina which is currently providing two research reactors and allied assistance to Peru.[20] Reportedly, India has been engaged in low-key nuclear supplier cooperation with Iraq, Argentina, Iran, Vietnam, and even Libya.[21] The most dramatic evidence of incipient regional nuclear cooperation for peaceful purposes came in May 1980 with the announcement of an agreement between Brazil and Argentina to conduct bilateral nuclear cooperation on a wide front.[22]

These LDC strategies reduce recipient vulnerability to pressures from advanced nuclear suppliers on nuclear policies, but the counterbargaining positions they create can be implicitly linked to other issues. For Brazil and Argentina, adjustments in nuclear policies and their recent commitment to direct bilateral peaceful nuclear cooperation are potentially useful for deflecting pressure from the U.S. on human rights grounds to liberalize their political systems. It is not unlikely that Chile and perhaps South Korea will also adopt similar approaches, and it is probably a consideration in the South African nuclear program.

Nuclear issue linkages for Mexico potentially focus on its growing role as an oil and natural gas supplier and industrialization options in which it hopes to benefit from its proximity to the U.S. and Canada but escape highly asymmetrical patterns of dependency. Hence it seeks to diversify not only its recipient relationships with nuclear suppliers but also its oil supply relationships with industrialized oil-importing countries. Deals in one sphere are made with an eye on the return flow of benefits in other spheres. Venezuela's relatively new interest in domestic development may reflect appreciation of Mexico's strategy of implicitly linking the two energy sources, in the interests of autonomy, industrialization and accumulation of regional influence.

LDCs which are rapidly industrializing but are deficient in conventional resources have to consider their autonomy not only from the industrialized countries but also from OPEC members. Although Argentina is favored by potentially self-sufficient domestic energy reserves of oil, gas and hydroelectric power, Brazil, India, South Korea, Taiwan, Israel and South Africa depend to a significant degree on petroleum imports. As the prices of internationally traded oil continue to spiral and security of access to supplies is disrupted by political instability such as the Iranian revolution, the balance of payments pressures and uncertainties cause setbacks to industrialization programs. Temptations mount in nuclear-capable LDCs to consider providing sensitive nuclear technology

---

19. John R. Redick, "Latin America," *op. cit.*
20. *Ibid.*
21. John Maddox, "Prospects for Nuclear Proliferation," *op. cit.;* Rodney W. Jones, "Nuclear Proliferation in South Asia?," *op. cit.,* and "Restraining Nuclear Proliferation in South Aisa" in Jones, *Next Steps After INFCE, op. cit.,* pp. 375–428.
22. *Financial Times,* January 30, 1980.

to oil-producing countries to stabilize prices and bilateral terms of access.

There have been reports of efforts by Iraq and Libya to use oil blackmail against Brazil and India, respectively, to obtain nuclear assistance that is presumably denied on policy grounds by established suppliers. Under these conditions, India, Brazil and others may try to exact their own price, for refusing to comply with blackmail, from those countries that have strong interests either in seeing the blackmail fail or in the efficacy of nonproliferation measures. Alternatively, an unregulated nuclear black market sponsored by LDC nuclear suppliers may expand and undermine international security associated with the nonproliferation regime.[23]

Security Strategies

It is the potential in nuclear technology for inflicting sudden massive destruction that makes nuclear policy exceptionally sensitive and rich in influence, even when the national capabilities seem quite embryonic. The fear of such consequences underlies the logic of nuclear deterrence, and explains the corresponding appeal of nuclear weapons to insecure countries. Whether the security gains from deploying nuclear weapons are worthwhile from this perspective may depend on various factors, including the numbers and orientation of other nuclear-armed powers in the environment, and the relative capacity of each to survive in some fashion the consequences of a nuclear exchange. Such factors are, of course, subject to change over time.

Theoretically, the desirable posture for a state which develops nuclear weapons for independent defense purposes is to procure a limited, survivable force and rely on the threat of credible retaliation, rather than preemption, so as to foster stable mutual deterrence. Achieving such a posture is conceivable for the larger or richer nuclear-capable LDCs against similar countries, but only after considerable time, effort and expense. Bear in mind, however, that the theoretical appeal of deterrence draws on the history of the two-way relationship between the superpowers. Despite the late emergence of a triangular strategic nuclear relationship among the US, China and the Soviet Union, it is clear that the Chinese leg is much shorter than the other two. There is little experience upon which LDCs therefore can draw to determine how stable the interaction of more than two antagonistic nuclear equals would be, not to speak of interaction among nuclear-armed LDCs in various stages of military evolution.

Since it is still difficult today for LDCs to rapidly achieve a posture of reliable nuclear deterrence, and because the path toward such a momentous decision also typically is fraught with high risks, uncertainty and indecisiveness, most experience thus far is with the halfway nuclear policies of LDCs. Such policies of "lingering on the threshold" tend to provide the state in question with the technical options to construct and usually to deliver nuclear weapons, and may go so far as to demonstrate the weapons option to the world in unmistakable terms — as India did with its 1974

---

23. Lewis Dunn, "Half Past India's Bank," *Foreign Policy,* No. 26, Fall 1979, pp. 71–88.

nuclear explosion. But such policies normally stop short of actually constructing and deploying nuclear weapons, and thus preserve an aura of ambiguity. That ambiguity is useful insofar as it avoids provoking a neighbor to take matching steps leading to a local nuclear arms race, deflects nonproliferation policy pressures mounted by the major powers, buys desired time to augment indigenous technological or military capabilities and permits the state in question to advocate arms control, nonproliferation or tension-reduction measures in international fora without facing charges of blatant hypocrisy.

Ambiguous policies also carry other potential advantages. They attract the attention and concern of the major and neighboring powers to the implied erosion of international security or the potential opportunities for gains in geopolitical influence that may redound to their opponents. Consequently, ambiguous nuclear policies put the host state into a new bargaining position where the major powers may have incentives to provide political support, security assistance and other benefits, or conversely to relax sanctions or policies of interference, in an effort to persuade the host state to refrain from open proliferation or acts of regional destabilization. Moreover, the gains from the adoption of ambiguous nuclear policies by one state have demonstration effects on others.

Ambiguous nuclear policies can also entail significant costs to the host state. Ambiguous policies risk precipitating *un*ambiguous nuclear program responses from less inhibited, anxious neighbors. Moreover, the major powers may or may not sympathetically responsive to the new bargaining chips of the host state. They may instead perceive their interests to lie in extending assistance or security guarantees to the opponents of the host state, to preserve some semblance of regional balance, or to face the host state with implicit threats of escalating costs in order to deter new steps across the nuclear weapons threshold. In short, ambiguous nuclear policies can have ambivalent consequences; they may ultimately increase rather than decrease the host state's dependence on external powers for its security and welfare.

Implicit LDC experimentation with nuclear security policies has been sufficiently extensive and varied to provide case illustrations of the following strategies and aims: (1) strategic deterrence of invasion or preemptive attack; (2) overcoming vulnerability to political blackmail by a nuclear-armed opponent; (3) fortifying regional preeminence and deterring direct or indirect superpower regional intervention; (4) compelling a sympathetic superpower to provide or maintain a local nuclear umbrella; and (5) bargaining for conventional military assistance.

While China best exemplifies LDC adoption of a classical independent nuclear deterrence posture, India and Pakistan in South Asia and Israel in the Middle East have moved in the same general direction. India's principal and long-range deterrent concern has been the potential nuclear threat from China and related fears of political blackmail.[24] After the US "tilt" toward Pakistan (to minimize the repercussions of the Bangladesh war

---

24. Wayne A. Wilcox, *Nuclear Weapons Options and the Strategic Environment in South Asia: Arms Control Implications for India,* Southern California Arms Control and Foreign Policy Seminar, June 1971.

in 1971), an additional Indian interest probably was to elevate the risks to the US of future intervention in the affairs of the subcontinent and thereby to consolidate India's preeminent regional influence.[25]

India's ambitions were complicated by Pakistan's quest for its own nuclear deterrent, which got underway soon after the events of 1971 (not waiting, as is often supposed, until after India's 1974 explosion).[26] Pakistan's recently disclosed secret effort to produce an atomic bomb with uranium enrichment technology seems likely to trigger a local nuclear arms race.[27]

Israel is presumed to have developed, for deterrent purposes, a small inventory of nuclear weapons after the 1967 war, and possibly contemplated threatening to use them in the 1973 war. In this case, the apparent deterrent utility is against conventional invasion, not an external nuclear threat. As the probable author of nuclear policy ambiguity, Israel is presumed to store unassembled nuclear weapons components instead of complete weapons in order to maintain its official posture that is will not be the first state to introduce nuclear weapons into the region.[28] Short air distances between Israel and key urban centers in neighboring states, combined with Israel's high performance aircraft and reputation for technical proficiency, make Israel's small nuclear deterrent highly credible. Should one or more Arab opponents develop a comparable capability, however, Israel's vulnerability due to its own urban concentration and small size (except for Jerusalem, which may be immune from nuclear attack for religious reasons) could diminish the credibility of Israeli resort to nuclear weapons in response to any attack other than a nuclear one.

Both cases also illustrate other policy purposes—of security in the broadest sense. Pakistan's drive for commercial-scale enrichment as well as reprocessing technology is allegedly for peaceful purposes, but it is hard to imagine how Pakistan's small nuclear energy program could absorb the output from either planned facility. Although the journalistic coverage of the notion of an "Islamic" bomb may have been somewhat exaggerated, it is not inconceivable that Libya or certain other Arab sources would help finance and encourage Pakistan to develop nuclear technology and services and produce surplus material that could be exported to the same Arab states, or that might be used some day against Israel. More likely, however, Pakistan would hint at such

---

25. Stephen P. Cohen, *Perception, Influence and Weapons Proliferation in South Asia,* Report for the Department of State, Bureau of Intelligence and Research/External Research, August 20, 1979 (mimeo).
26. Charles K. Ebinger, "U.S. Nuclear Non-proliferation Policy: The Pakistan Controversy," *The Fletcher Forum,* Vol. III, No. 2, 1979, pp. 1–21; D.K. Palit and P.K.S. Namboodiri, *Pakistan's Islamic Bomb,* New Delhi, 1979.
27. Richard Betts, "Nuclear Proliferation and Regional Rivalry: Speculations on South Asia," *Orbis,* Spring 1979, pp. 167–184.
28. Relevant literature on Israel includes Fuad Jabber, *Israel and Nuclear Weapons: Present Option and Future Strategies,* London, 1971; Allen Doty, "Israeli Perspectives on Nuclear Proliferation" in Johan Jorgen Holst (ed.) *Security, Order and the Bomb,* Oslo, 1972, pp. 142–151; Lawrence Friedman, "Israel's Nuclear Policy," *Survival,* May/June 1975, pp. 114–120; and Yehezkel Dror, "Small Powers' Nuclear Policy: Research Methodology and Exploratory Analysis," *The Jerusalem Journal of International Relations,* Vol. 1, No. 1, Fall 1975, pp. 29–49.

nuclear supplier possibilities mainly to entice support from the oil-rich Arab states to deal with its own energy, economic and conventional security problems.

An issue of long-standing concern to India has been the possibility — indeed there have been some specific precedents since 1965 — that portions of the sophisticated arms accumulated in the Middle East oil-producing states would be transferred to Pakistan for use against India in the event of future war on the subcontinent. Using nuclear supplier leverage is, of course, a strategy that India can also use, and indeed has used on a minor scale, in the Middle East to assure oil supplies, win construction contracts, employ surplus technical and skilled personnel, and probably to preempt growing sympathy and support in the region for Pakistan.

Nuclear-tinged rivalry between India and Pakistan for favors from the Middle East predated but has probably been intensified by the repercussions of the Iranian revolution and the Soviet invasion of Afghanistan. The latter development also magnified the bargaining opportunities for India and Pakistan in their relations with the superpowers in at least two ways. On one hand, the Carter administration's stepped-up nonproliferation policy pressures which affected the economic interests of both south Asian countries were somewhat relaxed in January 1980. On the other hand, the superpowers hastened to offer new packages of military assistance — the US to both countries, and the Soviet Union to India. The Indo-Soviet arms deal announced in May 1980 was a heavily subsidized, $1.5 billion equipment package. The nuclear factors in the subcontinent, of course, do not explain the main thrust of these superpower actions, but they are part of the perceptions in Moscow and Washington of the climate of risks and opportunities for their interests in the region. Moreover, the possession of nuclear capabilities in India and Pakistan probably increases the self-confidence of their decision-makers in pressing, despite newly alarming circumstances, for concessions from the superpowers on terms that maximize rather than encroach on their autonomy. Rather than jump at new US offers of limited conventional military assistance, Pakistan, for example, has stoutly held out for larger quantities and a differently composed package.

Although Israel's main nuclear rationale may be deterrence of an all-out Arab military assault (at the point Israel's ordinary defenses are on the verge of collapse), there may be other nuclear contingency plans. It is conceivable, for example, that Israel could seek to influence US crisis-management by signaling its readiness to launch a nuclear attack on Soviet expeditionary forces, in the event they are ever deployed in the local combat zone. If Israel is believed to possess such a capability, it not only could itself inhibit direct Soviet military intervention but, more importantly, would put great pressure on the US to use preventive diplomacy with the Soviet Union to avert such an escalation-prone scenario from the start, thereby enhancing Israel's peacetime security and wartime freedom of maneuver. Similarly, while Israel may want the deterrent capability *per se*, the prior purpose it serves is to compel US arms resupply, to cope with conventional attrition and preclude reaching the desperate situation in which Israel would actually decide to use nuclear weapons. Needless to say, such confrontation states as Iraq probably believe that some of Israel's bargaining potency might be nullified if they too acquired nuclear weapons capabilities.

Other LDCs that are vulnerable to invasion and enjoy a close military security relationship with one superpower — such as South Korea and perhaps Taiwan with the US, or Cuba with the Soviet Union — may perceive incentives to develop nuclear weapons on grounds analogous to those just hypothesized for Israel, the general thrust of which are to strengthen or guarantee the security commitments of the superpower in question. States such as South Africa that are ostracized by all the major powers have little scope for maneuver. It is difficult to determine how South Africa intends under foreseeable circumstances to use its expected nuclear weapons capability. The most potent threat it is likely to face is internal, and external threats probably would be organized and deployed for guerrilla warfare. It is possible, however, that a tactical airborne nuclear force would discourage Cuban regular combat force deployment from adjacent territory in open warfare against South Africa. Alternatively, South Africa may believe that its present policy of ambiguity still provides some leverage on the major Western powers to assist in diplomatically moderating UN majority support for extremist solutions, to resist enactment of oil and economic sanctions, or even to covertly enable South Africa to import conventional arms.[29]

Nuisance Strategies

A few states actively support or provide sanctuary for international terrorist organizations, sometimes — as seems to be true of Libya — quite indiscriminately. A somewhat larger number of states have employed nuisance strategies of a different sort, the expulsion of "boat people" from Vietnam and Cuba, or the tacit promotion of opium traffic — though the latter is typically for economic reasons. That one or two idiosyncratic governments might collude with terrorist organizations to conduct acts of nuclear terror or sabotage for one or another political cause is no longer inconceivable,[30] perhaps no more improbable than the seizure in Teheran of US diplomats as hostages.

Most LDCs are unlikely ever to sponsor nuclear terrorism of this sort. The penalties that would eventually be brought to bear would be much too high. But there may be a minority of LDCs that would secretly relish rare incidents of nuclear terrorism occurring in powerful, privileged, unresponsive or intimidating countries, either as humbling experiences or as compulsions on such states to pay an economic or diplomatic price to LDCs in exchange for multilateral cooperation or energetic measures to prevent any recurrence of those incidents. Such incidents are unlikely to be initiated, for example, by the kinds of LDC grievances expressed in the demands for a new international economic order, but it is not difficult to imagine the spur that would be given to rich-

---

29. See Chester Crocker, "Current and Projected Military Balances in Southern Africa," in Richard Bissell and Chester Crocker (eds.) *South Africa into the 1980s,* Boulder, Colorado (forthcoming), and Richard K. Betts, "A Diplomatic Bomb for South Africa?," *International Security,* Vol. 4, No. 2, Fall 1979, pp. 91–115.
30. See Mason Willrich and Theodore B. Taylor, *Nuclear Theft: Risks and Safeguards,* Cambridge, Mass., 1974.

country responsiveness in the North-South dialogue if the impression got around that a recent flurry of nuclear incidents was somehow related to the desperate poverty in certain LDCs.

Conclusions

Singling out the nuclear factor in the foreign policies of LDCs has dangers as well as virtues. The danger is that it may convey exaggerated impressions of the current foreign policy importance of the nuclear factor in developing areas. The virtue is that by drawing attention to and comparing those cases where it is important today, it not only enlarges our understanding of contemporary affairs but provides clues to how prospective nuclear-capable LDCs may behave as their nuclear assets grow.

To limit the dangers of exaggeration, three points should be made. First, with the possible exceptions of Israel and recently Pakistan, it is doubtful that non-weapon LDCs rank independent possession of nuclear arms nearly as high in their security policy calculations as the traditional nuclear weapon states. The policies of nuclear ambiguity (or of a weapons "option") are present in at least half a dozen other LDCs, but those policies suggest almost by definition that the nuclear arms factor is not of supreme importance in their current defense or foreign policy postures. A strong case can be made that nuclear arms currently is a minor consideration, if it exists at all, in the remainder of our list of nuclear-potential LDCs. Second, LDCs that have well-established civilian nuclear energy or research programs still represent a small proportion of the total number of LDCs. For most LDCs, therefore, the nuclear factor is not prominent in foreign policy calculations yet, although it may gradually become so over time. Finally, even in those LDCs where nuclear power development is prominent, the degree to which it affects foreign policy undoubtedly varies and there is no case, in this observer's opinion, in which it normally dominates an LDC's foreign policy considerations. Nevertheless, the same could be said for most developed countries.

On a relative scale of priorities, on the other hand, it is possible that nuclear issues generally carry more weight in the foreign policies of such LDCs as India, Pakistan, South Africa, Brazil and Argentina than they do in the foreign policies of at least the non-weapon developed states. This issue probably cannot be settled by the present evidence and may deserve further empirical study.

It does seem to be true that nuclear-capable LDCs — those with substantial research or power programs — perceive foreign policy utility in what they do with their nuclear assets, are learning to use influence derived from their nuclear policies more self-consciously and with increasing sophistication, and probably perceive that part of this influence depends upon anxieties about proliferation and threats to international or regional security. Since the same anxieties about proliferation are present in the nuclear-capable LDCs as well as in LDCs generally (not merely in the nuclear weapon states or industrialized countries), the nuclear factor in LDC foreign policies normally trades on ambiguities. In some cases, nuclear weapons motivations or covert capabilities are present and in other cases they are not, but in

Atomic Diplomacy in Developing Countries

Attributes of Nuclear-Potential LDCs

	Domestic Political Structure		External Affairs Orientation		Nuclear Program Characteristics			Military Option	Perceived Threat Environment	
	Orientation	Stability	Alignment	Militancy	Civilian	International Safeguards	Cooperation		Intensity	Nuclear
Large Nuclear-Capable										
India	Plural Democratic	Moderate	N-A (S)	Moderate	Complex	Partial	Diverse	Demonstrated	Variable	Yes
Pakistan	Military	Low	Ambiguous	Variable	Rudimentary	Partial		Proximate	High	Yes
Yugoslavia	Socialist	Fragile	N-A (S)	Moderate		NPT		N.A.	Variable	Yes
Argentina	Military	Moderate	Hemispheric	Low	Complex	Partial	Diverse	Proximate	Low	No
Brazil	Military	Moderate	Hemispheric	Low	Complex	Comprehensive	Diverse	Probable	Low	No
Medium Nuclear-Capable										
Israel	Plural Democratic	High	West	High	Negligible	None	Clandestine	Presumed	High	Contingent
South Korea	Military	Fragile	U.S.	Low	Complex	NPT	Diverse	Probable	High	Contingent
Taiwan	Authoritarian	High	U.S.-Informal	Low	Complex	NPT		Probable	Variable	Yes
South Africa	Apartheid	High	Pariah	Moderate	Complex	Partial	Diverse	Proximate	High	No
Prospective Nuclear-Capable										
Iraq	Authoritarian	Fragile	Radical Arab	Moderate	Rudimentary	NPT		Remote	High	Contingent
Iran	Theocratic	Low	N-A	High	Rudimentary	NPT	Diverse	Remote	Variable	Contingent
Cuba	Communist	High	Soviet bloc	High	Rudimentary	None	U.S.S.R.	Remote	Variable	Contingent
Chile	Military	Moderate	West	Moderate				Remote	Low	No
Mexico	Quasi-Democratic	Moderate	West	Low	Complex	NPT	Diverse	Remote	Low	No
Egypt	Authoritarian	Moderate	Variable	Variable	Rudimentary			Remote	Moderate	Contingent
Libya	Authoritarian	Fragile	Radical Arab	High	Rudimentary		Clandestine	Uncertain	High	No
Vietnam	Communist	High	Soviet bloc	High	Rudimentary	None		Remote	High	Contingent

either case it seems to be useful to convey the impression that they could be.

The growing sophistication in using such influence lies in policy linkage in international relations. In some cases, the linkage is quite narrow, falling within the confines of peaceful nuclear cooperation, but using influence to diversify sources of supply to alleviate nuclear energy resource or technological dependency, and to become new suppliers of nuclear technology, fuel, or services. In other cases, the linkages are broader, reaching to satisfy other foreign policy goals. In the foreign economic policy area, these can include assured oil supplies or stable oil prices,

	Nuclear Delivery Systems	Defense Program Conventional Arms Production	Superpower Security Commitment	Non-Nuclear Energy Resources		
				Petroleum	Gas	Coal
Large Nuclear-Capable						
India	Missile/Aircraft	Major	USSR-Cooperation	Limited	Limited	Abundant
Pakistan	Aircraft	Negligible	US-Cooperation	Limited	Significant	Limited
Yugoslavia	Aircraft	Major	US-Informal	?	?	?
Brazil	Aircraft	Major	Hemispheric	Limited	?	Limited
Argentina	Aircraft	Major	Hemispheric	Adequate	Adequate	
Small Nuclear-Capable						
Israel	Aircraft/Missile	Sophisticated	US-Informal	Negligible	Negligible	Negligible
South Korea	Aircraft/Missile	Major	US-Defense Treaty	Offshore potential	Offshore potential	Negligible
Taiwan	Aircraft	Major	US-Cooperation	Offshore potential	Offshore potential	Negligible
South Africa	Aircraft	Major	Uncertain	Nil	Synthetic	Abundant
Prospective Nuclear-Capable						
Iraq	Aircraft	Negligible	USSR-Cooperation	Abundant	Abundant	?
Iran	Aircraft	Negligible	Uncertain	Abundant	Abundant	?
Cuba	Aircraft	Negligible	USSR-Defense Treaty	Nil	Nil	Nil
Chile	None	Minor	Hemispheric			
Mexico	None	Minor	Hemispheric	Abundant	Abundant	
Egypt	Aircraft	Potential	US-Cooperation	Abundant	Abundant	Nil
Libya	Aircraft	Negligible	None			
Vietnam	Aircraft		USSR-Defense Treaty			

economic or financial assistance on favorable terms, and marketing opportunities for manufactured products, valuable engineering and other services, or surplus skilled labor. The cultivation of such technical and economic interchange contributes in turn to political and security goals of foreign policy by enlarging internal allocatable resources, establishing regional influence and local dependencies, and generating actual or potential allies against current or foreseeable threats.

Similar linkage approaches also appear to improve LDC political and security bargaining opportunities with the superpowers or other major suppliers of military equipment, technology and assistance, for protective umbrellas, provision of conventional arms, training and technical assistance, recognition of regional status, and even understandings about non-interference in regional disputes or domestic political issues.

At present, the linkage and enhanced bargaining opportunities appear to be much greater in bilateral relationships between nuclear-capable LDCs and other countries than in multilateral or global institutional settings, and the most rewarding future relationships may remain bilateral. The development of the NPT regime, however, multilateralized certain LDC anxieties and grievances about arms control, nuclear cooperation and technology transfer, and there are signs of embryonic coordination among nuclear-capable LDCs on these issues as they relate at least to energy resources and development objectives. Such coordination may eventually lead to more explicit LDC linkage of the nuclear issues with the New International Economic Order concerns, or process of collective North-South bargaining, prompted perhaps by incidents of nuclear terrorism. LDC coordination of nuclear issues on regional, religious or ideological lines may also emerge some day, as nuclear capabilities spread.

How the industrialized world, the West, or the US should respond to these developments is outside the scope of this essay. But any debate about responses will benefit from a sober effort to understand the political and security as well as economic and technical dimensions. Even as the bloom of nuclear energy fades somewhat in the industrialized world, the economical satisfaction of energy requirements is becoming more difficult. Nuclear energy is not only likely to hold its own in the global supply picture, but to expand with industrialization in LDCs. Thus the LDC foreign policy use of the nuclear factor is more likely to spread and intensify than disappear, and to become more complex over time. The analysis of the broader LDC foreign policy patterns that may emerge is only beginning.

I wish to express my appreciation to William G. Young, my assistant at the Center for Strategic and International Studies, to Manfred Hamm, a doctoral candidate in political science at Georgetown University, for research and editorial assistance with this article, and to Peter Clausen of the Department of Energy for his thoughtful readings and comments on the draft. Final responsibility for the views expressed and any remaining defects are the author's alone.

5. External Financing of Development: Challenges and Concerns

ROGER S. LEEDS

The problem confronting an increasing number of developing countries[1] is simply stated: how to finance mounting current account deficits without seriously impeding national growth and development? In the early years of the last decade, prior to the quadrupling of oil prices that occurred in the four-month period between October 1973 and January 1974, the combined current account deficits of the non-OPEC countries averaged approximately $7 billion per year. In 1980 the deficit for these countries surpassed $60 billion, an increase of about 800 percent in less than a decade. Nations, like households and corporations, must finance a large portion of their shortfalls by obtaining access to external sources of funds, either in the form of grants or loans. Thus, it comes as little surprise that the external debt of LDCs increased dramatically after the oil crisis. Between the end of 1974 and 1977, the external debt of developing country governments doubled in real terms—from $113 to $231 billion—and is expected to jump to approximately $348 billion by 1985 (see Table 1).

Concurrent with this increase in the size of LDC debt, there was a significant change in the way that these countries obtained funds from external sources. The primary source of capital shifted from the public to the private sector. Official aid from industrialized countries declined from 44 percent of the total financial flow to developing countries in 1970 to about 30 percent at the end of the decade.[2] Conversely, private commercial bank lending to Third World countries experienced tremendous growth. The inflow of publicized medium- and long-term Eurocurrency credit* increased from a yearly average of approximately $9 billion in the 1969–1973 period, to $12.5 billion in 1975, immediately after the oil crises, to approximately $39 billion by the end of the decade.[3] It is projected that by 1985 developing countries will owe approximately $438 billion to their private creditors, as opposed to a relatively insignificant $32 billion in 1970. Thus in a short time span private financial institutions have become the single largest supplier of capital to developing countries.

The purpose of this essay is to examine this dramatic growth in external debt of developing countries, particularly since the onset of un-

---

The views expressed in the article are those of the author and do not necessarily represent those of the International Finance Corporation.

1. Throughout this essay the terms "developing country," "less developed countries," and "Third World" are used interchangeably. No difference in meaning is implied by changes in usage.
2. Organization for Economic Cooperation and Development, *Development Cooperation, 1979 Review*, Paris, 1979, p. 66.
3. World Bank, *Borrowing In International Capital Markets*, Report EC-181/784, Washington, D.C., 1979, p. 17.

*The predominant source of external private borrowing for LDCs.

TABLE 1
Developing Countries: Medium- and Long-term Debt Outstanding and Disbursed at Year-end, 1979–1990
(Billion current US dollars)

	1970	1977	1985	1990
To Private Creditors	32	155	438	771
Low Income Countries	2	10	16	19
Middle Income Countries	30	145	422	752
To Official Creditors, including Multilateral	37	104	302	507
Low Income Countries	15	39	108	183
Middle Income Countries	21	66	194	324
Total	68	258	740	1,278
Total at 1975 Prices	113	231	348	449

Source: The World Bank, *World Development Report*, August 1979, p. 29.

precedented increases in the price of oil in 1973. It will trace the recent growth of private international lending and examine some of the problems that have emerged as a result of the increasingly dominant role played by private banks in developing countries. Then the present decade will be discussed with an eye toward explaining the magnitude of the financing problems confronting developing countries in the future. The prospects for non-OPEC developing countries must be examined in the wake of recent oil price hikes and the shifting priorities of the private international banking community. And finally, this analysis will review what adjustments the international financial community might undertake to alleviate some of the debt pressures that threaten to undermine the growth and stability of this important group of nations.

This is not a subject to be studied in vacuum; it must be examined within the realistic context of contemporary international political and economic affairs. Policy pertaining to such issues as food and agricultural production, defense and national security, energy, and North-South relations—all are linked to the issue of developing country access to international capital markets. For example, even a cursory examination of international events in the final weeks of the last decade reveal that there is an undeniable relationship between the external debt problems of developing countries and other subject matter examined in this volume. No one would deny, of course, that the debt problem is inextricably related to the steady increases in the price of oil. But there are other linkages as well. Turkey, a country of vital strategic interest to the West, has been teetering on the brink of the interrelated disasters of financial bankruptcy and serious political instability for over a year as the international financial community deliberates over an appropriate rescue package. The assassination of South Korea's President Park adversely affected that country's international credit rating. Inflation in the United States was a factor in the erosion of the value of the dollar in foreign exchange markets, which directly affects the cost of borrowing for developing countries. Political turmoil in Central America limited the access of countries in that region to international capital markets. And events in Iran not only jeopardized that country's access to the international market place, but they also caused reverberations throughout the Eurocurrency markets that are likely to have adverse consequences for *all* developing countries.

Nor is the subject of the financial well-being of relatively poor countries a mere academic curiosity. United States economic interests are as dependent upon the solvency of developing countries as they are on the prosperity of the industrialized world. It is estimated, for example, that about 800,000 American jobs in the manufacturing sector alone depend on exports to developing countries. With approximately 35 percent of all merchandise exports destined for Third World nations, United States' exporters receive more revenue from these relatively poor countries than from all of Western Europe. And on the import side of the ledger, Third World countries supply the United States with 93 percent of its tin, 85 percent of its bauxite (the essential ingredient for aluminum production), and virtually all the natural rubber consumed.[4] These figures are merely representative of the magnitude of the interdependence between US national interests and Third World economic well-being.

It is little wonder, therefore, that even a staunch conservative Congressman like Henry J. Hyde (Republican, Illinois) is a supporter of foreign assistance to developing countries. Representing a district that includes the factories of some of the largest corporations in America, Congressman Hyde does not justify his advocacy of foreign aid on humanitarian grounds. "I listen to the entrepreneurs in my district," he explained, "and they benefit directly from the sale of their goods to the Third World."[5]

What the Congressman did not mention was that if a country is teetering on the verge of bankruptcy, unable to gain access to international sources of credit, those goods produced in his Illinois district will not be purchased. When a nation reaches an alarmingly high level of external debt and is unable to generate sufficient foreign exchange revenues from exports, it rapidly becomes isolated from its traditional sources of credit. The country is caught in a so-called debt trap: As the debt problem becomes more severe, credit markets become more inaccessible, and without access to credit, investing in projects that stimulate growth and development becomes increasingly constrained. An unremitting process of financial strangulation begins to occur as the trap slowly closes.

The subject of LDC debt has a potentially awesome significance for the entire international financial system, which faces a dilemma no less formidable than the developing countries themselves. On the one hand, if the banks curtail their lending to developing countries the deficits will only grow worse and increase the likelihood that the banks will not receive timely repayment of previous loans. But, if the creditors continue lending in line with the patterns established during the last decade, they may soon be in the precarious position of having loan portfolios that are unbalanced and excessively risky. Under such circumstances, one or two major defaults could create serious problems for the entire international banking system.

The Growth of Private Debt[6]

The 1973–1974 oil crisis was a watershed in the history of capital flows to developing countries. Prior to that time most of the external financial resources channeled to the Third World came either from of-

---

4. US Department of State, Bureau of Public Affairs. Speech by Secretary of State Cyrus Vance before National Urban League Annual Convention, "America and the Developing World," July 23, 1979, p. 2.
5. Thomas B. Edsall, "Constituents' Economic Interests Lead to Conservatives' Switch to Foreign Aid," *Baltimore Sun*, July 24, 1979, p. 1.
6. Portions of this section are excerpted from an earlier monograph written by the author entitled "Cofinancing for Development: Why not More?" *Overseas Development Council Monograph*, Washington, D.C., February 1980.

ficial sources, such as domestic agencies for international development (e.g., US AID) and multilateral aid organizations (e.g., World Bank), or from direct private investment, which steadily increased during most of the decade of the 1960s. Even in 1970 the role of the private banking community as a source of capital for developing countries was minor relative to what it would become before the decade ended.

In the 1970s the sources of development financing began to change. On the private side, the enthusiasm of corporate foreign investors waned as the risks became more self-evident. Some developing countries, stung by what they perceived to be the excessive repatriation of profits and exploitation of finite natural resources, instituted protective legislation that attempted to impose the terms on which foreign direct investment could be made. In some cases these measures had the effect of discouraging prospective foreign investors. In other countries—for example, Chile, Angola, and even Iran—the risks of foreign investment were more manifest, with the painful realization that an entire venture could be lost as a result of expropriation or outright war. The enthusiasm of foreign investors during the earlier years was replaced by caution and, in some cases, an attitude that the risks simply outweighed the profit potential. Consequently, private companies in many instances resigned themselves to foregone revenues, and the developing countries retained control of their natural resources at the cost of having to seek out new sources of technical assistance and financial resources. As a result, between 1970 and 1977, direct foreign investment declined in relative terms from 13 percent to 8 percent of total capital flows from external sources to non-oil-exporting developing countries.[7]

At the same time, official sources of economic assistance also began to decline relative to total capital flows to developing countries. Unreliable in the best of times because it depended on the beneficence of a handful of wealthy countries that could grant or withhold funds on the basis of political as well as socioeconomic motivations, bilateral assistance steadily contracted as a percentage of grantors' GNP. For example, in the years immediately after World War II, when the United States was committed to European economic recovery, an astounding 2.7 percent of gross national product was allocated to external assistance. By 1965, the figure had fallen dramatically but was still a respectable 0.50 percent. In the 1970s, the flow of economic assistance from industrialized countries to the Third World has deteriorated from bad to worse. By 1979, according to the OECD, official aid from all developed countries as a percentage of GNP had dropped to 0.34 percent, and for the United States alone the ratio plummeted to 0.19 percent—ranking the United States sixteenth out of seventeen donor countries, just ahead of Italy.

Under these circumstances it is little wonder that former Secretary of State Cyrus Vance referred to this performance as "disgraceful" in a commencement address at Harvard University. Nor is it surprising that a major Third World spokesman, noting this same trend, claimed in a tone of bitterness and exasperation that "the sorry record of foreign assistance in the last two decades is beginning to convince me . . . that the developing world would have been better off without such assistance." And, he continued, "the developed countries have

---

7. Nagy Pancras, "It's Time to Call In the Commercial Banks," *Euromoney*, February 1979, p. 120

neither the will nor the imagination to offer such assistance."[8]

But as these traditional sources of foreign capital began to diminish in relative terms, there was a spectacular increase in Eurocurrency lending to developing countries by commercial banks, particularly after the 1973-1974 oil crisis. Once the Organization of Petroleum Exporting Countries made the decision to increase the price of oil by more than 400 percent, the private banks became the recipients of an unprecedented inflow of deposits—the flood of so-called petrodollars. It is estimated that OPEC oil revenues increased from $28 billion in 1973 to $106 billion the following year, and that the OPEC current account surplus soared from $6.5 in 1973 to $68 billion in 1974.[9] According to the Bank for International Settlements, nearly $30 billion of this surplus flowed into private banks in the major international financial centers in 1974 alone, before declining to a range of $10 to $13 billion in the years 1975-1977. Most of these surplus funds became available for lending in the Eurocurrency markets at the same time that several other factors were beginning to influence the utilization of private international capital markets by developing countries.

The middle income nations[10] were characterized at that time by the high priority they attached to rapid, energy-intensive industrialization as the most appropriate strategy for achieving widespread national development. Unfortunately, they also were among the countries most heavily dependent on petroleum imports (see Table 2). For them, the enormous oil price increase presented the unpalatable choice of cutting back on their ambitious development plans, borrowing on the external capital market, or drawing heavily on cash balances and limited reserves of foreign exchange to pay for their

TABLE 2
Petroleum Import Bill for Oil-Importing Developing Countries 1973-1980 ($ Billion)

	1973	1975	1977	1979	1980
Low Income	.06	1.8	2.0	2.7	3.3
Middle Income	6.1	20.3	26.1	40.4	54.5
Total	6.7	22.1	28.1	43.1	57.8

Source: *The Times* (London), March 16, 1980, p. 16.

energy needs. Therefore, the dilemma—reduced to its simplest terms—was whether to opt for slower growth and development, or to risk serious balance of payments disruptions, or to embark on a program of heavy external borrowing. As Table 1 has illustrated, they chose the latter strategy on the belief that the development gains would be sufficient to ensure repayment of the debt and not cause unacceptable strains on their balance of payments.

The situation in Brazil was a case in point. Between 1967 and 1973, Brazil's economic growth increased at an impressive annual rate of 11 percent in real terms. This period of rapid growth was led by a 13 percent annual expansion of industrial output—an enviable performance by any standard. Even though Brazil was poorly endowed with petroleum resources (importing more than 80 percent of its needs), before 1974 petroleum accounted

---

8. Mahbub ul Haq, *The Poverty Curtain: Choices For The Third World,* New York, 1976, p. 45.
9. OECD, "External Indebtedness of Developing Countries: Present Situations and Future Prospects," Paris, January 19, 1979, p. 6 (mimeo).
10. Although the term is somewhat arbitrary, it refers to countries with an annual per capita income above $1,135 and a level and rate of economic development that is considerably higher than other Third World nations.

for just over 10 percent of total imports. After the 1973-1974 oil crisis, this figure rose to more than 33 percent, with predictable consequences for overall growth and balance of payments developments. Rather than sacrifice enterprising development objectives, Brazil opted for borrowing in external private credit markets as a significant component of its 1974 strategy.

At the same time that the developing countries were grappling with the numerous internal difficulties, there was a marked deterioration in the balance of trade between rich and poor countries. Caught in the throes of the worst recession in the post-war period, the industrialized countries reduced their demand for traditional developing-country exports, such as raw materials. Moreover, for those developing countries committed to the vigorous pursuit of rapid economic growth, it was difficult to reduce the level of imports—primarily of capital goods—from the West. The imbalance of trade that resulted from this series of events further complicated the decision on whether or not to opt for rapid growth and development. With the likelihood of lower revenues from exports and higher expenses for imports, the demand for external sources of credit began to mount rapidly.

Another manifestation of the post-oil crisis recession was a contraction of demand for credit by the industrialized countries. Low or negative growth rates coupled with high inflation and soaring interest rates curbed the appetite of many borrowers to take on additional debt. The wealthier participants in the credit markets could, of course, afford to wait for better times, but developing countries intent on rapid development could not. It is not surprising that the private banks—highly liquid and without the normal levels of demand from their traditional customers—readily acquiesced to satisfying demands for credit emanating from the developing world.

As a result of this series of events, the international financial flow of funds underwent a dramatic change in a relatively short period of time. Not only did the OPEC countries suddenly become a dominant supplier of funds to the international capital markets, but developing countries became major borrowers. The net inflow of medium- and long-term credit to these countries from private sources increased from a yearly average of approximately $7 billion between 1969 and 1973, to more than $20 billion in the 1976-1978 period; and at the end of 1980 the figure exceeded $40 billion. As a result of this increase, which occurred at the same time as the relative decline of official sources of assistance, private lenders currently provide the bulk of all external capital to middle-income developing countries. In 1978, for the first time ever, the net external borrowing of developing countries from private capital markets exceeded the net flow of funds from official sources. In less than a decade, therefore, private financial institutions became the principal source of external capital for a large group of countries, supplanting the role previously played by direct foreign investment and official development assistance.

The developing countries now comprise the single largest category of borrower on the Eurocurrency markets. For those country borrowers deemed sufficiently creditworthy by the private lending community, the Eurocurrency market is often more attractive than resorting to official sources of credit, such as the International Monetary Fund (IMF), the World Bank, or one of the regional development banks. Because the market is highly competitive and

TABLE 3
Commercial Bank Claims on Developing Countries, 1976–79

	Percentage composition of amounts outstanding[a]			
	1976	1977	1978	June 1979
Brazil	16.7	16.6	16.2	16.1
Mexico	16.2	13.4	11.4	11.7
Venezuela	6.2	6.0	6.9	7.5
Spain	6.6	7.6	6.5	6.5
Argentina	3.0	3.2	3.4	4.8
Subtotal, 5 largest borrowers	48.7	46.8	44.4	46.6
Next 5 borrowers	17.4	18.7	18.8	18.0
Next 10 borrowers	20.4	19.6	19.9	19.2
All others	13.5	14.9	16.9	16.2
All developing countries	100.0	100.0	100.0	100.0
Amount (billions of dollars)	110.5	151.1	203.9	221.5

Source: World Bank, *World Development Report, 1980*, August 1980, p. 1-29.

[a] Excludes offshore banking centers (e.g., Bahamas, Bahrain).

relatively free of restrictions or onerous regulations, a creditworthy borrower is likely to obtain funds efficiently and with a minimum of time-consuming bureaucratic exigencies. Even when rates are higher on the open market, as they usually are, borrowers frequently prefer to pay the premium in order to avoid restrictive conditions and close surveillance that accompany most loans from official sources.

Although the data appear encouraging on the surface, the record of developing country access to private international capital markets in the seventies was mixed. Out of the 96 countries that the World Bank classifies as developing, only a fraction became active customers of private creditors. At the end of 1978, for example, 10 countries accounted for approximately 63 percent of total commercial lending to developing countries and 20 nations took about 83 percent. On balance, most Third World countries did not have ready access to this huge pool of capital simply because most private creditors, accountable to shareholders for their profitability and understandably concerned about the safety of their investments, did not judge them to be sufficiently creditworthy. This banker's jargon, reduced to its simplest form, means that in most Third World countries the risk that interest and principal will not be repaid on time outweighs the potential reward, given alternative lending opportunities.

Nevertheless, most analysts claimed that in the wake of the 1973–1974 oil crisis the private international financial community did a reasonably proficient job of recycling the flood of petrodollars that suddenly entered the marketplace. Contrary to the pessimistic forecasts of the period, the OPEC current account surplus declined from $68 billion in 1974 to less than $5 billion at the end of 1978 and the adjustment mechanism functioned well. Regardless of how these funds ultimately were distributed throughout the world, it is undeniable that a large portion flowed to developing countries relative to the period preceding the oil crisis. Moreover, contrary to some doomsday analysts,[11] the high external debt levels that were incurred by some developing countries did not result in widespread defaults that some believed would undermine the stability of the

---

11. See, for example, US Senate, Committee on Foreign Relations, Subcommittee on International Economic Policy, *International Debt, the Banks and US Foreign Policy*, Washington, D.C., August 1977.

entire international financial system. Although there have been a handful of notable exceptions, most countries have continued to make on-time debt repayments and there has not been a single case of bank failure due to difficulties with loans to developing countries.

Prospects for the Eighties

Although the international banking system functioned well in the 1970s, it is difficult to be as sanguine regarding prospects for developing country access to international capital markets in this decade. At one end of the equation, receipts from oil revenues are likely to soar to new heights. After declining to a marginal $5 billion in 1978, the OPEC current account surplus came to nearly $68 billion in 1979 and exceeded the $100 billion mark in 1980. With a barrel of OPEC oil selling at an average price of slightly more than $32 in the Spring of 1981, the real price of petroleum has increased by more than 100 percent since the end of 1978. Moreover, as a result of the fall in oil production following the upheaval in Iran, coupled with the expressed desire of other OPEC countries such as Libya and Kuwait to limit their output levels, oil prices are not likely to decline in real terms during the next few years as they did in the 1975–1978 period.

If this prognosis is accurate, the current account outlook for the non-oil-exporting LDCs is bleak. According to one analyst,[12] the combined current account deficit for this group of countries may mushroom from its already dangerous level of more than $60 billion to over $200 billion in 1986. This staggering growth would increase LDC debt to private lenders from the present level of approximately $150 billion to almost $800 billion by the end of the decade, or $450 billion in 1980 dollars.

Even if the accuracy of these projects is called into question, the magnitude of the problem is of sufficient proportion to suggest that the future debt financing task confronting the LDCs is massive.

But there are a variety of developments that could affect the validity of this and numerous other forecasts. If, for example, the politico-economic situation in Iran deteriorates further, or another major OPEC producer is subjected to a similar outburst of turmoil, oil supplies to the West could be further curtailed and prices would be likely to rise at an even faster rate than in 1979. Supply lines are also threatened in a more general sense by heightened Cold War tensions that have the potential to erupt into a major conflict that would have major global repercussions.

It is also conceivable that the future will evolve more favorably and oil prices could rise less rapidly than anticipated. In the spring of 1981, for example, oil consumers were treated to a rare dosage of encouraging news when some oil producing countries announced a small reduction in their oil prices. If the rate of growth of world oil consumption continues to decline, or if oil output from non-OPEC sources (e.g., North Sea, Mexico, Alaska) continues to increase, then the price outlook may become more favorable. According to a study prepared by two analysts at the Hudson Institute, non-OPEC free-world oil production has been growing at the impressive annual rate of 6 to 8 percent. If this growth is sustained, according to the analysis, by 1985 non-OPEC free world output will exceed production of the 13 nation cartel, whereas in 1975 it was only

---

12. Adam Parkin, "The LDC Debt Burden May Be Impossibly Heavy By 1986," *Euromoney*, March 1980, p. 118.

half. And, of course, prices are likely to be affected by the success or failure of stepped-up efforts to develop non-oil energy sources, such as natural gas coal, and nuclear power. All of these factors will influence the future supply and demand for oil in the world, and the magnitude of developing country balance of payments deficits.

In addition to the uncertain outlook for energy prices, there are other differences between the current situation and the 1970s. For example, in the earlier period the OPEC countries managed to spend almost $500 billion on the importation of goods and services, which amounted to roughly 75 percent of total OPEC receipts from petroleum exports.[13] Although OPEC expenditures for imports are likely to remain relatively high in the 1980s, it is improbable that these countries will sustain this high level of absorptive capacity. This is particularly true of Iran (crippled by the upheaval that erupted in 1979), which managed to spend a staggering $14 billion on imported military equipment alone between 1972 and 1978. Thus, with the likelihood of a lower rate of spending on imports the OPEC current accounts surplus should increase in relative terms, and the combined deficits of the non-petroleum-exporting developing countries would, of course, increase by a substantial margin.

Limits on the System

Even if the OPEC surplus remains at relatively high levels, it is questionable whether in the foreseeable future a substantial portion of the funds will flow through the private banking system into the coffers of developing countries, as occurred after the last rise in oil prices. Although there is little doubt that developing country borrowers will continue to be strong demanders of funds, the OPEC suppliers may not rely as heavily on the banks as they begin to seek out alternative havens for their windfall riches.

For understandable reasons, OPEC countries are not as singularly committed to the Eurocurrency market as the dominant target for their investments as they were in the past. Approximately 75 to 80 percent of the market consists of dollar denominated assets and liabilities. Throughout the 1970s investors helplessly stood by and witnessed the decline in the value of their dollar-denominated assets as inflation and depreciation took their toll. Without any large-scale viable alternative to the US currency, OPEC investors grew increasingly frustrated. Although it may not be a conscious part of OPEC investment strategies, there have been unmistakable signs in recent years that a relatively greater portion of the OPEC surplus is finding its way into more tangible assets, such as gold and other commodities, real estate, and direct equity investments in non-OPEC private enterprises.

In addition to the dollar's instability, the Eurodollar market was shaken to its core in November 1979 when President Carter suddenly declared a freeze on all dollar-denominated Iranian assets in US banks. This action was taken in response to indications that the post-Shah government of Iran would not honor all of the debts to foreign banks that were incurred by the previous regime. Regardless of the ostensible wisdom of these retaliatory measures, one effect was to undermine investor perceptions of the safety of placing funds in the Euromarkets. Although fears that the Euromarket might collapse beneath the pressure of widespread defaults proved

---

13. Morgan Guaranty Trust Company, "World Financial Markets," December 1979, p. 1.

to be unfounded, events were sufficiently unsettling to suggest that the market would never again function as it had prior to events in Iran. Mr. Jawad Hashim, President of the Arab Monetary Fund, summed up the sentiments of many large holders of dollar-denominated assets when he stated, "The attitude of some American banks has shaken the confidence and trust placed in them, especially as regards the future." And another longtime observer noted that Iran demonstrated that

> the cozy club atmosphere in which Euromarket business has been transacted for the past two decades is unlikely to survive. The smooth running of any club is dependent upon its members upholding the rules. As far as the Euromarket is concerned, it appears that the rulebook has been torn up.[14]

These events provided still another incentive for OPEC nations to be wary of depending heavily on the Eurocurrency banking system to recycle their surplus funds.

The oil producers also are likely to take into consideration suggestions that they undertake a greater volume of direct lending to developing countries, rather than rely on non-OPEC international banks to recycle the funds.[15] The heavy LDC demand for external sources of credit is in part a result of substantial increases in their energy-related imports. For example, the World Bank estimated that in 1980 the oil import bill for LDCs was more than double the 1978 figure, reaching $75 billion or 7 percent of their GNP. Thus many developing countries reason that the OPEC countries should play a more active role in the recycling process, preferably in such a way that brings relief to the oil importers (e.g., lower prices or preferential interest rates).

But even if OPEC countries do alter their investment strategy, the private banks still will be the depository for large sums of petrodollars. One projection estimates that the amount of OPEC deposits in the international banking system would reach $30 to $40 billion in 1980 alone.[16] However, unlike the period after the first large increase in oil prices, there are a number of constraints that will impede the ability of the banks to lend large portions of their funds to those who have a desperate need—the developing countries.

One problem results from the heavy lending by the banks to a limited number of countries in the last decade. Consequently, outstanding loans to developing nations are concentrated in a small number of borrowers. Two countries—Brazil and Mexico—accounted for 25 percent of total outstanding bank claims to developing countries at the end of 1979, and 50 percent of total claims were on only five borrowers. As a result, some of the largest private lenders must now exercise restraint, or run the risk of violating one of the cardinal rules of banks: diversify risk by avoiding a high concentration of loan activity in a single category of borrower. Thus the future lending activity of some of the largest banks is likely to be constrained by their adherence to prudent banking practices.

Similarly, banks are concerned that it is precisely

---

14. "International Insider," Brussels, December 10, 1979, p. 1.
15. See, for example, recent public statement by Henry Wallich, Member of the Board of Governors of the Federal Reserve System, and Rimmer de Vries, Senior Vice President of Morgan Guaranty Trust Company.
16. Morgan Guaranty Trust Company, "World Financial Markets," January 1980, p. 12.

these same countries that borrowed so heavily in the 1970s that are likely to have the most serious balance of payments problems in the 1980s. Even before the end of the last decade a number of the largest LDC borrowers, such as Zaire, Turkey, and Peru, had encountered severe repayment problems, and others currently loom on the horizon as presenting serious problems for their international creditors. Brazil, for example, which was one of the most sought-after LDC borrowers in the 1970s, now has more than $50 billion in external debt and a debt service ratio that recently surpassed 60 percent. In 1980 Brazil's total expenditures on imported oil ($10.2 billion) plus external debt service ($13 billion) were greater than estimated revenues from exports ($20 billion). This unfortunate turn of events prompted one observer to comment, "It's just as if you spent your entire salary on oil, gas and your mortgage."[17]

Although the Brazilian case is somewhat extreme, it is little wonder that many international banks that were aggressive lenders to LDCs in the 1970s are now demonstrating greater restraint in the international arena. As Gabriel Hague, former Chairman of the Board of Manufacturers Hanover Trust, observed, "Bankers are becoming increasingly selective in their foreign lending. . . . They look with inquisitive eyes for the continued existence of creditworthiness."[18]

Bank lending to LDCs also is likely to be somewhat constrained by mounting concern for the adequacy of their capital. For many of the larger banks that were aggressive lenders in the 1970s, their capital base has failed to expand as rapidly as their growth in assets. In the case of the large US banks, for example, the ratio of their equity capital to total assets declined from 4.5 percent at the end of 1972 to less than 3.5 percent by September 1978. During the same period, the proportion of foreign assets to total assets for this group of banks rose from about 11 percent to 33 percent, and reached as high as 50 percent for a few of the largest international lenders.[19] In 1979 the ten largest US banks derived 42.6 percent of other combined earnings from their international operations,[20] a figure that did not go unnoticed by the regulatory authorities. Moreover, the same type of concern has been noted in Germany, Britain and Japan where efforts are underway to implement reforms that will permit more prudent control of the capital adequacy of their financial institutions.

This evidence suggests that the banks have continued to increase their lending activity without a commensurate expansion of their capital base. For a financial institution this capital base serves as a vital protective cushion against unexpected loan losses. Although there is no consensus among bank regulators regarding the meaning of "adequate" capital relative to earning assets, it is widely recognized that a steadily declining ratio is cause for concern. Under present circumstances, the expansion of the international lending activity of many banks will be adversely affected by the sluggish growth of their capital base. This sentiment was con-

---

17. Quotation attributed to Rimmer de Vries, Morgan Guaranty Bank's senior economist, in article by Hobart Rowen, "Monetary Time Bomb," *Washington Post*, June 5, 1980, p. 20.
18. Speech delivered at International Monetary Conference, Tokyo, May 1977.
19. Morgan Guaranty Trust Company, *op. cit.*, December 1979, p. 6.
20. Salomon Brothers, "Lending in LDCs: Mounting Problems," April 2, 1980, p. 2.

firmed recently when Chairman of the Federal Reserve Board Paul Volcker declared, "One potential danger . . . that we must avoid as far as possible is the overloading of the commercial banking system."[21]

It should be noted that these developments in the banking industry are not occurring only with US institutions. The problem of capital adequacy, for example, is actually more severe for some of the largest European and Japanese banks that traditionally have been permitted to operate in a more forgiving regulatory environment. In 1979, the Japanese government became so concerned about the rapid increase in the international lending activities of Japanese banks that it temporarily curtailed their medium- and long-term international lending. Thus many of these non-US lenders are also beginning to slow the pace of their international operations.

As if these problems for LDC borrowers were not sufficient, lending terms have begun to turn against them. As banks have become more reluctant to increase their international loan portfolios, they have raised the cost of borrowing. Maturities on Eurodollar loans that averaged nine years in the late 1970s recently began to shrink for many borrowers. More significantly, the spreads between LIBOR (lending institutions' borrowing rates) and the lending rates, which effectively determine the profit margin for lenders, began to widen in the early months of the 1980s. Whereas the average spread over LIBOR narrowed from 1.25 percent in 1976 to the .5 to .75 percent range in 1979, it now appears headed back toward the previous levels. All of these factors signal a tightening of credit availability for less creditworthy borrowers, and there are no indications that this unattractive environment will change in the foreseeable future.

These trends suggest that most banks may slow down their international lending of their own volition. Self-imposed prudent banking practices are likely to serve as an effective check against the possibility of irresponsible lending that could threaten to undermine the foundations of the international banking system. But even if this assumption proves overly optimistic, the system is likely to be closely watched by the regulators. The US Congress, the Federal Reserve, the Comptroller of the Currency, and a host of state regulatory bodies recently have increased their surveillance of the international activity of US banks. In other countries where financial institutions conduct a large portion of their business abroad (e.g., England, Germany, Japan), there is also evidence of mounting concern that the banks proceed with caution. And even the Bank for International Settlements recently announced that due to the "greater risks" now threatening the international banking system, it too will take special precautions to monitor the overseas lending activities of the private banks. If the banks are not prone to take a more conservative view of overseas lending on their own, this flurry of regulatory activity will most likely hasten the process.

The implication of this scenario for the developing countries is somber. Even though the OPEC current accounts surplus is likely to be larger than ever before, the flow of funds to deficit-ridden LDCs may be constricted. Due to a series of internal and external constraints it is unlikely that the private banking system will be positioned to perform a dominant role in the financial intermediation process as it did in the aftermath of the 1973–1974 oil crisis. Thus the

---

21. *American Banker,* March 14, 1980, p. 9.

key issue is not whether there will be sufficient funds available to finance non-oil-exporting developing country deficits, but what alternative channeling mechanisms can be established in lieu of heavy dependence on traditional private bank lending.

Alternative Financing Mechanisms

If the private banks cannot be depended upon to shoulder as large a portion of the recycling burden as in the past, attention must focus on other institutional participants that have the requisite financial resources and the will to assist in the adjustment process. The two most obvious candidates are the multilateral institutions (e.g., the IMF, the World Bank, regional development banks) that have a clear mandate to provide financial assistance to developing countries and arrangements that permit the OPEC nations themselves to play a more direct role in channeling their surplus funds to the deficit countries. Clearly, the magnitude of the financing that must be undertaken is so great that no single cure-all will suffice. Rather, a variety of mechanisms must be implemented in such a way that the preponderant role played by the private credit markets in the last decade will be more evenly distributed in the eighties.

The most obvious choice to play a more active role in balance of payments financing is the International Monetary Fund. Although the liquid resources available for lending are small relative to the network of international banks, the Fund is capable of playing a more extensive role than it has in the past. With approximately $13 billion of lendable assets in its ordinary account and an additional $17 billion in special accounts that include the so-called Witteveen Facility, which was established to provide balance of payments financing to non-OPEC LDCs, the Fund has resources that are specifically earmarked for balance of payments assistance. Moreover, it would be relatively painless for OPEC members and other industrial countries to allocate additional funds to the IMF, as opposed to creating an entirely new institution to accomplish the same purpose. The first step in this direction was taken in the Spring of 1981 when Saudi Arabia agreed to lend the IMF approximately $10 billion over a three-year period.

But even though the interest rates charged on balance of payments loans from the IMF are considerably below market rates, LDC borrowers traditionally have preferred to go to the private market rather than tap this source of funds because of the tough credit conditions that are often attached to IMF loans. In 1979, 37 countries borrowed $1.8 billion from the IMF, only a small portion of which was tied to specific conditions. IMF members are entitled to draw down a portion of their borrowing quota without acceding to Fund conditions, but additional borrowings are contingent upon meeting the terms established by the officials of the Fund.

Jamaica provides a recent example of the difficulty that many financially strapped LDCs have with the IMF. In 1972, just before the first oil crisis, the country imported $49 million worth of oil—or 9 percent of total imports in that year; in 1979, the sum increased to $200 million, which was fully 25 percent of the total import bill.[22] Not surprisingly, foreign exchange revenues from Jamaica's exports did not rise anywhere near as rapidly as the increase in the price of oil, and consequently the balance of payments deficit skyrocketed. In addition, the island economy

---

22. *Financial Times*, April 3, 1980, p. 3.

was struggling with extremely high unemployment, double digit inflation, declining productivity, and an uncertain political climate. These symptoms, of course, are not unique to Jamaica.

The foreign exchange crisis that developed from the balance of payments deterioration left the Caribbean island with few options. An untenable economic situation, coupled with former Prime Minister Michael Manley's publicly expressed antipathy for traditional Western solutions, created an environment in which the private banks became increasingly unwilling to serve as a source of funds. The only alternative was to approach the IMF for help. For almost three years the Jamaican government and the IMF negotiated over what conditions would be attached to the requested balance of payments assistance. The IMF remedy did not diverge from the norm for similar circumstances: a combination of currency devaluation and deflationary measures such as curtailed government spending and wage controls.

In March 1980, the Jamaican government abruptly broke off negotiations with IMF officials despite the serious financial difficulties that the country was encountering. Former Prime Minister Manley severely criticized the IMF for demanding such large cutbacks in government expenditures as a prerequisite for a $180 million loan. In an election year he could ill-afford to appear to be succumbing to external pressures that would result in additional short-term economic hardship for significant portions of the electorate, even if the trade-off was balance of payments assistance.

But the upshot of the Prime Minister's action enhanced the likelihood that Jamaica would edge closer to the precipice of bankruptcy. Without the support of the IMF, the private bankers publicly announced their reluctance to extend further credit to the country. Although the banks had approximately $375 million in loans outstanding, they made the judgment that the future of their Jamaican assets would be seriously in doubt unless the country received the IMF assistance *and* acquiesced to the reforms demanded by the multilateral lending institution. But the Manley government remained adamant. After meeting with a group of important international bankers who rejected Jamaica's plea for additional loans, Finance Minister Hugh Small stated, "we have told the bankers that when it finally comes down to a choice between feeding our people and paying off the loans, we will advise them of our decision."[23]

The Manley government's approach to international finance was repudiated in November 1980 when the Jamaican electorate went to the polls and elected his arch rival, Edward Seaga. The new Prime Minister immediately reopened negotiations with the IMF and the private banking community. Within six months of Seaga's inauguration he succeeded in obtaining a $700 million assistance package from the IMF and a major debt rescheduling from the country's private creditors.

The Manley government had received support from another Third World leader who in the past had been explicit in his criticism of the IMF. In a New Years Day speech in Dar es Salaam to the diplomatic corps, Tanzanian President Julius Nyerere lashed out at the Fund for what he interpreted as the "repugnant" manner in which it "interfered in the management of our economy."[24]

---

23. *The Washington Post,* April 10, 1980, p. A27.
24. *Daily News* (Tanzania), January 3, 1980, p. 4.

Although he conceded that certain adjustments in the domestic economy were justified, he balked at the traditional solutions suggested by the multilateral institution:

> Tanzania is not prepared to devalue its currency just because this is the traditional free market solution to everything and regardless of the merits of our position. It is not prepared to surrender its right to restrict imports by measures designed to ensure that we import quinine rather than cosmetics, or buses rather than cars for the elite.[25]

To the Manleys and the Nyereres of the Third World, the IMF's policies are indicative of efforts of the rich nations to dominate the poor ones, and the pressure is mounting for the Fund to alter its operating procedures to better reflect these concerns. Even so respectable a publication as *The Economist* warned that unless the Fund becomes more flexible, "it is in danger of fading off the world scene."[26]

So far IMF officials have successfully resisted efforts to impede its capacity to impose strict conditions on its loans. They claim, with some justification, that the purpose of IMF financing is to provide temporary assistance that permits countries in difficulty the time needed to undertake structural adjustment programs. In order for this type of assistance to have a reasonable chance for success, they argue, certain economic policies must be adopted. Thus, although Managing Director Jacques de Larosier asserts that the Fund "stands ready to assume an increasing role in recycling," he reminds listeners that, "we do expect that countries to which the fund lends in relatively large amounts or for unusually long periods will be prepared to meet certain conditions."[27]

But possibly there are alternative mechanisms that could be established within the Fund that would permit easier access by developing countries. For example, suggestions have been made that the oil exporting countries channel a portion of their surplus into a special IMF Oil Facility that would lend to LDCs on easier terms. Others, most notably Walter Levy, have suggested that the IMF sell special long-term bonds to the OPEC governments and use the revenues for balance of payments assistance to the poorer nations. And A. W. Clausen, when he was President of Bank of America, proposed that the IMF set aside some of its funds to support an insurance pool for private banks that lend to developing countries. The objective of these and other similar suggestions is to alter the recycling process by having the IMF assume a portion of the role that was played by the commercial banks in the mid-1970s.

Another category of proposals focuses on establishing new institutions to deal with the problem. Austrian Chancellor Bruno Kreisky, for example, in a recent speech at the United Nations advocated the creation of a new Fund for Economic Cooperation and Structural Adjustment. In a similar vein a group of US legislators led by former Senator Jacob Javits recommended the establishment of a $50–100 billion pool of OPEC funds that would be invested in developing countries. Another proposal calls for an international insurance company that would guarantee debt to developing countries, with membership along the lines of the World Bank or

---

25. Ibid.
26. *The Economist*, 22–28 March, 1980, p. 21.
27. Reprint of speech by Mr. de Larosier before the Economic and Social Council of the UN, Geneva, July 4, 1980, *IMF Survey*, July 7, 1980, pp. 205–206.

the IMF. One advantage of this proposal is the relatively small capital outlay required. And the much-heralded Brandt Commission, which is composed of eminent leaders from the developed and developing countries, wrote a report entitled "North-South: A Programme for Survival," which proposed the creation of a well-endowed World Development Fund that would receive its capital from a novel system of international taxation. But skeptics of these proposals point out that it makes little sense to add to the proliferation of international bureaucracies, rather than strengthen existing institutions. Moreover, there is an urgency to the problem that cannot be addressed by proposals that would require many years to implement.

For those who oppose establishing new institutions there are still numerous options, ranging from simply providing the multilateral banks with more money,[28] to expanded use of co-financing and/or other guarantee schemes that would induce the private banks to step up their lending activity in the Third World. One proposal that figures prominently on any roster of suggestions is to broaden the mandate of the World Bank to include a lending program aimed at alleviating payments deficits by channeling funds directly to activities that contribute to export expansion or import substitution.

In the early years of the World Bank's existence, in the aftermath of World War II, the emphasis was on providing assistance for the reconstruction of the war-ravaged countries of Western Europe. At that time the bulk of the Bank's financing was in the form of program loans earmarked for widespread structural assistance. Since that early phase, virtually all of the Bank's activity has shifted to Third World countries, where concessional loans are extended to finance large-scale projects and specific sectoral assistance that is considered essential for national development (e.g., health delivery systems, roads, hydroelectric plants, public housing). But recently, as the balance of payments problems of non-oil-exporting LDCs have begun to loom larger than ever before, the Bank has undertaken a fundamental operational change that would permit it to provide a different type of financial and technical assistance to its membership.

Under the new scheme, so-called structural-adjustment lending would reemerge as a significant parcel within the Bank's portfolio. By shifting some resources from specific projects and sectoral assistance to this more general type of lending program, the Bank once again would focus attention on some of the underlying causes of serious external payments imbalances that currently plague so many developing countries. Thus, for example, loans would be made to increase import substituting capacity or export generating capability of a country suffering from chronic current accounts difficulties. The assistance provided under this type of program would occur over an extended period of time and would be expected to result in specific structural adjustments that hopefully would have a lasting impact on the balance of payments.

Although this new lending program bears a resemblance to the type of assistance provided by the IMF, there are significant differences. Although a balance of payments crisis might precipitate World Bank involvement, the objective would be to assist the recipient government to initiate long-range programs that involve fundamental economic changes.

---

28. The Board of Directors recently approved a resolution calling for doubling of the World Bank's capital to approximately $80 million.

Rather than function as a fire-fighting operation, it would address structural problems in the economy that require prolonged attention (e.g., design and implementation of incentives to promote growth and diversification of exports).

Of course, like IMF assistance or even private bank loans, the actual disbursement of funds would be conditional on the recipients' willingness to undertake certain changes. However, if the loans are flexibly administered there should be ample room for agreement between borrower and lender. Moreover, because structural-adjustment lending is designed to address structural problems rather than immediate crisis situations caused by severe foreign exchange shortfalls, the Bank expects that program will avoid the controversy that occasionally surrounds IMF assistance. Nevertheless, the success of the new lending program to a large extent hinges on the willingness of the recipient government to undertake specific policy actions deemed necessary to achieve a particular set of structural reforms.

Another type of activity undertaken by the multilateral development finance institutions that could alleviate some of the balance of payments pressures is co-financing.[29] This lending mechanism permits official institutions, such as the World Bank or the Inter-American Development Bank, to enter into a formal agreement with a group of private creditors for the purpose of making a loan to a developing country for a specific project.* On the surface, co-financing arrangements provide clear benefits for all three participants—the recipient country, the private banks and the official lenders. For the borrower, the loan may increase the flow of external capital needed to promote growth and development. For the official lender, co-financing is noteworthy because of the prospect that additional capital may be channeled into projects identified as being of a high developmental priority. Not surprisingly, therefore, the OECD suggested that "by mobilizing liquid funds under the umbrella of the multilateral development lending institutions, [co-financing] could add significantly to their total capacity to support investment activities."[30]

But, at a time when the recycling process is facing its most formidable challenge, the benefits derived from the co-financing mechanism may be most significant for the private bank, which might be reluctant to make a loan in the absence of participation by an official institution. For example, there is the attraction of added protection for the private lender that results from the so-called cross-default clause in the official loan agreement. This covenant stipulates that default or prolonged delay of repayment by the borrower to the private creditor is sufficient cause for the official lender to suspend disbursements or accelerate repayment. Because most LDC borrowers would be extremely reluctant to trigger the displeasure of the official lending institution, the private creditors gain a form of protection that is not present in ordinary loan agreements.

Another inducement for the private banks to partake in co-financing agreements is access to otherwise privileged information. The official lender, with

---

29. For additional information on the pros and cons of co-financing see the author's recent publication "Co-financing For Development: Why Not More?" *op. cit.*
*Co-financing can also refer to a loan agreement between two or more official lending institutions, without the participation of private banks.
30. Organization for Economic Cooperation and Development, "A Program For Stepped-Up Investment In Developing Countries," Paris, July 20, 1978, p. 13 (mimeo).

the consent of the borrower, may provide the co-lender with detailed information about the country and the project that would not ordinarily be divulged. The private bankers also have a valued opportunity to take advantage of the in-depth project analysis that invariably is performed by the official lending institutions prior to approving a loan. Because of these factors private bankers have stated repeatedly that, particularly in developing countries (where real and perceived lending risks are greater than in traditional markets) they feel more confident when one of the multilateral lending institutions is directly involved.

Despite these apparent advantages co-financing has not gained widespread acceptance in its initial years of operation. In the case of the World Bank, for example, between December 1975 and the end of 1979 there were only 23 examples of formal co-financing arrangements with private banks.[31] In the 1970s, when LDC debt levels were not alarmingly high and the banks were flush with petrodollars, the incentives to enter co-financing agreements were not sufficient to trigger a rush by the private banks. However, under present circumstances, with many private bankers concerned about the future prospects of lending to developing countries for the reasons described earlier, co-financing may be one mechanism that could offset their inclination to reduce their capital outlays to the Third World.

More lenient conditions attached to IMF loans, expanded use of program lending by the World Bank, a larger role for co-financing between official and private lenders — all of these suggested remedies will help to redress the imbalance in the global flow of funds. But in large measure the solution to the impending crisis depends on mechanisms that will induce those that are endowed with surplus capital to channel it to those who are not. All proposals hinge upon the willingness of the oil exporting nations to play a major role — whether they channel funds through official and private banks, or whether they bypass the financial intermediaries in the West and lend directly to deficit-ridden developing countries.

It cannot be said that the OPEC countries have ignored the poor in the past. In the last decade, while the industrialized countries were allocating only .35 percent of GNP annually to development assistance, since the 1973-1974 oil boom OPEC aid has been between 1.1 and 2.7 percent of the combined GNP of its membership.[32] In addition to the large deposits of petrodollars in private banks that became available for recycling, OPEC commitments directly to the multilateral development institutions were substantial throughout the last decade. In the case of the IMF's new $10 billion Witteveen Facility, for example, Saudi Arabia alone had pledged $2.5 billion, which is considerably more than any other country, including the United States, Japan, and West Germany. In addition, most of the OPEC countries have separate bilateral aid programs that provide funds on concessional terms, such as the Kuwait Fund for Arab Economic Development, the Iraq Fund for External Development, and the Abu Dhabi Fund for Arab Economic Development. These countries also make a significant contribution through their regional aid agencies, such as the Vienna-based OPEC Fund with assets approaching $4 billion and the Arab Fund for Economic and Social Develop-

---

31. Leeds, *op. cit.*, pp. 18-19.
32. World Bank, *World Development Report, 1980*, Washington, D.C., August 1980, p. III-37. It should be noted that when measured as a percentage of GNP, OPEC aid has been declining in recent years.

ment located in Kuwait. Although some of these agencies limit their lending to other Muslim nations, their financial contribution has been significant at a time when other sources of official aid have not been as dependable as in the past.

This aid performance by OPEC countries is sufficiently impressive to refute critics who claim that the oil exporting countries reap all the windfall profits without assuming any of the responsibility for achieving a semblance of global balance of payments equilibrium. Moreover, those who suggest that some of the pressure could be taken off the international banking system if those countries would do more direct lending to LDCs ignore an important factor. Although these countries are suddenly flush with funds, they are still underdeveloped in many respects. For example, they have a serious lack of experienced personnel who can conduct sophisticated project analysis and administer these massive foreign assistance programs. These wealthy countries are in need of a type of non-financial assistance that cannot be implemented quickly, namely higher education and manpower training programs.

Nevertheless there are ways that the major oil exporting nations could play a more substantial role that would not be particularly taxing on their limited pool of experienced manpower. For example, they could serve as the guarantor of credit extended to LDCs by private banks, or assume the major financial responsibility for the international insurance facility noted previously; they could offer concessional prices or extended payment terms to LDC buyers of their oil; or the OPEC nations could participate in co-financing arrangements with an official lending institution or a syndicate of private banks. These and various other proposals would permit the surplus nations to assist the developing countries without creating a drain on their limited human resources.

Regardless of which additional steps are taken, it appears fairly certain that the adjustment process for non-oil-exporting countries in the eighties will be more painful than it was during the last decade. As one respected observer noted, "it is our expectation that the amount of rescheduling will be far greater and considerably more difficult than in the 1976–1979 interval."[33] Unlike the earlier period, when the success of the recycling process allowed most creditworthy LDCs (e.g., Korea, Philippines, Brazil) to obtain the loans needed to maintain the pace of their growth, this time it appears that banks will assume less of the total burden and, as a result, LDC growth rates will be pushed lower. Austerity measures, such as currency devaluations, import restrictions, and cuts in government expenditures, will most likely be unavoidable for some countries, while others will have to dip heavily into coveted reserves in order to meet debt payments. Henry Wallich, a member of the Board of Governors of the Federal Reserve System, expressed this view in testimony before Congress: "I believe that many countries will have to place greater emphasis than in the past on adjustment of their economies to the higher oil bills rather than on financing enlarged deficits."[34]

Looking back on events of the last decade, it is possible that analysts were too quick with their plaudits for recycling. For although disaster was avoided, little was accomplished to reduce the

---

33. Salomon Brothers, *op. cit.,* p. 2.
34. *Federal Reserve Bulletin,* January 1980, p. 16.

likelihood that the underlying imbalances would reemerge in the same fashion—or worse. As Federal Reserve Board Chairman Paul Volcker observed in a speech at New York University, "In a sense, we muddled through the post-1973 period without really dealing effectively with the problems, and we lost some of the sense of urgency for doing so because no disasters occurred."[35] Most preliminary signals indicate that in the early 1980s it will be considerably more difficult to "muddle through." Rather, in order to avoid widespread disruptions that could affect the developed world as severely as the stricken Third World, there will be a need for an unprecedented amount of cooperation and innovation in the international financial system. The challenge to the system is formidable; the outcome is uncertain.

---

35. *American Banker, op. cit.*

6. Industrialization, Trade and the International Division of Labor

LUCIANO TOMASSINI

Problems and Strategies

At the end of the Second World War the Western powers—prompted by the United States—determined to avoid the protectionism which had prevailed with such disturbing effects in the 1930s and to establish free trade on a lasting footing. The 1944 meeting at Bretton Woods laid the basis for the new system, setting up two institutions for the purpose of promoting international financial and monetary cooperation: the International Bank for Reconstruction and Development (IBRD), which in a first stage would devote itself to supplying the financial assistance required for the economic recovery of Europe and Japan, and the International Monetary Fund (IMF), responsible for watching over the stability of the exchange rates and for the maintenance of international liquidity, all of which was to stimulate the growth of world trade. Originally this system included the creation of an International Trade Organization (ITO), formally agreed upon in the Havana Charter of 1948, but this remained unratified by the United States Congress. Some of its terms were incorporated in the General Agreement on Tariffs and Trade (GATT) with its more limited scope, and so it has remained up until the present the focal point of the multilateral trade negotiations. It was never possible to implement many of the objectives assigned to the ITO, including the organization of commodity markets along the lines suggested by John Maynard Keynes during the Second World War. The Bretton Woods system consequently did not reflect the fundamental interests of the developing countries—not surprising in a world in which only around 50 States were represented in the newly created United Nations Organization.

During the next few years, however, the interest of the international community in the underdeveloped countries began to increase. Various developing regions had contributed to the war effort, supplying the allied powers with raw materials and natural resources, so that the latter powers had acquired greater familiarity and established new economic links with those regions. On the other hand, the fact that the theatre of war had spread to very remote regions caused deep-rooted politcal changes in those societies and forced them into international politics, giving rise to a progressive process of decolonization extending from the independence of India in 1947 to the present day, when more than 150 independent States—the majority of them developing countries—have been incorporated into the United Nations.

A series of theories have emerged as regards the nature of underdevelopment and the most appropriate strategies for overcoming it. Their common denominator is to be found in the assimilation between the concepts of "development" and "modernization." Development was conceived of as a univocal road, which of necessity passes through certain stages, which all countries must similarly traverse. The difference between development and underdevelopment was due to the fact that some started on this road earlier, while others were still in the initial stages. International cooperation — basically identified with external aid — was to contribute to bridging the gap between the two groups of countries and bringing modernization to the backward societies. However, the international cooperation programmes implemented on the basis of these hypotheses did not lead to the expected results, and the stage which lasted until the end of the 1960s concluded with an unalloyed feeling of disillusion vis-à-vis aid, which was reflected in a series of reports prepared at the end of this period.[1]

The approach to development in the 1950s had the drawback of being profoundly unhistorical. It implied that development constitutes a process which occurs independently in different countries at different moments in time and consists in reproducing, under different circumstances, the model coined by the countries which were the protagonists of the Industrial Revolution. The state of underdevelopment in which the backward countries lived could be overcome insofar as they incorporated the traits of modernity corresponding to advanced societies. This would be achieved with the contribution of external aid and the trickle down effect induced by the growing prosperity of the industrialized countries. In turn, this process would contribute to building a safe world for the growth of the industrial civilization created by the great powers and their main agents, the transnational corporations. The consensus in the developed countries did not then entertain the possibility that the situation of the underdeveloped countries was due precisely to the structure of their relations with the industrialized countries. It was the disillusion vis-à-vis aid in the 1960s which led these countries to entertain this suspicion:

> Donors and recipients alike tended to view the modernization and development of low income countries as an attempt to repeat the Industrial Revolution in quick time. They also tended to expect too much too soon from aid supplementing the national development efforts. A dramatic change in the life of hundreds of millions of people was expected from a relatively modest flow of resources, much of which was offset by unfavorable trends in the terms of international trade.[2]

The motto of "trade not aid" which emerged from this analysis, as a form of reaction against previous policies, did not take the developing countries by surprise. In fact they had long attributed the causes of underdevelopment to the structure of their relations with the developed countries, and they had been pressing to restructure these relations. These ideas had been developed since the beginning of the 1950s by the United Nations Economic Commission for Latin America (CEPAL) and its influential Executive Secretary, Dr. Raúl Prebisch, who gave them world importance when he became the first Secretary-General of UNCTAD in 1964.[3]

---

1. See, for example Pearson, L., *Partners in Development,* New York, 1969; CEPAL, *Estudio Económico de Américana Latina 1949,* Santiago, 1950; Prebisch, R., *Problemas Teóricos y Prácticos del Crecimiento Económico,* Santiago, 1952.
2. Pearson, *op. cit.* pp 5-6.
3. CEPAL, *op. cit.;* Prebisch, 1952, *op. cit.;* Prebisch, *Towards a New Trade Policy for Development,* New York, 1964.

According to this analysis, the "center" (comprising the developed countries) had established an international division of labor in which it reserved for itself the production of manufactures and capital goods, allocating to the "periphery" (the underdeveloped countries) the role of producers of food and raw materials. For a group of reasons which will be reviewed below, this type of specialization implied that the market functioned in opposition to the interests of the developing countries, giving rise to a long-lasting trend towards the deterioration of their terms of trade, and ultimately, their import capacity, and persistent situations of external disequilibrium.

This trend consisted of a long-term decline in the prices of primary products in the export of which the periphery countries specialized in comparison with the prices of manufactures and capital goods imported from the center. This reflected a failure by entrepreneurs and workers of the industrialized countries to transfer the benefits of increased productivity resulting from technological innovations to the developing countries through lower priced exports. Instead they kept prices high and retained high profits. Secondly, it was assumed that the demand for primary products is relatively inelastic, as a result of Engels' Law, which holds that as a society's income increases (a process which is concentrated in the industrial countries), the smaller is the proportion of that income which the consumer devotes to food and commodities, so that demand for this type of product grows slowly and irregularly. Finally, there appeared to be biases characteristic of modern technology, which tends to lead to the generalized substitution of synthetic for natural products and production processes based on the saving of materials. The protection which the industrialized countries have traditionally given to their primary sectors, in impeding access to their markets of the commodities in which the periphery specializes, accounted for the remaining effects which were seen as prejudicing the developing countries' terms of trade.

The new trade strategy of the Third World was increasingly based on this analysis. From the standpoint of the developed countries, it was natural to expect that its theses should be controversial. For example, the tendency for the terms of trade to deteriorate has more than once been questioned in the light of empirical evidence.[4] All in all, the essential lines of the argument continue to be influential, particularly if its validity is not measured so much in terms of the real evolution of commodity prices but it terms of the evolution which the developing countries had expected.[5] In order to consider the strategy which was constructed on the basis of this theory, rather than assess its intrinsic validity, it should be asked whether the circumstances in which its main hypotheses were based continue to be in force.

This theory was based on the assumption that both the place assigned in the international division of labor to the periphery countries — that of producers of raw materials — and the tendency

---

4. Ellsworth, P.T., "The Terms of Trade between Primary Producers and Industrial Countries," *Inter-American Economic Affairs,* X, Summer, 1956; Flanders, M.J., "Prebisch on Protectionism: An Evaluation," *Economic Journal,* June, 1964; Morgan, Th., "Economic Relationships among Nations," Hoselitz, B. (ed.), *Economics and the Idea of Mankind,* New York, 1965.
5. Fishlow, A, et al., *Rich and Poor Countries in the World Economy,* New York, 1978.

towards the disarticulation of their economies with respect to the international economy, expressed in their decreasing share in world trade, would be irreversible insofar as they trusted in the forces of the market. The industrialization of the periphery countries and the drawing up of commodity agreements appeared in the light of this analysis to be the two paths which would allow these countries to obtain a larger proportion of the benefits of technical progress, with changes in their specialization in the international division of labor and the improvement of their terms of trade. The plummeting value of their exports as the result of the crisis of the 1930s, and the additional difficulties of making imports caused by the war, supplied these countries with new incentives to adopt policies of protection and stimulus for the creation of an industry which, in its first stage, was based on "inward-directed growth" and on import substitution, and to insist on the need to regulate the markets for raw materials. The assumption that the disarticulation of the periphery countries in regard to the international economy would be maintained without further changes was based, *inter alia,* on the existence of an extremely rigid international hierarchy, whose predominant objectives related to security rather than economic interests (a hypothesis linked to the Cold War) and on the existence of an international economy far less integrated than it later came to be, in which the mobility of factors was much lower than that of merchandise.

These hypotheses changed in the next few decades, as evidenced by the following trends:

- the relative weakening of the rigidly bipolar scheme which emerged after the Second World War and the tendency towards dispersion of world social-economic power contributed to reinforcing the trend towards the diversification of markets and sources of supply of capital goods, technology and financing available to the developing countries, and fostered their integration into the international system (see Kolodziej and Harkavy in this issue);

- the fact that economic interests came to be of increasing importance in international negotiations, compared with security-linked objectives, has also contributed to making the participation of the developing countries more flexible in the international system, and has encouraged them to seek a greater degree of autonomy, since economic power is relatively less concentrated than political and military power;

- the tendency towards the formation of a transnational economic system based on growing interdependence among the national societies, in which the transnationalization of industrial production and services has followed that of trade and the production of raw materials, made a still greater contribution to incorporating these countries into a global system experiencing an accelerated process of consolidation.

The lengthy period of growth experienced by the industrial center during the 1950s and 1960s constituted the background which made the expansion of this system possible and hence the progressive integration of the periphery countries into the world economy. This in turn implied more or less profound changes in their external economic relations. The fact that in the course of time this international system showed signs of crisis only shifted this trend marginally but could not reverse it.

Before returning to and expanding on these considerations in the concluding sections of this essay, I shall review the main concerns of the developing countries in the fields of the commodity trade, the access of their manufactures to the markets of the industrialized countries, and their share in world industrialization.

The Commodity Trade

Although the economic progress of many developing countries increasingly depends on their exports of manufactures, the commodity trade continues to be of decisive importance for them. Most of their export earnings come from commodities: 57 percent in 1978, or 81 percent including oil. Moreover, in many cases these earnings depend substantially on a very limited number of products. At the beginning of the 1970s more than half the non-oil-exporting developing countries obtained over 50 percent of their export earnings from only one or two products of agricultural or mineral origin, and many depend basically on only one, such as Cuba and Mauritius on sugar (84 percent and 90 percent, respectively), Gambia on ground nuts (85 percent) and Zambia on copper (94 percent). This structure exacerbates the impact on the economies of the developing countries of the violent fluctuations to which commodity prices are subject as a result of typically cyclical expansions and contractions of output.

In addition the developing countries oscillated between a policy of defense of their commodity exports and a policy aimed at industrialization based on import substitution, with very little integration between these two policies. The main link between them consisted in the fact that primary export activities functioned in practice as the capital goods sector which the industrialization process required, since this supplied them with the necessary foreign currency to purchase these goods abroad. Until a few years ago there was little call for patterns of industrialization more closely linked to the natural resource base possessed by each country and therefore aimed at profiting in a dynamic form from the comparative advantages offered by these resources, or for completing the formation of a basic industry which could in turn favour the development of other industrial activities on more autonomous bases. As one report noted:

> Industrialization based on import substitution gave rise to an incomplete structuring of the Latin American economies. It may be said that the increased development of Latin America's natural resources constitutes a field which may easily be considered to be of common interest for all the countries of the continent. Moreover, it should be recognized that the processing of raw materials in the region is not only a requisite of their sovereignty, but constitutes an essential foundation for completing the industrial base of these countries and increasing their employment generating capacity and at the same time the value-added of their exports.[6]

National policies in this area, however, and their results are conditioned by how the international commodity markets are organized. In essence, since the Second World War to date the opportunity has been lost of improving the markets for raw materials, probably due to the fact that they appear to be functioning 'well,' or at

---

6. Foro Latinoamericano, "Los Estados Unidos en el Desarrollo Autónomo de América Latina," *Estudios del Tercer Mondo,* 1 March, 1978.

least considerably better than before the war. But they were functioning well for the industrialized countries, which controlled them implicitly, both through their transnational corporations and through their governments, which sporadically and unilaterally intervened in the markets through various activities such as the imposition of quotas (in the case of oil), tariffs (in the case of copper and sugar) and increases or reductions in their strategic stocks.[7]

Reference has already been made to the violent fluctuations experienced by the prices of primary products and consequently the earnings of the exporting countries, particularly in the case of developing economies. Account must also be taken of the fact that the developed countries are important producers of raw materials, and that in many cases they defend these sectors from external competition by means of subsidies, domestic price policies or trade barriers (eg. EEC agricultural policy), while the rest are less affected by price fluctuations owing to the fact that their dependence on these products is relatively smaller or the progress they have made in processing them is greater — all of which hinders the access of developing country commodities to the markets of the industrialized countries. At the same time, the tariff structure of the developed countries impedes the processing of the natural resources of the developing countries, since tariffs rise according to the value-added of imports. For example, while raw rice is exempt from tariffs in the EEC and the United States, in its processed form it is taxed by between 13 and 15 percent; unworked timber has free entry to Australia, while sawn timber pays a tax which recently increased from seven to 14 percent. This tariff scaling constitutes a serious obstacle to the increase in exports of manufactures by the developing countries and to industrial redistribution at the international level, to which the last two sections refer.

In view of the persistence of these and other problems, the objectives of the developing countries in the sphere of commodities should be defined more broadly than they have in the past, when excessive concentration was placed on designing machinery to control their prices. Simplifying a very complex subject to the extreme, it could be said that there are three main objectives which commodity policy should pursue, particularly if its aim is to reconcile the interests of the developing countries with those of the developed countries: the improvement of prices (of primordial interest for the former), price stabilization (obviously of mutual interest) and the development of natural resources (a topic which to date has been raised largely by the developed countries).

The Integrated Programme for Commodities (IPC) which during the last few years has constituted the central concern of UNCTAD (and of the Third World in general), endeavours to respond to these objectives. Its central element is the Common Fund which will be used to finance buffer stocks, designed to intervene in the market so as to ensure prices which would be "remuner-

---

7. Tironi, E., "Politicas Nacionales y Comercio de Productos Bàsicos," Hill, E. and L. Tomassini (eds.), *America Latina y el Nuevo Orden Economico Internacional*, Nuevo Santiago, 1979.

ative and just to producers and equitable to consumers," and to stabilize them. According to the main lines of the programme, in order to constitute these buffer stocks International Commodity Agreements must be negotiated for each of ten commodities identified by UNCTAD as the most important (core commodities) from the point of view of the earnings of developing countries. Past history shows that in the course of this century more than 50 commodity agreements have been tried out. Since 1964 UNCTAD has vigorously advocated agreements which would include both producers and consumers, an example of which is the International Coffee Agreement, formalized that year, and later renewed in 1975. In recent years efforts have been made to set up producers associations, following the spectacular example of OPEC, and this has given rise to such organizations as the International Bauxite Association, the Intergovernmental Council of Copper-Exporting Countries and the Association of Iron Ore-Producing Countries, *inter alia*.[8] UNCTAD IV at Nairobi in 1976 adopted in principle the Integrated Programme for Commodities and the procedures which would have to be followed by subsequent negotiations relating to the Common Fund and the Commodity Agreements. In March 1979 consensus was achieved as regards a Common Fund provided with two windows. The first would be used for the constitution of buffer stocks by means of purchase and sales on the market, and would consist of US$ six billion, of which one third would come from direct contributions (paid-in capital), while the rest would be obtained through loans. The original proposal of the Group of 77 required that the first third should be contributed by the governments, which in fact only undertook to contribute directly the sum of US$ 400 million, while the rest (US$ 1.6 billion) would have to come from contributions made by the Commodity Agreements. The object of the second window is to promote the development of natural resources and its funds amount to US$ 370 million. Behrman endeavoured to assess the results which could be achieved by applying this instrument in the case of eight out of the ten core commodities by simulating market performance *vis-à-vis* the operations carried out on the basis of the buffer stocks anticipated in the programme. Reviewing past history, he comes to the conclusion that in the past the prices of these commodities have undergone greater fluctuations during periods when agreements existed than when there were none, with the exception of wheat and tin-in both cases largely due to stockpiling-operations carried out by the United States and Canada. Efforts to raise prices have been less successful; they would rather require the intervention of producers cartels, the successful functioning of which implies conditions which do not often obtain, such as a high degree of concentration of the market, high barriers to the entry of new producers, a high degree of homogeneity of the commodity and little possibility of its substitution by another product. Behrman finds that the amount of the Fund is inadequate to finance the operations which

---

8. Behrman, J., "International Commodity Agreements: An Evaluation of the UNCTAD Integrated Commodity Programme," *Overseas Development Council Monograph,* No. 9, Washington, D.C., 1977.

would be required to maintain price fluctuations between ten and 15 percent above or below market trends. On the other hand such a margin of fluctuation would benefit both producers and consumers in reducing uncertainty as regards prices, and would increase the earnings of the producers by US$ 5.4 billion over ten years. Although this figure is not spectacular, it should be borne in mind that these are "static" profits, since the study could not calculate the dynamic effects which would stem from a greater stabilization of prices as a result of the increase in investments and a better planning and development of natural resources both in producer and consumer countries. Lastly, as regards the distribution of these profits, it should be borne in mind that three quarters of world exports of the ten UNCTAD core commodities come from developing countries, which is precisely the group of products which can yield the largest profits.

An important complement to the commodity agreements are the income stabilization systems or compensatory financing facilities, particularly in the case of agricultural products which cannot be stored or which have experienced a poor harvest or even, in the case of other commodities, when the price stabilization mechanisms have failed. Between 1976 and 1979 the operations of the compensatory financing facility of the International Monetary Fund accounted for nearly half of the total credits granted by this body to the developing countries. However, this facility still suffers from some restrictions, and the UNCTAD Secretariat is studying the possibility of proposing reforms which will make its application more efficient, including the feasibility of setting up a new facility. Within the context of the Lomé Convention which groups the EEC and a number of Asian, African and Pacific countries in a preferential scheme, the Stabex system carries out the same functions. Although some people stress the advantages of this compensatory facility, which contributes to stabilizing the earnings of the developing countries in terms of commodity exports without incurring the costs to which a system based on market intervention may lead, this facility should essentially be considered to complement the others.

It has already been said that the third objective of the developing countries in this field concerns the development of their natural resources, including improvements in the productivity of their extractive activities, a greater degree of local processing of these resources, and more participation in their marketing and distribution channels and in the corresponding profits. The second window of the Common Fund is precisely aimed at financing research and development activities, and other operations aimed at promoting these objectives. The appearance of bottlenecks in the supply of a variable number of strategic materials in the 1970s has given rise to the fear that we might be entering a period of scarcity or one of the broad cycles identified by the Russian economist Kondratieff,[9] a fear which has determined that the development of natural resources has become the center of world concern. In 1976 the United States unsuccessfully proposed to UNCTAD IV the setting up of an international resources bank. This idea was reiterated in the

---

9. Rostow, W. W., *Getting from Here to There: America's Future in the World Economy*, New York, 1978.

Inter-American context, but in 1980 the Assembly of Governors of the Inter-American Development Bank rejected an initiative aimed at setting up a guarantee fund for foreign investment in the field of natural resources. On the other hand, it has been reported that the World Bank is preparing to set up a fund for the development of energy resources (see Leeds and Mossavar-Rahmani in this issue). Depending on the breadth of the approach to these types of programmes, and the aspects dealt with through them, an area of mutual interest between developing and developed countries could be found here.

It would seem that the developing countries should balance the stress which in the past they have laid on prices against a greater concern for the development of their commodities. From another standpoint, referred to in the next section, an increasing number of people consider that the results which could be achieved through the Commodity Agreements (and preferential systems for the access of manufactures from developing countries to the markets of developed countries) could be less significant than those which might be expected from a generalized liberalization of trade.[10] In any case, in a dynamic perspective like that which is emerging in the present international division of labor, the extraction trade in and processing of natural resources should be considered in the context of a broader view of the development process which includes industrialization and trade in manufactures.

Industrialization and Trade in Manufactures

It has already been observed that at the beginning of the 1950s no one placed great hopes in the development and industrialization of the periphery countries coming to pass through their progressive integration into the world economy, and industrialization policies by import substitution and the regulation of international markets in raw materials were advocated.

During their early stages of industrialization many developing countries endeavoured to substitute domestic production for imports of manufactures. Import substitution was to increase the proportion of national consumption covered by local production. The immediate motives for the adoption of this strategy lay in the chronic balance of payments crises through which the developing countries passed owing to the structural situation of external bottlenecks such as their capital goods requirements. This strategy also responded to the political objectives pursued in the long term by the national governments. Indeed, on the one hand this permitted these countries to speed up their industrialization, by reducing their expenditure in foreign currency. On the other hand, this strategy provided the governing elites with a way of satisfying the nationalist pressures generated by the emerging middle class and labor sectors through a policy which at the same time fostered growth, income redistribution and employment. This strategy could be termed an effort to win the domestic market away from foreign producers. As domestic demand was able to give rise to the creation of new industries which some day — and this consideration has nowadays come to be very impor-

---

10. Fishlow, op. cit.; Cline, W.R., *Policy Alternatives for a New International Economic Order: An Economic Analysis*, New York, 1979, Introduction and n. 14.

tant — would become competitive with the displaced foreign producers, it was possible to justify the levels of protection applied at that time by using the arguments brought out in favour of infant industry in the past. Naturally, as this latter condition did not come to pass, the import substitution strategy — which in practice only replaced imports of consumer goods by imports of capital goods and inputs required for the functioning and growth of the new industrial structures — had to find its own limits. In other words, either industry began to generate the foreign currency required for its later development, or its growth rate adjusted to the available means of payment abroad generated by primary production (which had had a secondary priority allocated to them in the framework of these strategies). In the course of time, many countries came to realize that the tendency to use (without generating) foreign currency is not inherent to the manufacturing sector. One after another they reached the conclusion that it was necessary to place less stress on protection and give more importance to efficiency, competitiveness, and export promotion. Since the mid-1960s — and even before in the cases of economies not endowed with large populations, markets, or availability of natural resources — new strategies, based on the liberalization of the domestic market and on opening up these economies to the outside met with application at different paces and in different forms. Noteworthy examples include, of course, Singapore, Taiwan and Korea, as well as Brazil and Ivory Coast.

Although because of their theoretical training, their age or their lack of historical vision, many economists have converted this transition into a struggle between rival schools, given the perspective of time it will certainly be possible to appreciate that in practice these stages were not put forward as alternatives, but rather as complementary processes. For many Third World countries the import substitution strategy represented the sole valid option at that time, in view of the stage of development and the existence of an adverse external framework. Often it served as the basis not only for industrialization but for the formation of national economic awareness. On the other hand, not only is there no necessary contradiction between the domestic and external markets, but frequently the former served as a jumping off point for reaching the international markets. Although it is true that there were changes in the growth strategies and the forms of external relations of the developing countries during the period indicated, it is no less true that these changes did not take place overnight.

> They cannot accomplish these changes suddenly; but since the 1960s many developing countries have moved towards strategies to promote exports and to offset disadvantages due to the isolation of their domestic markets.... A number of countries which have introduced export oriented policies had been able to exploit their comparative advantages in world markets. They include some Latin American countries with a fairly long history of national independence and some island and city-state economies which were from the outset obliged to rely on export demand. Once industrialization has taken root, it is not only in labor-intensive industries like clothing or leather-work, but also in moderately capital-intensive industries like electronics, steel, and shipbuilding, that they can become highly competitive in world markets.[11]

---

11. Independent Commission on International Development Issues, *North-South: A Program for Survival*, London, 1980, p. 164.

It is against this background that the performance of exports of manufactures by the developing countries during the most recent period can be appreciated. During the last twenty years these exports grew at a very rapid pace. From 1960 imports of manufactures from developed countries originating in the markets of developing countries grew more rapidly than their industrial imports from the rest of the world. Between 1970 and 1976 exports of manufactures from developing countries to developed market economy countries increased at an annual rate of around 14 percent, i.e., twice as fast as total imports of manufactures by these countries, including reciprocal trade, and twice as fast as the industrial output of developed market economy countries.[12] The share of manufactures in total exports by developing countries (excluding petroleum) increased therefore from ten percent in 1955 to 20 percent ten years later, and 40 percent in 1975.

The efforts of the developing countries to obtain access to the markets of the developed countries began to take shape during the first UNCTAD meeting in 1964. To begin with they concentrated on the adoption of a Generalized System of Preferences by the industrialized countries (GSP). At that time, the developing countries did not look kindly on the liberalization of trade among developed countries which was taking place as the result of the negotiations held within GATT, since they considered that they undermined the preferences claimed under the GSP. This was a rather limited system, which excluded some countries and certain sensitive products (such as textiles, footwear, oil and agricultural products), or which restricted the value which could be achieved by preferential imports of specific products or goods from specific countries. A recent estimate for 1974-1975, which includes both manufactures and agricultural products, arrives at the conclusion that the earnings of the non-oil exporting developing countries derived from the increase in their exports owing to the application of the GSP must be around US$ 1.1 billion annually, which is not very significant, since it only represents slightly over one percent of their total exports.[13] Despite the emphasis which the developing countries have placed on the GSP, therefore, some consider that the benefits which the developing countries could obtain from the results achieved through the multilateral trade negotiations, which have progressed another step with the end of the Tokyo Round, should not be ignored.

It is true that these benefits are distributed very unequally in the developing countries, in view of their level of income and the degree of diversification of their economic systems, and that the newly industrialized countries (NICs) tend to absorb an extraordinarily high proportion of the increase in LDC's exports of manufactures (see Rothstein in this issue). However, it should be borne in mind that a country's degree of economic development tends to change dynamically, and that it is probable that an increasing number of countries will in the future meet with the necessary conditions to have access to these

---

12. UNCTAD, *Exámen de la Evolución y las Tendencias Recentes del Comercio de Manufacturas y Semimanufacturas*, TD/B/C2/190, 1978.
13. Birnberg, Th.B., "*Trade Reform Options: Economic Effects on Developing and Developed Countries*," Overseas Development Council, Washington, D.C., 1978.

markets. Once the appropriate adjustments have been made the abolition of the trade barriers put up by the industrialized countries which have an inhibiting effect on the industrial development of the poorest countries will tend to stimulate in them the emergence of new manufacturing activities. In this sense the NICs would seem to be anticipating the evolution which other developing countries could experience in the future.

It is also true that the opportunities which have been opening up to developing countries in terms of industrialization and trade in manufactures, could be restricted by the resurgence of protectionism in the developed countries. Precisely as the result of the growing competition in developing countries and the recession, unemployment and permanent balance of payments problems experienced since 1974, the developed countries began to abandon the liberal principles adopted at Bretton Woods, which had made possible the exceptional growth of international trade and the rapid growth of the industrial economies during the postwar period. Protectionism is not a new phenomenon in the economic policy of the developed countries. It reached its critical point in the 1930s with disastrous consequences for the international economy and for world peace. However, in recent years the protectionist phenomenon has acquired new magnitudes and characteristics. These include its systematic nature, its permanence and its selectivity — i.e., its discriminatory application against products which are becoming highly competitive, including the main industrial goods which the developing countries are in a position to export.

The new forms and instruments of protectionism are ceasing to be isolated measures -if ever they were- to become a coherent system which heavily limits imports from the developing countries. They are tending to become institutionalized in clear, explicit rules of the game by means of international agreements, which systematize and stabilize them. The relative importance of tariff barriers is declining, while restrictions of other kinds are growing in importance: these are more effective and presumably will be applied normally rather than exceptionally within the legal framework which appears to be coming into being.[14]

On the one hand the tariff reductions agreed on by the developed countries in the context of the multilateral trade negotiations mainly benefit advanced technology products, which are fundamentally negotiated among industrialized countries, while higher tariffs are kept for the manufactures exported by the developing countries. This is in addition to the tariff scaling according to the degree of processing of the products exported by the developing countries, maintained by the industrialized countries, as has already been said. On the other hand, in recent years restrictions of a non-tariff nature have proliferated, the results of which are frequently more effective or insidious than that of the tariff barriers. These include quantitative restrictions which range from a prohibition on imports of specific products (such as meat in the case of the EEC), to the imposition of quotas (such as those on food and vegetables in the EEC and of sugar–and more recently steel–in the United States). They also include the imposition of countervailing duties on exports from developing countries which the industrialized countries consider to be "subsidized", a type of

---

14. CEPAL, *América Latina en el Umbral de los Años 80,* Santiago, 1979.

measure which has been abused in recent years, with particularly adverse effects since it tends to frustrate the export promotion policies which the developing countries have after a long time been putting into practice with great effort. Also part of this context are several types of agreements to restrict trade, noteworthy among which are what are known as the orderly market agreements signed between exporting and importing countries with the object of restricting trade in specific products (the most conspicuous example is the Multifibre Arrangement), and the "voluntary restrictions" which are usually agreed on bilaterally by the exporting and importing countries, by imposition of the latter, and without any possibility of appeal since formally the developed country has not adopted any measure or violated any principle of international trade.

Behind this phenomenon can be found the tendency towards the loss of competitive capacity in developed countries in a growing number of branches of industry, which at the same time is giving way to a process of redistribution of these activities as a consequence of the factors reviewed in the next section.

Industrial Redistribution

The loss of competitiveness of some sectors of industry in the developed countries is the result of a combination of factors. In the first place there is the tendency for their industrial costs to rise as a consequence of the wage levels and the amount of public expenditure predominating in those societies. Another factor is represented by the loss of dynamism of the investment process in the developed countries, as a consequence of the deterioration in the rates of return prevailing in them, and the reorientation of these investments towards more economically worthwhile areas. Other factors associated with the foregoing are to be found in the relative saturation of the markets for durable goods and in the reduction of the pace of technological innovation in the traditional sectors. The need to conserve the environment vis-à-vis the deterioration caused by specific industrial activities, and the consequent increase in the cost of the respective investments, constitutes another factor with a similar effect. Insecurity in supply and the rise in the prices of oil and certain natural resources on which some critical industrial inputs depend, are added to the inflationary pressures stemming from an accumulation of factors. The oligopolization of societies, due to vertical and horizontal conglomeration of different productive units, raises costs and exacerbates inflation. Pressures from labor organizations in the industrialized countries, the effects of state regulations, and the change in workers' preferences push in the same direction. In more general terms, the deep-seated change experienced in individual values or preferences in the industrial societies and the incipient emergence of a system of values which has come to be termed "post-industrial," to distinguish them from those which were to be found at the bases of the economic growth of the industrialized countries during the postwar period, would seem to be reorienting the demands of the public in a direction which is not very favourable to economic growth, efficiency and productivity as these concepts have been understood during the last few decades.[15]

---

15. See among other studies which document these trends, that of OECD, 1979.

All of this has not only made the manufactures which the developing countries are in a position to export more competitive, but at the same it is giving rise to a process of industrial redistribution of a scope which for the moment is difficult to anticipate. It should be borne in mind that as a result of the international division of labor established by the powers which carried out the industrial revolution, more than 90 percent of manufactures and production is concentrated at the present time in the developed countries, which gives an idea of the magnitude of the target proposed by UNIDO in Lima in 1975, that at the end of this century the share of the developing countries in world industrial output should increase to 25 percent. The measures taken by the international community to facilitate the process of industrial redistribution mentioned above will contribute decisively to achieving this goal.

Industrial redistribution is understood to be the transfer of an existing industry from one location to another in response to market factors and government intervention. In fact, this process has already begun, and is growing rapidly. From the end of the 1960s the share of the developing countries in world industrialization began to grow and to take on new forms which made it possible to absorb an increasing number of industrial activities previously located in developed countries — both in the United States and to a larger extent in the EEC (particularly West Germany) and Japan. The branches in which this trend is most strongly seen not only include the traditional labor-intensive industries (like textiles and apparel), but also heavy industries (iron and steel, refining, petrochemicals and fertilizers), shipbuilding, metal working and machinery, and certain polluting activities such as the chemical industry and the pulp and paper industry.

One of the factors which has most contributed to boosting this process is to be found in the tendency towards industrial complementarity or subcontracting, in which transnational firms of the developed countries share their production with subsidiaries or independent enterprises located in developing countries, making the most of the advantages which they offer in terms of wage levels, tax treatment, availability of natural resources, less strict environmental regulations or the direct granting of subsidies. At the same time this process obtains for the transnationals better international distribution for their products. An active exchange of parts and components and a close complementarity between the production processes required for the manufacture of the respective final products have thus been developed, a phenomenon which constitutes one of the central features of international trade at the present time.

It is interesting to quote the testimony of a member of the Brandt Commission, from the South, in this respect, when he says that what has most surprised him "in the form in which the Western European countries (and also Japan) perceive the world and their relations with the developing countries has been their sensation of systematically being losing industrial sectors in which they previously believed themselves paramount, owing to the competition from some developing countries"[16]

---

16. Botero, R., "La Comisión Brandt: Una Perspectiva Latinoamericana," *Estudios Internacionales,* 48, October-December, 1978.

Naturally, in this process the newly industrialized countries of Southern and Eastern Europe, Eastern Asia and Latin America play an outstanding role; in recent years they have developed a great capacity for producing highly competitive manufactures in the world markets, a phenomenon which has been described as "the emergence of two or three Japans" in the field of trade.

This new international division of labor makes it possible to rationalize certain inefficient industries in the developed countries and also to promote the industrialization of the developing countries, permitting the achievement of mutual benefits, and providing a response to the protectionist tendencies of which the former are giving strong signs.

Mutual North-South Interests

It was mentioned at the beginning that the appreciable growth experienced by many developing countries in recent years was generally speaking accompanied by a large-scale intensification of their links with the world economy. This is what the Executive Secretary of CEPAL said as regards Latin America in a recent declaration:

> It is a fact that the Latin American countries have developed within the context of growing integration in the international economy. Although external factors have always been of decisive importance in the evolution of the region, the present extent and characteristics of its external relations are new... The existence of an open world economy and the establishment of an international division of labor which is more in keeping with the capacities of each country, large or small, have become an increasingly important requirement for the development of the Latin American Countries.[17]

From this point of view a strategy based on the delinking of the developing countries from the international economy, as has been proposed in some intellectual circles, does not seem very realistic. A symposium on Latin America and the New International Economic Order, held at the beginning of 1979, arrived at the following conclusions:

> Latin America aspires to a type of development fully integrated with the international economy. Generally speaking, it is thought that the countries of the region do not adhere to those options which could encourage a separate road to development. This strategy seems historically alien to the options which the majority of the Latin American countries have already selected in practice. This does not mean that there is a single road for the countries of the region to become integrated into the international economy. There is a multiplicity of means for this purpose. These will depend on the dimensions, the economic structure, the political orientations and the traditional external links of each country. It is also thought, however, that this multitude of means does not exclude the possibility of their arriving at an increasing concertation of their external policies, and that the countries of the region would be in a better position to negotiate with the industrial centres through action in solidarity, instead of choosing a solitary road.[18]

The developed countries for their part are becoming aware of the importance which the economic growth of the developing countries implies for the prosperity of their own economies. A study which served as a focal point at the latest meeting of the North-South Round Table of the Society for International Development upholds

---

17. Iglesias, E.V., "Preliminary Balance of the Latin American Economy in 1979," *CEPAL Information Service*, Santiago, January 1980.
18. Mill and Tomassini, *op. cit.*, pp. 10-11.

the proposition that the economic progress of developing countries now affects the economic performance of industrialized countries to a greater degree than at any time in the past and that this impact will continue to grow[19]

These new realities indicate the possibility of restructuring the relations between the developed and the developing countries on the basis of a search for mutual interests between both groups of countries. From the 1950s, assuming the existence of an irreversible trend towards the growing marginalization of the world economy, the developing countries readily welcomed a strategy which fostered the adoption of different types of machinery for market intervention (ICP) or non-reciprocal measures of a preferential nature (GSP). Without denying the importance of this type of measure to correct the asymmetries which may be observed in the functioning of the international economy, it is possible to recognize today that the developing countries would have a great deal to gain from a more active participation in the international markets, and a greater liberalization of international trade. As former Chancellor Willy Brandt noted in his introduction to the report on North-South relations prepared recently by the Commission over which he presided:

It would be dishonest to gloss over different convictions, and foolish to disguise conflicts of interest. But it would also be extremely unwise if we failed to balance and link interest wherever a common denominator can be found. North and South have more interests in common on a medium and long term basis than many have so far been able to recognize. An experience shows that durable solutions are often found only after confrontation has been brought to an end.

Naturally a strategy based on the active participation of the developing countries in the international markets would have to be accompanied by intensive negotiations aimed at inverting the protectionist trends which have re-emerged with vigour in the developed countries, and which selectively tend to discriminate against developing countries, and to achieve the acceptance of structural reforms which will make it possible to eliminate the numerous imperfections from which the international markets suffer at the present time.

---

19. Sewell, J., "Can the North Prosper without Growth and Progress in the South?", McLaughlin (ed.), *The US and the World Economy,* Agenda 1979, ODC, New York, 1979.

7. Multinational Corporations and Developing Countries

JOSEPH LAPALOMBARA
STEPHEN BLANK

Few issues have generated more rhetoric in recent years than the relations between multinational corporations (MNCs) and developing nations. Extensive debate has resulted in little agreement among the defenders and opponents of the MNCs in the developing world. For some, like former Secretary of State Henry Kissinger, the multinational corporation is seen as "one of the most effective engines of development"; for others, such as Ronald Müller, co-author of *Global Reach*, the MNC is "one of the most powerful impediments to Third World development."[1]

The purpose of this article, which draws upon research conducted by the authors for The Conference Board in 1976–78, is to throw light on an important dimension of international relations that is likely to affect increasingly the foreign policy framework in many developing nations. While the scope and nature of private multinational corporate involvement varies greatly throughout the developing world, governments in almost every developing nation have been active in establishing guidelines for these companies that seek to enhance benefits provided to host countries. As issues of economic development and national security become less distinct, analysts of foreign policies of developing countries must give closer attention to how governing elites view the role of MNCs. Before turning to this topic, however, we want to look briefly at the general pattern of foreign direct investment in the developing world.

Foreign Direct Investment in the Developing Countries

Most MNC activities are located in the developed, not the developing world. This is so notwithstanding the proliferation of developing nations since World War II, and notwithstanding the location of natural resources and population growth in the Third World. In fact the imbalance seems to be increasing. Table I depicts the global distribution of foreign direct investment (FDI) of the developed market-economy nations. In 1975, more than 40 percent of all developed-nation foreign direct investment was located in four host nations: the United States, the United Kingdom, Canada and the Federal Republic of Germany.

The share of the global stock of foreign direct investment located in the developing nations fell from 31 percent in 1967 to 26 percent in 1975. Three percent of the investment going to the

---

1. Address by Henry R. Kissinger on "Global Consensus and Economic Development"; delivered by Daniel P. Moynihan, US Representative to the United Nations, Seventh Special Session of the UN General Assembly, September 1, 1975; Ronald Müller, "The Multinational Corporation and the Exercise of Power: Latin America," in Abdul A. Said and Luiz R. Simmons, eds., *The New Sovereigns: Multinational Corporations as World Power*, Englewood Cliffs, N.J., 1975, p. 55.

TABLE 1:
Stock of Direct Investment Abroad of Developed Market Economies, by Host Country, 1967–1975

Host Country and Country Group	1967	1971	1975
Total value of stock (billions of dollars)	$105	$156	$259
Distribution of stock (percentage)			
Developed market economies	69%[a]	72%[a]	74%
Canada	18	17	15
United States	9	9	11
United Kingdom	8	9	9
Germany (Federal Republic)	3	5	6
Other	30	32	33
Developing countries	31	28	26
OPEC countries[1]	9	7	6
Tax havens[2]	2	3	3
Other	20	17	17
Total	100%	100%	100%

Source: United Nations Economic and Social Council, *Transnational Corporations in World Development: A Re-Examination,* E/C. 10/38, March 20, 1978, p. 237.

1 Algeria, Ecuador, Gabon, Indonesia, Iran, Iraq, Kuwait, Libya, Nigeria, Qatar, Saudi Arabia, United Arab Emirates, and Venezuela.
2 Bahamas, Barbados, Bermuda, Cayman Islands, Netherlands Antilles, and Panama.
a Details do not add to 100 percent because of rounding.

indicate that in 1967 about three-quarters of the affiliates of MNCs headquartered in the developed nations operated in the developed world. The UN data show that between 65 and 75 percent of U S-based MNC affiliates were located in the developed market economies, as were 68 percent of the British, 82 percent of the German, and 60 percent of the French.[2] Japan is the exception to this rule in that more than half of its direct investment stock was in developing nations in 1975, although this proportion, like that of other developed nations, was lower than in 1967.[3]

Research carried out by the Harvard Comparative Multinational Enterprise Project confirms the United Nations' findings. The Harvard group found that 60 percent of the foreign manufacturing subsidiaries of large US MNCs are sited in the developed nations and in the less-developed nations of Europe (which the UN counts as developed). For Britain, the share is 55 percent; for Germany, 62 percent; and for France, 57 percent.[4]

In 1957, 41 percent of the book value of US direct investment overseas was in the developing nations; by 1973, the figure was only 24 percent (see Table 2). The British pattern is similar: 28 percent of British foreign direct investment was sited in the developing Commonwealth nations in 1962 and only 15 percent in 1974 (see Table 3).

developing nations in 1975 was directed to tax-haven countries such as Bermuda and the Netherlands Antilles, and was often routed back to the developed nations; six percent went to the OPEC nations—leaving only 17 percent of the global stock of foreign direct investment in all of the other developing nations.

Data gathered by the United Nations in 1972

2. United Nations, *Multinational Corporations in World Development,* St/ECA/190, 1973, p. 147.
3. See United Nations, *Transnational Corporations in World Development: A Re-Examination,* E/C. 10/38, March 20, 1978, p. 40.
4. Lawrence G. Franko, *The European Multinationals: A Renewed Challenge to American and British Big Business,* Stamford, Conn., 1976, p. 108.

TABLE 2:
U.S. Direct Investment Position Abroad at Year-end (Million US$)

Country or Area	1957 Amount	Percent	1962 Amount	Percent	1967 Amount	Percent	1973 Amount	Percent	1978 Amount	Percent
All Countries	$25,262	100%	$37,226	100%	$56,583	100%	$100,675	100%	$168,100	100%
Developed Countries	13,905	55	22,618	61	38,708	69	72,214	70	120,700	72
Developing Countries	10,316	41	12,960	35	14,928	26	25,266	24	40,500	24
Other	1,041	4	1,647	4	2,947	5	6,195	6	6,900	4

Sources: 1957, *U.S. Business Investment in Foreign Countries,* US Department of Commerce, 1960
1962, *Survey of Current Business,* US Department of Commerce, August 1964
1967-73, *Revised Data Series on US Direct Investment, 1966-1974,* US Department of Commerce, 1974.
1978, *Survey of Current Business,* US Department of Commerce, August 1979

Latin America has by far the largest regional stock of foreign direct investment from the developed nations, although its share of the global stock of FDI dropped slightly between 1967 and 1972. Asia's share increased significantly during this period, while the African and Middle Eastern proportions both declined marginally.

Working with OECD data, an International Labor Organization research team analyzed the distribution of foreign direct investment in the

TABLE 3:
United Kingdom Overseas Direct Investment, Location and Growth, 1962-1974[a]

Country or Area	Book Values (£ million) 1962 Amount	Percent	1970 Amount	Percent	1974 Amount	Percent	Average Annual Percent Increase 1962-1969	1970-1974
Developed Commonwealth (including Canada)	£1,470	43%	£2,759	43%	£3,961	37%	12%	9%
Developing Commonwealth	936	28	1,300	20	1,633	15	4	7
United States	301	09	762	12	1,678	16	16	32
EEC (the six)	272	08	808	13	2,095	20	24	37
EFTA (the seven)	82	02	182	03	373	04	14	25
Other	344	10	593	09	883	08	10	11
Total	£3,405	100%	£6,404	100%	£10,623	100%	11%	15%

Source: John M. Stopford, "Changing Perspectives on Investment by British Manufacturing Multinationals," *Journal of International Business Studies,* Fall-Winter, 1976, p. 15.
[a] Excludes oil, banking, insurance

TABLE 4:
Developing Countries, 1970—Breakdown of Foreign Private Investment (by region and type)

Region	Type of Foreign Investment			Total	
	Exploitation of basic products (percent)	Penetration of protected markets (percent)	Exploitation of cheap labour (percent)	Million US Dollars	Percent
Africa	60%	34%	6%	$ 7.9 m.	20.8%
Latin America	33	62	5	20.8	54.6
Middle East	91	9	—	3.6	9.4
Asia	30	36	34	5.8	15.2
Totals (in million U.S. dollars)	$16.6	$18.0	$3.5	$38.1 m.	
Percent of overall total	44%	48%	9%		100%

Source: Computed from Y. Sabdo and R. Trajtenberg in collaboration with J.P. Sajhau, *The Impact of Transnational Enterprises on Employment in the Developing Countries.* Geneva, Switzerland: International Labour Organisation, 1976, p. 2.

developing nations (including Southern Europe) by type and region of investment (see Table 4). Three basic types of investment are categorized: exploitation of basic products; penetration of protected markets; and exploitation of cheap labor. Table 4 shows that overwhelmingly the largest share of FDI in the Middle East and the largest share in Africa was of the basic product variety. In Latin America, import substitution programs provide the incentives for FDI. Although the three types of incentive are evenly distributed in Asia, it is noteworthy how relatively important the incentive of cheap labor is for that region.

Available data may underestimate the amount of foreign investment flowing into the developing countries, and into the OPEC nations in particular. For one thing, data on investment flows from several major developed nations—Germany, for example—are probably incomplete. Secondly, through the use of management contracts, licenses and other similar arrangements, the presence of the multinationals in developing countries undoubtedly is greater than figures on direct investment alone suggest.

These data also omit the rising flow of foreign direct investment within the developing world. Nations such as India, Mexico, Argentina, Taiwan, Hong Kong and Singapore are growing sources of foreign investment, and multinationals headquartered in developing nations are increasingly active in their own regions and even globally.[5] Brazilian investors are found throughout Nigeria, for example, and Singapore remains the leading source of foreign investment in Malaysia.

These additional sources of investment not-

---

5. See articles by Louis Wells and Carlos F. Diaz-Alejandro in Agmon and Kindleberger, eds., *Multinationals from Small Countries,* Cambridge, Mass., 1977.

withstanding, investors in the developed nations by and large have been progressively less attracted to the developing nations since World War II, relative to their enormously increasing interests in other developed nations. The attitude of many MNCs toward the developing world is well summarized by Peter Drucker. He observes that in a group of 45 major multinationals he has studied, "75 to 85 percent of all growth, whether in sales or profits, in the last 25 years, occurred in the developed countries." He argues that

> for the typical twentieth century multinational, that is a manufacturing, distributing or financial company, developing countries are important neither as markets nor as producers of profits.[6]

Increasing Differences within the Developing Nations

Even where by global standards the amount of investment, the size of MNC affiliates, and the scale of their operations are small, foreign direct investment is still frequently a critical factor in a developing nation's economic life. What may be a small investment in a relatively minor operation by New York or London boardroom standards can be of crucial importance to the economy of the host nation. Peter Drucker, in the article previously cited, emphasizes that the discrepancy can be a key source of tension between MNCs and developing country governments:

> Within the developing country the man in charge of a business with 750 employees and eight million dollars in sales has to be an important man. While his business is minute compared to the company's business in Germany, Great Britain, or the United States, it is every bit as difficult — indeed it is likely to be a good deal more difficult, risky and demanding. And he has to be treated as an equal with the government leaders, the bankers, and the business leaders of his country — people whom the district sales manager in Hamburg, Rotterdam, or Kansas City never even sees. Yet his sales and profits are less than those of the Hamburg, Rotterdam, or Kansas City district. And his growth potential is, in most cases, even lower.

That foreign investment or the activities of foreign companies often give rise to severe tensions between home and host company governments, or between host countries and foreign firms, is no surprise. Nor are such tensions a recent phenomenon. Expropriation, nationalization and armed intervention to protect foreign-owned property were not uncommon long before the era of the multinational corporation. But the rapid emergence of so many politically independent countries (in 1950, 37 developing countries were members of the United Nations; in 1977, there were 110); the growing concern in these nations with economic development and with the economic aspects of independence; and the expansion of the multinational corporation in the world economy have all focused attention on the role — positive and negative — of the MNC in national development and internal economic relations.

Tensions between multinational corporations and developing nations often reflect the deep feeling of ambivalence regarding industrialization in the developing nations. Almost all are commit-

---

6. Peter F. Drucker, "Multinationals and Developing Countries: Myths and Realities", *Foreign Affairs*, October 1974, pp. 121–122.

ted to the goal of industrialization, even as they acknowledge the social and political cost of development. Leaders in these nations are unsure about the means of economic development. Does external assistance — through foreign aid or the participation of multinational corporations — lessen or increase social costs?

Differences of opinion such as these frequently lead to ambivalent responses to the presence of foreign corporations. On the one hand, Charles Kindleberger observes, "... 'uncompromising nationalism and economic populism' and the aim to 'terminate dependence on the United States' or the developed world seem... to characterize the environment in which the multinational corporation has had to operate *vis-à-vis* developing governments in the last decade or so."[7] On the other hand, governments of the developing nations (especially in the corridors of their own ministries) urge greater MNC participation and investment. MNC executives complain that leaders of developing countries take a different line on foreign investment for each audience, and policies toward the foreign investor become stakes in host country politics.

Although the share of the world stock of foreign direct investment located in the developing nations has declined, the absolute amount of investment in these nations has increased substantially, according to UN data, from $32.8 billion in 1967 to $68.2 billion in 1975.[8] Aggregate figures such as these, however, obscure more fundamental changes taking place within the developing world — in particular, the increasing differentiation within the group according to the rate and structure of economic development. The fact is that a relatively small group of Asian and Latin American countries can no longer be considered "less developed" at all. These are the NICs, the newly industrializing countries,[9] which while heterogeneous with regard to geography, per capita income and development policies are all "characterized by rapid growth in the level and share of industrial employment, expansion of export market shares in manufactures and real per capita income levels which are approaching those of some of the advanced industrial countries."[10]

The NIC role is especially prominent in industrial production and in the worldwide export of manufactured goods. Between 1963 and 1977, the developing countries' share of world industrial production increased from 14 to 19 percent, and between 1965 and 1974, the developing countries' manufactured exports rose from five to eight percent of the world trade in manufactured goods. Even in aggregate terms, these apparently modest LDC gains include some remarkable achievements. In 1977, for example, 49 percent of the US and 34 percent of EEC imports of

---

7. Charles P. Kindleberger, "The Multinational Corporation in a World of Militant Developing Countries," in George W. Ball, ed., *Global Companies: The Political Economy of World Business,* Englewood Cliffs, N.J., 1975, p. 71.
8. UN, *Transnational Corporations in World Development, op. cit.,* p. 254.
9. Those considered to be NICs include Brazil, Hong Kong, Mexico, Singapore, South Korea, and Taiwan; Argentina and India are also often included in this group.
10. Helmut Führer, "The Industrialisation of the Third World", *OECD Observer,* January 1980, p. 24.

miscellaneous manufactures, including clothing and shoes, came from developing countries; with regard to manufactures based on raw materials, 22 percent of US and 24 percent of EEC imports were produced in the developing world.[11]

A disaggregation of these statistics by source of exports is still more impressive. They are heavily concentrated in a few nations. Bradford, in the paper cited, calculated that the 22 second-tier developing nations exported only 20 percent of the NIC total in manufactured goods in 1976. While the real growth in manufactured exports from North America was about nine percent per year between 1965 and 1974, from Western Europe ten percent and from Japan, 16 percent, Korea's exports of manufactures grew by 37 percent a year in this period, Taiwan's by 29 percent, Brazil's by 25 percent and Mexico's by 21 percent.

One result of the widening gap between the NICs and poorer developing nations has been to strain the unity of the developing world on many key issues in the global economy. The developing nations have struggled to maintain a common front in recent negotiations with the developed nations, although they have adopted more moderate positions on several key issues than in the past. Efforts by the developed nations to split off the non-oil producing developing nations from the OPEC countries have not been successful (See Mossavar-Rahmani and Rothstein in this volume). Wealthier developing nations, such as Brazil, have taken a line, possibly to demonstrate their solidarity with the poorer members of the developing world. But despite heroic efforts by the Group of 77 to maintain a common front, and the concern of the richer developing nations to keep in step, the heterogeneity of the nations of the developing world and the variety of their interests and needs are increasingly evident.

Much of this heterogeneity rests on basic "givens." Some of the developing nations are plentifully endowed with natural resources; petroleum, minerals and, of growing importance, soil and climate suitable for extensive agricultural production.

The history and experience of a developing nation constitutes another crucial "given." Because colonial powers drew borders between countries without reference to ethnic, tribal, religious or linguistic factors, every African nation today embodies an inherent source of instability as an element of its colonial heritage. The British predilection for "indirect rule" provides one legacy; the French approach to colonial rule another. The large number of university-educated Nigerians is an aspect of its colonial legacy — a condition for which the newly independent Nigeria was not responsible. Zaire, the former Belgian Congo, received quite a different legacy. Literally, no native of the Congo was awarded a university degree during the era of colonial administration.

Asian cultures seem to have been more resilient than African in the face of European domination, while the Indian cultures of South America all but disappeared. Colonial systems altered entire social structures. The British brought Chinese to work in the tin mines of what is now Malaysia and

---

11. Führer, *op. cit.*, and Colin I. Bradford, Jr., "The Newly Industrialising Countries in Global Perspective", unpublished paper, June 1980.

also carried the seeds for the rubber tree from Brazil to Malaysia. European and American slavers mined the west coast of Africa for human cargoes and violently altered social, economic and political structures there.

The level of political and economic development at the time of independence constitutes another "given." Were there cadres of trained local administrators? Had there been some experience with local self-government? How well-developed was the economic infrastructure? Were there railroads, ports, communications? Had efforts been made to develop the entire local economy, or merely one sector — or none of it at all?

What did the country face to win its independence? A long and violent struggle or a more gradual process? Were patterns of trade with the former colonial nation maintained or sharply interrupted? Were long-term economic and assistance agreements laid down at independence, or was the newly independent nation determined (or forced) to fend for itself? Did the new nation plunge immediately into internal strife; rebellion, civil war, partition? What about external pressures? Rapacious neighbors? Did it become a pawn in the Cold War?

The effect of these "givens" has been heightened by policy choices for development. The public sector's role in the economy is substantial in all developing countries, given the demands of modernization and industrialization. But while some nations have opted for a high degree of centralization, administrative discretion, and a large segment of public ownership in the economy, others seek to lessen the role of government and to emphasize private sector growth. While few nations have chosen a Chinese model of development — excluding foreign corporations — the degree of acceptance of foreign corporations varies considerably. All developing nations would like to have the technology, capital and managerial skills multinational corporations provide — but not all are willing to pay the cost involved in terms of providing stable investment regulations, provisions for rapid remittance of profits and capital, and so on. Developing countries are more or less capable of exploiting the growing competition among MNCs, particularly as they come increasingly from different home countries. They also differ in their capacity to negotiate favorable terms with foreign corporations.

Resources are a necessary but not sufficient element of success. Countries with substantial natural resources have failed to develop coherent national development policies and programs and have squandered their wealth. Others with less natural endowment (for example, Singapore and the Ivory Coast) have devoted intense efforts to development and to the maintenance of a favorable investment and business climate.

Development is self-reinforcing; success breeds success. Critical managerial and entrepreneurial skills acquired in one sector are spun off to another; lessons learned become guidelines for the future. As Bradford observes, "Once Korean manufacturers learned how to penetrate the US market for electronic calculators in a major way, they could move on to color television sets with greater ease than other countries who have been marginal exporters.[12] Success also attracts external interest. International banks and multinational

---

12. Bradford, *op. cit.*, p. 28.

corporations are primarily interested in those countries with the best track records. Indeed, there is a further self-reinforcing characteristic of this interest: once foreign banks and companies commit themselves heavily to a particular country—such as Brazil—it is even more difficult for them to decrease their involvements (see Leeds in this volume).

A recent study of the NICs carried out by the Royal Institute of International Affairs lists several factors which support the recent rapid economic development in these nations.[13] The first is the educational revolution: several NICs now have literacy rates very close to levels in developed nations. Even where literacy rates are still lower, as in India or Mexico, large numbers of highly trained (often in the US) public and private sector managers staff key positions throughout the economy.

Improvements in global communications, secondly, have given the NICs access to the developed nations' economies. Third is the improved planning capabilities in the NICs, as well as the commitment of leaders in most of the NICs to effective economic planning systems. Another factor listed in the Chatham House study is the improved access of the NICs to international finance. "In the past," Turner and his associates observe, "Third World countries had to rely on foreign direct investment or aid to finance large industrial projects. Now, the expansion of the Eurocurrency markets means that leading Third World countries can borrow directly from the international banking system."

Finally, technology is now far more readily available than in the past. In few industries do a small number of companies now effectively control key technical processes. Rising levels of skills in the NICs, together with heightened competition among multinational corporations from different nations, mean that for the most part no effective limits exist to the spread of technology in most mainstream industries.

The impressive economic gains recorded by the NICs in no way suggests that all problems of development have been solved. Indeed, initial stages of economic development may, in fact, be easier to achieve than later stages that are closer to self-sustaining growth. As development proceeds, the easy decisions have all been taken and the early, high-return investments (basic communication systems or port development, for example) all made. Profit margins are narrower and the social costs of mistakes may be higher. Development targets can no longer be framed in terms of such general goals as miles of road completed or number of elementary schools constructed. Choices made at this stage with regard to policies which favor import substitution or the development of export capacities, which channel manpower development in one or another direction, or which put in place this or that technology will determine whether or not development aspirations are achieved.

Governments at this stage must also begin to confront some of the social costs of development. Development strategies must be reformulated to include policies to create a better distribution of income; to deal with imbalances in rural and urban development; to establish more effec-

---

13. Louis Turner et al., "Living with the Newly Industrialising Countries", The Royal Institute of International Affairs, London, 1980, pp. 3–5.

tive social welfare protection for newly urbanized workers and their families; and to regulate local business practices. As certain nations approach the goal of self-sustaining growth, their economic policies may become more conservative. They are playing the game and beginning to win. They now have much more to lose by seeking to change the rules.

For some of the developing nations, the achievement of political and economic stability seems within reach. For others, even some with great natural resources, it is a goal that cannot be obtained. Nations of South America, which have been independent since the early 19th century, may experience continuing political turmoil, but their existence as nations is not in doubt. But many delegations now sitting at the United Nations represent countries without historic or cultural identities. Some of these new nations may never achieve adolescence, let alone maturity. Strife between ethnic groups in a developing nation, even open internal warfare, might create fissures in society so wide that they can never be bridged, or it might be the catalyst for national unification. Success in coping with these problems underlies further achievements; failure decreases confidence in existing institutions and political arrangements and leads contending groups to seek alternative solutions all the more vigorously.

Patterns of Developing Country Policy Toward Multinational Corporations

If leaders of developing nations are hesitant, even fearful, about industrialization, momentum in that direction is too strong to halt. The pressures of population and poverty often impel governments to be less discriminating than they might be where there is an overwhelming need for capital, technology, managerial know-how, and access to foreign markets.

The capacity of these governments to negotiate with multinational corporations has increased sharply as the skills of their administrative cadres have improved and as competition among multinationals from different countries has increased. In addition, after a period of intense preoccupation with the multinationals, in the mid-1970s many leaders in developing countries saw that the multinational corporation was only one — and not the most important — dimension of the problems that confronted their nations. Critical problems of the global economy, of North-South relations, and of economic development were not caused by the multinationals and, while the MNCs remain a convenient symbol of these problems, hammering the multinationals has done little to provide solutions.

In all countries in which MNCs operate, the network of regulation and control has become more and more dense. National legislation relating to multinational corporations (reports a recent United Nations survey) focuses on four broad areas.[14] The first is foreign-investment decision making. This includes procedures for the selection of foreign investment and the screening of foreign investment proposals, control of takeovers, establishment of sectors reserved for local firms or in which foreign participation is restricted, and

---

14. United Nations Centre on Transnational Corporations, *National Legislation and Regulations Relating to Transnational Corporations*, New York, 1978.

incentive schemes designed to attract foreign investment interest, particularly in certain regions of the country or in certain sectors of the economy.

The second focus of national foreign investment legislation is ownership, management and employment: restrictions on foreign ownership involving either specific local participation requirements or a requirement for eventual divestment; requirements regarding local participation in management; and restrictions relating to employment creation and the use of expatriates. The third area is taxation and financial transactions. This includes the determination of taxable income (often in the form of bilateral double-taxation agreements) and the regulations of corporate financial transactions — particularly the repatriation of capital and profits and debt financing by foreign enterprises.

The fourth area of regulation deals with the administration and supervision of national foreign investment legislation. The report suggests that in the developing countries such legislation is increasingly administered by interministerial investment boards or commissions, or by special agencies established for the purpose of coordinating all matters relating to foreign investment. This is one dimension of a tendency among the countries studied toward the coordination and integration of legislation relating to private investment in general — and foreign direct investment in particular.

The United Nations report surveys the foreign investment laws and regulations of 37 developing countries. It states that, in nearly all of these countries, major investment proposals are thoroughly scrutinized either at the time the foreign enterprise is established or in connection with an application for incentive benefits. It notes, however, that criteria for screening investment or incentive applications, although numerous, are often not precise enough to serve as a fixed standard for evaluation. Although there is a tendency in developing countries to encourage local equity participation in foreign enterprises, the proportion of those countries studied that require majority local ownership is still small (6 out of 37). The movement toward increased local equity participation is nevertheless apparent.

In most countries, foreign direct investment in certain sectors of the economy is prohibited or restricted. Such sectors include defense-related production, nuclear power, public utilities, inland transportation, telecommunications, radio, television and the press. Commercial banking and insurance are increasingly included among the closed sectors, and wholesale and retail trade are often reserved for local entrepreneurs.

Investment incentives constitute an important part of most developing nations' private investment policies. In a few cases, regulation may be limited to foreign firms receiving incentive benefits. Elsewhere, benefits may be designed to encourage local equity participation by being limited to joint ventures or to enterprises with a minority foreign participation. Investment laws tend to deal with the financial aspects of investment in general terms. When they are more specific, they frequently take the form of a limitation on the proportion of profits that can be repatriated. In most financial aspects of foreign investment and in the determination of taxable income, host country regulations are vague and general.

Arrangements for supervision and control after the establishment of a foreign enterprise are frequently unsatisfactory, the UN report concludes. Disclosure requirements may vary among government departments, and coordination of ministerial or departmental regulations is normally poor. Problems also tend to arise in connection with registration or licensing, the expansion of an enterprise or its merger with another company. The settlement of disputes between host countries and foreign enterprises constitutes one of the most sensitive areas of the relationship. Virtually all Western hemisphere developing nations (and some in Asia and North Africa) insist on local jurisdiction for investment disputes, membership in the International Centre for Settlement of Investment Disputes notwithstanding. Some regional agreements (such as the Andean Common Market, ANCOM) also cover the settlement of disputes.

The UN report suggests that while foreign investment legislation is too complex to permit generalizations beyond these, three general patterns of foreign direct investment regulation are discernible. One general pattern prevails in most African and certain Asian nations, as well as in the Central American Common Market (CACM), and is characterized by relatively few regulations and restrictions and a greater number of incentives. The pattern found in the Asian Middle East and North Africa is similar, except that most of these countries have established local participation quotas. The South American pattern is characterized for the most part by greater restriction and control. The three patterns are summarized in Exhibit 1.

The Brazilian Model

Our research suggests that there are good grounds for believing that another pattern or model of MNC-host country relationship is now coming into existence, particularly in the most industrially advanced developing nations. We call this the Brazilian model, and suggest that, within limits, one can think of Brazil as constituting a model of the kinds of demands, bargaining posture, and regulations multinational corporations will encounter in other developing nations. The model cannot be generalized even to all of the NICs. Hong Kong and Singapore, for example, cannot gain the leverage Brazil has with its size and muscle in the world economy. Few developing nations can aspire to be in Brazil's class. Most will never weigh as heavily as Brazil in their dealings with multinationals.

Despite such obvious caveats, the concept of the Brazilian model is appealing. In its basic posture toward foreign investment, Brazil seems to fit what many observers would expect from nations as they develop economically and politically. The Brazilian case makes it perfectly clear that a developing nation can introduce a wide range of stringent policies and regulations without turning off the flow of foreign direct investment. Brazil seems also to represent a novel middle ground between *laissez-faire* capitalist and socialist assumptions about the need and value of foreign investment—and what form such investment should take.

The Brazilian model is usefully considered along the following major dimensions:

Ideology. Preconceptions are less rigid about capitalism and socialism, or about the relative

EXHIBIT 1:
Patterns of Foreign Direct Investment Regulation in Selected Developing Countries

	Parameter	Pattern 1 (mostly Asia — excluding India — Africa, CACM)	Pattern 2 (mostly Middle East, North Africa)	Pattern 3 (mostly South America)
I.	Administration	Case-by-case screening largely restricted to award of *incentives* (non-discriminatory).	Case-by-case screening at establishment (degree of discrimination varies).	Separate administration for foreign investment. Screening at establishment.
II.	Investment screening criteria	Emphasis on functional contributions of investment. Little indication of extensive cost/benefit analysis. Screening largely for award of incentives.	Emphasis on functional contributions and conditions of investment. Little indication of extensive cost/benefit analysis.	Criteria formulated for cost/benefit analysis, often extensive. Includes social cost criteria in some cases.
III.	Ownership	Few requirements. Few sectors closed to foreign investment.	Joint ventures prevalent.	Strict regulations on ownership and investment (exc. Brazil). A large number of closed sectors.
IV.	Finance	Few repatriation limitations.	Few repatriation limitations.	Repatriation ceilings in most areas (exc. Mexico). Screening of foreign loans. Special control of payments to parent company.
V.	Employment and training	Announced indigenization policies but little headway in practice.	Local quotas for work force. Few local quotas for management.	Specific across-the-board indigenization requirements.
VI.	Technology transfer	No controls.	No controls.	Screening and registration of all technology imported.
VII.	Investment incentives	Long-term tax incentives for establishment.	Establishment incentives limited to five years — in most cases non-renewable.	Incentives tied to specific contributions, but incentives may be curtailed for foreign-owned firms.
VIII.	International dispute settlement	Adherence to international dispute regulation. Regional investment regulation: UDEAC, OCAM, EAC, OAMP.	Same as Pattern 1. Regional investment regulation: Arab Economic Union	Local adjudication and regional harmonization of investment regulation: ANCOM, CACM.

Source: U.N. Commission on Transnational Corporations, *National Legislation and Regulations Relating to Transnational Corporations*. (Report of the Secretariat) (NY: United Nations. 1976; E/C. 10/8–12.1.76), pp. 21–22.

superiority of private or public ownership of the instruments of production. However, most leaders agree that the state constitutes a major factor in the economy — as a source of investment capital, as entrepreneur and producer, as planner and regulator of industrial and agricultural enterprise.

Some degree of centralized planning is accepted. The need for coordinating the Brazilian public and private sectors, as well as the private foreign investment sector, is widely acknowledged. Also the need to bring into harmony developmental plans and policies of governmental units throughout the federal system is conceded.

Attitudes Toward FDI. Attitudes are favorable but not uncritical. The basic commitment is to encourage a continuous flow of foreign capital, to treat the foreign investor fairly, and to accept modes of resolving conflict typical of the industrial world. A growing commitment is that the kind and levels of FDI should be more consciously attuned to the developmental needs and priorities of the nation.

The multinationals are seen as major factors regarding a range of problems of great concern to Brazilian interest groups, political leaders, and policymakers. These include the balance of payments, servicing foreign debt, import substitution, exports, rationalization of national industry, and so on. Because of this, regulation and control of the multinational is considered a prime requisite of effective internal economic management.

Significant Actors. In the normal negotiations and day-to-day operations carried on by the multinationals in places like Brazil, the most significant host-country actors are found in the upper reaches of the military and civilian bureaucracies. Key figures in these sectors seem to be permanent; they generally manage to survive many changes of presidents, cabinets and governments. They also probably account for most of the policies directed toward the multinationals and their administration. Among the strategic elite categories of host countries, this one is the most important.

These actors in Brazil are *tecnicos* — well-trained professionals who, by and large, know what they are doing. Their internal economic and political managerial capability is high. They approach multinationals with self-confidence. Their praise and criticism of the foreign direct investor, their demands and concessions are, more often than not, likely to be based on direct experience.

Significant actors are not limited to the military or civilian bureaucracies. As the political system is liberalized, they will appear increasingly at the head of labor unions, the mass media, and political parties. Within the universities and other intellectual circles, there are always those whose views about the foreign direct investor are more than marginally important. It must be taken for granted that actors from these categories will often make the multinationals the objects of much of their criticism of society. On the whole — and for a variety of reasons — such criticisms are likely to remain circumscribed within bounds that will not seriously threaten the foreign investor.

Indigenous industrialists and entrepreneurs are also significant actors. They are neither merely potential "sleeping partners" for foreign companies nor necessarily natural allies of the multinational corporation. They are also potential competitors, often highly influential, who may try to keep some foreign investors out; and they are potential partners in joint ventures who will want to share management control. By and large, the impact of these groups is favorable both to the preservation of the private sector and to the encouragement of a continuing but regulated flow of FDI.

Bargaining Style. Because the stakes are high, Brazilians seek to drive hard bargains. As the world's tenth largest economy, Brazil will no doubt escalate the demands its makes not only on foreign investors, but also on international banks whose offshore lending practices are considered demeaning or offensive.

Brazilians are also pragmatic negotiators. This means that, despite what may appear as formal legislation or regulation, they prefer to deal with issues on a day-to-day, case-by-case basis. They prefer not to stand too rigidly on legalistic formulations. Their bargaining style is indirect, opaque, nuanced and polite.

Bargaining Strategies. The basic strategy is to keep the other side off balance, but to do so within a context that clearly implies a rational and pragmatic approach to negotiations. Beyond pragmatism, Brazilians are empiricists; they want to gather and analyze the relevant facts. They are likely to be as capable at arranging data to suit their own arguments and purposes as those they deal with.

They emphasize that their policies and their implementation will be coherent, predictable and efficient. In exchange for this, Brazilians will demand much greater efforts by foreign investors to integrate their business plans into Brazil's developmental schemes.

Managerial Capability. As the foregoing suggests, managerial capacity is high, and no doubt much higher than in many Third World countries. There is also extensive interaction and collaboration among elites in government and in the private economy. Brazil has undoubtedly been a leader in this development—what some have called the "new corporatism." For this reason, the kind of authoritarian political system that exists there today must not be confused with the more historically typical form of military or authoritarian political systems. Brazil, many feel, is in this basic sense very much the wave of the future.

Political Stability. High-level managerial skills may reduce the probability of explosive political developments but they will not entirely remove it. This is especially so where economic development brings about extreme levels of inequality, as it has in Brazil. Indeed, the history of nations since World War II suggests that the more open the political system, the greater the probability of economic turmoil, political fragmentation, and political repression (military or otherwise).

Levels of current inequality in Brazil, measured by class, geography and race, are acknowledged to be excessive. If the real wages of industrial workers in the cities have been steadily decreasing for some years, their income, on average, is still four times that of the agricultural peasant. If inflation has battered purchasing power in Brazil's industrialized Southwest, rising prices of food and other necessities have been devastating in the countryside. If Brazil can boast the largest black population outside Africa and many truly remarkable achievements in racial integration, it cannot escape the fact that groups at or below the poverty line are overwhelmingly black or Indian.

Brazil's political leaders acknowledge that better wage, price and taxation policies would reduce existing extremes of inequality. Some effort to develop such policies is under way. On the other hand, the leadership wants to resist populism or falling into the easy trap of thinking that the level of inflation can be reduced without austerity.

Brazil's leaders believe the way to resolve current economic problems is through continued economic growth. They say that if they are to succeed in this mission, they will require a high degree of understanding and cooperation from the international banking community and from the multinational firms operating there.

Brazilians, in short, understand the implications of integration into the world market and the interdependence this implies. They wonder whether those who provide capital and direct investment from the developed nations also understand these implications. The dialogue they want to pursue, as well as the policies they put in place, will certainly attract imitators throughout the developing world.

Concluding Thoughts

The fate of foreign-owned multinational enterprise is guided or influenced for the most part by the attitudes and behavior of the host country's strategic elites.[15] With variation from country to country, these elites are the leaders of political parties and trade unions, influential industrialists and educators, opinion makers in the mass media, highly placed officials in the executive and legislative branches of government and, above all, the civilian and military managers who occupy the commanding heights of public bureaucracies. Not riots or revolutions but the attitudes, policies and behavior of these elites toward the multinationals is what affects most of these companies in most countries most of the time.

Strategic elites in almost every developing nation tend to be ambivalent toward multinational corporations. This is true even of those who wish to encourage foreign direct investment, and who acknowledge that its continuing flow is a necessary condition for economic growth. Essentially all national leaders would prefer that a nation be able to move forward under its own power. When dependence on the outside world is focused on them by the nature of the international economy, it is unrealistic to expect that they will be unqualifiedly grateful.

The following patterns and tendencies summarize our findings with regard to elite attitudes toward multinationals in the developing world:

(1) The most generalized suspicions of the MNCs are likely to exist in countries at the lower levels of economic development, especially those that have only recently become independent. Here foreign capital has been traditionally associated with extractive industries and has domi-

---

15. For a brief overview, see Joseph LaPalombara and Stephen Blank, *Multinational Corporations and National Elites: A Study in Tensions,* New York: The Conference Board, 1976, Appendix.

nated the cash economy. Their leaders will typically have had limited experience with the multinational firms, and it is predictable that the foreign investor will be viewed as essentially exploitative.

(2) Almost by definition, the least developed countries are also in greatest need of outside inputs of capital and managerial, organizational and technological know-how. Thus, suspicion is matched by felt need. The frustration this engenders will sometimes lead to aggressive policies and behavior toward the foreign investment community.

(3) Where developing countries possess significant capital resources of their own, it is natural to expect more demanding and stringent regulation of the foreign investor. Nigeria is a good example and Mexico, visibly flexing its new-found economic muscles, is another.

(4) It would be premature to suggest, however, that as Third World countries discover new resources, or reach higher levels of economic development, their attitudes toward the multinationals will become more hostile. An equally plausible hypothesis is that the development of the economy will lead to more integration of these nations into the world economy, to more economic and financial interdependence, and, therefore, to a mature and sophisticated approach to the foreign investor.

(5) Brazil provides strong evidence that the latter is the more probable tendency. The Brazilian case suggests that more sophisticated approaches to the multinationals should not be equated with a more liberal or permissive climate of regulation. Brazilians have a precise understanding of how the multinational firm works, and what place it should have in the economy. One result is that foreign investors in Brazil are spared not only sweeping negative judgements, but also the kinds of general laws that raise anxiety levels among those investors. Another result is that the more knowledgeable and experienced Brazilian elites have produced a wide array of specific regulations designed to cope with the multinational-related problems they have pinpointed for attention.

(6) Far from causing high anxiety or panic among investors, policies and regulations of this kind might be welcomed. They suggest not only that governmental elites know what they are doing, but also that, within limits, they perceive foreign investment problems as predictable and manageable. Moreover, insofar as regulations result in unanticipated consequences for either side, they are open to further discussion and negotiation — although administrative elites in all of the countries studied claim to be more rational and pragmatic than they believe they are judged to be by multinational corporate managers.

(7) Although host-country knowledge of industrial enterprise varies by sector and country, it is apparent that the knowledge gap is narrowing almost everywhere. Horror stories about bureaucratic corruption of inefficiencies should not be too readily generalized for all of the Third World, or reported as if they do not find counterparts in the West. It is generally a mistake to assume that one's business is so complex that no one in the host country can understand it.

(8) Elites in these nations are not of one mind

regarding the role of the public sector in the ownership and management of enterprise. Many are committed to maintaining a dual economy in which the market and the private sector remain fundamental. Even in those cases where leaders advocate direct public ownership in certain sectors, there is usually recognition that private property, free markets, and profitability are necessary to attract foreign direct investment. Nevertheless, these same leaders do not anticipate that state-ownership trends will be reversed; and they believe that central planning of economic development is not only desirable but essential.

(9) Bureaucratic elites in particular defend the entrepreneurial role of the public sector. Those who manage state-owned enterprises will not passively accept efforts to return these firms to the private sector. In tomorrow's world, they will find allies at many points in the political and interest-group spectrum. The multinational firm must, therefore, be prepared to deal with the public managers not only in their traditional regulatory roles, but also as potential competitors, joint-venture partners, and so on.

(10) Nationalism should not be confused with xenophobia. It means nothing more than greater self-consciousness on the part of elites of host countries that they can — and should — secure the greatest benefits for their countries that bargaining circumstances will allow.

It is doubtful that in dealing with governmental officials abroad multinational firms will be able to overpower them with the underlying logic — the so-called imperatives — of industrial enterprise conducted on a global scale. These and other local leaders will resist accepting truncated subsidiaries; they will insist on full-scale production, on production for export, on a wide range of conditions that restrict the freedom of the corporate center to optimize its worldwide operations.

(11) When elites think about the benefits multinationals bring, the transfer of technology tops almost everyone's list. There is no way around this issue with host-country leaders who are increasingly able to tell whether the "black box" has anything of value in it. The problem of discussing technological value added becomes exceedingly complicated where host-country pressures are high and where, as in Brazil, local joint-venture partners intend to share in the management and control of the firm. More than ever in the past, negotiations will center on this issue and, therefore, may well require modified corporate negotiating strategies and skills.

8. The North-South Dialogue: The Political Economy of Immobility

ROBERT L. ROTHSTEIN

The North-South Dialogue is virtually moribund, appearances or rhetoric to the contrary notwithstanding. Immobility and stalemate have become the norm, tempered by occasional counterfeit agreements designed primarily to provide some illusion of progress and to keep the game going.[1] Neither the South's desire to institute and accelerate a major restructuring of the international economic order for its own benefit nor the North's desire to justify its preference for moderate, case-by-case reforms and to educate the South about the North's political and economic problems have been very persuasive — a classic dialogue of the deaf between interlocutors with different premises, needs, and goals.

Both sides are extremely unhappy with this state of affairs, although they attribute responsibility differently, and disagree about what needs to be done to engender real progress.[2] The unhappiness reflects more than the absence of substantive results and the consequent feeling that scarce resources — especially time and money — have been wasted. There is a feeling on the part of some developed countries that many developing countries are using the Dialogue — which incorporates the demands for a new international economic order but also concerns broader questions of future North-South relations — to divert attention from their inability or unwillingness to undertake far more crucial, but politically dangerous, domestic change. Instead, inflated expectations of external salvation have come to dominate a realistic sense of what can legitimately be expected from changes in the international system. Conversely, many developing countries argue that this criticism disguises or rationalizes an unwillingness to admit the inequities built into the existing system and the degree to which external developments (e.g., worldwide inflation), for which they bear little responsibility but from which they are disproportionate sufferers, can undermine even wise and effective domestic policies. There is much to be said for both arguments, so far as they go, but the inability to move toward some degree of shared consensus about their interrelationships results only in rhetorical posturing.

The critical question that arises is not whether the Dialogue will "survive" — for in some form it will be part of our political universe for generations to come — but whether it can survive in a

---

1. Some would argue that keeping the game going *is* the Dialogue's triumph. There is a minor point here, but no more. Failure to achieve real progress is not merely costly in its own terms; disguising the failure delays necessary adjustments in behavior.
2. "Both sides" is obviously rather an oversimplification, for there are groups within each side quite content with the persistence of stalemate: for example, some conservatives in the developed countries, who are convinced developing country demands are irrational and unjustified; some radicals in the developing countries, who feel that progress in the Dialogue will only delay revolution and self-reliance.

form that encourages the negotiation of meaningful substantive agreements or whether it degenerates into a meaningless (and cynical) charade. An attempt to answer this question necessitates some understanding not only of the political and economic dynamics within the various multilateral settings of the Dialogue but also some understanding of the relationship between what happens, in, say, Geneva and New York and what happens in, say, New Delhi, Lima or Abidjan.

A large degree of conflict and confrontation is inevitable in the North-South arena. The participants have different values, different needs and priorities, and different interpretations of past, present, and future. Nevertheless, they also have some shared and converging interests. As in the Cold War, sharp conflict should not preclude serious negotiations over mutual interests. Indeed, the very existence of both conflicting and common interests insures that the negotiating system — the means of achieving acceptable compromises — will be critical.

THE VIEW FROM GENEVA AND NEW YORK

One needs to begin with the Third World's widely and strongly shared belief that unity is its strongest weapon.[3] As President Nyerere declared to the Arusha meeting of the Group of 77, "... unity is our instrument — our only instrument — of liberation."[4] Only unity presumably prevents, or at least inhibits, successful implementation of divide and conquer tactics by the developed countries. In the abstract this is an unassailable argument. In practice, however, the critical question is whether a rather weak form of essentially procedural unity is the best tactic for the developing countries if the most likely outcome is substantive stalemate in negotiations with the developed countries.

As Nyerere himself has emphasized, unity among over one hundred countries, split every which way in economic, social, and ideological terms, is inherently fragile. The resulting unity

> "is basically a unity of opposition. And it is a unity of nationalisms. For it was our separate nationalisms which caused us to come together, not the ideals of human brotherhood, or human equality, or love of each other."

---

3. The discussion of the bargaining process in multilateral settings draws upon my *Global Bargaining: UNCTAD and the Quest for a New International Economic Order,* Princeton, 1979.
4. Nyerere's speech was reprinted as an appendix to the Arusha Program of the Group of 77, dated February 1, 1979. The Arusha meeting was the Group of 77's major preparatory meeting for UNCTAD-V. Subsequent quotations of the Nyerere speech are from the same source. See *Arusha Programme for Collective Self-Reliance and Framework for Negotiations* (Geneva: UNCTAD, TD/236, May 1979). There is obviously an element of hyperbole in some of the Third World's "one for all, and all for one" descriptions of unity. In any case, the concept of unity needs to be taken in a "more or less," not an "either/or" sense. The defection of one or a handful of relatively uninfluential states would not mean that "unity" would no longer be important in the bargaining process. For example, Burma left the Non-Aligned Movement after the Havana summit, but the effect was minimal; if Egypt had been expelled or all the disaffected had quit, the effect would have been quite profound. In short, all are equal, but some are more equal than others; thus interpretation and judgment are always necessary to determine how much unity there is and whether it will be strong enough to withstand pressure.

The fashionable analogy between the Group of 77 and an international trade union of the poor — poor countries, not people — is also suspect, not only because the interests of the members are not always congruent but also because, as Nyerere notes, they lack a strike fund — that is, few can afford the risks implicit in a strike. If Zambia is asked to withhold its copper exports, many Zambians will starve. But the point at which unity is likely to become increasingly weak and rhetorical will probably fall well short of the extreme: even the offer of a reasonably good deal by the developed countries is bound to be tempting.

How is unity to be achieved and maintained in these circumstances? What has evolved in the UN Commission for Trade and Development (UNCTAD) and other institutional settings is the group system. The primary justification for the group system is that it is the only alternative to chaos — how else could so many developing countries negotiate with so many developed and socialist countries? In any case, for the Group of 77, the three regional sub-groups caucus on an issue and develop a common position, the leaders of the regional groups then caucus together — with the addition of the leadership of the Group of 77 itself and the leadership of the institution dealing with the issue (if that leadership is considered friendly) — and what emerges is a common Group of 77 position. This is then presented to the developed countries, which meanwhile have been establishing their own group position in a similar fashion — if usually only as a response to expected Group of 77 demands, and not as a completely independent position on the issue. The two positions are then either compromised during meetings of relatively small "contact groups" or the issue is left in suspension until a later meeting — the bridge usually being an innocuous verbal formula designed to keep lines open.

One needs also to emphasize that the increasing institutionalization of the Group of 77 plays an important role in keeping pressure on the developing countries and in keeping potential dissidents within the Group of 77 itself in line. Very frequent meetings of the Group, of the regional groups, of various functional committees, and of the political and intellectual leaders of the Third World have been deliberately scheduled not only to maintain the common position but also to thwart the tactic of "institutional shopping" by the developed countries. As the Secretary-General of UNCTAD once noted, the developed countries can no longer hide from the developing countries by shifting discussions away from an unpopular institution like UNCTAD.

This description is accurate, so far as it goes, but decidedly insufficient, for it disguises some of the main characteristics of the bargaining process. For present purposes, it may suffice to note briefly two of these characteristics and their implications for the negotiation of viable substantive agreements:

1) The package proposal that emerges from Group of 77 deliberations is exceedingly complex since agreement can be achieved only at a very broad level of generality. The issues themselves are, of course, intrinsically complex, but the real difficulty is the operating principle that guides the quest for agreement: as Nyerere notes, successful Group of 77 packages must provide "equal benefit for all the participating Third World coun-

tries in each package of cooperation." It hardly needs emphasis that this is virtually impossible, since interests on many issues are barely compatible, if not in overt conflict. Consequently, each agreement is burdened, implicitly or explicitly, with promises of side payments or compensation for potential losses — none of which have been, or probably can be, accurately calculated. More critically, the process of reaching agreement within the Group of 77 is extraordinarily difficult since consensus can be blocked by any country or sub-group that chooses to do so. As a result, internal conflicts are not really resolved: each set of particular demands is simply added on to the others. Moreover, negotiations on details with the industrial countries are very difficult because the package is always threatening to come apart, especially when the discussion moves from the level of grand generalities to the specifics of who gets what and when. The process of reaching agreement within the Group of 77 is also so time consuming that very little time is left over to worry about what the developed countries might see as in their interest — the commitment to Third World unity prevails over the need to achieve agreement by detailed bargaining with the developed countries. Another important byproduct of the process is the inflation of expectations that it creates among many developing countries — easily convinced that the international system is solely responsible for all their problems and that external salvation will result if only unity is maintained. But even if all the demands in the New International Economic Order were accepted, the benefits for the developing countries would not be revolutionary, and they would be distributed inequitably.[5]

2) The process of consensus formation within the Group of 77 may appear cumbersome, but nonetheless democratic. There is less here, however, than meets the eye: in fact, the process — setting the agenda, forming proposals, determining tactics — is dominated by a small oligarchy of key Third World delegates and key staff members of a few international institutions. This is hardly surprising — if the many are indeed to speak as one — and it is not necessarily improper or maligning, but it does create problems that need to be recognized.

The leadership and the staff of institutions like UNCTAD are critical actors in the North-South arena because they are indispensable. Many Third World countries lack the technical skills necessary to devise policies on complex issues like commodities or the reform of the international monetary system and they must rely on external expertise. Moreover, the explosion of meetings, confer-

---

5. Thus William R. Cline notes that if virtually all the changes the LDCs demand were enacted, "the result still would be only a moderate increase in the per capita income of the poor countries. For example, the full list of measures might amount to increased benefits to the less developed countries of $35 billion or more . . . for comparison, the aggregate GNP of the poorest countries . . . is approximately $500 billion; and if the middle-income developing countries . . . are included, the total rises to about $800 billion (1974 figures)." See "A Quantitative Assessment of the Policy Alternatives in the NIEO Negotiations," in William R. Cline, ed., *Policy Alternatives for a New International Economic Order: An Economic Analysis,* New York, 1979, p. 52.

ences, special sessions and the like overwhelms the capacity of many poor and weak governments to cope. Policy, virtually by default, must come from external experts. The staffs are even more critical in putting together a technically acceptable program for the whole Group of 77: they thus play both a technical role in developing proposals and a political role in packaging the elements, in selling them to the various parties (initially within the Group of 77 and, after acceptance, to the developed countries), and in indicating the boundaries of acceptable compromise. The central point is not that the leadership and the staff *determine* outcomes in the bargaining process — for they can and have been overruled by government officials — but that their influence has not been properly understood. What needs special emphasis is the importance of their role in the early and middle stages of the process. They are especially critical in deciding what issues will top the agenda and what form the ensuing debate will assume. The political leaders (from *both* sides) who enter the debate in its late stages (for example, at an UNCTAD conference) are left frequently to haggle over programs that were determined months before. In effect, to get into the bargaining game only at, say, the UNCTAD-V Conference in Manila is to get in too late and to be required to play by someone else's rules.

The specific proposals that emerge from this process tend to have a number of characteristics that make substantive bargaining particularly difficult. They are usually excessively ambitious, perhaps beyond the current state of the art in both politics and economics, for they must promise too much to too many — as with UNCTAD's demand for global resource management in commodities, or with the demand for a legally binding code of conduct for the transfer of technology (which may help the transnational corporations more than the LDCs), or with the original demands in debt (which might, again, have done more harm than good for the critical debtors). The proposals also are frequently badly designed because they seek primarily a single goal — restructuring to facilitate development, usually by a transfer of resources. This is not only too narrow a goal for developed countries with interests and needs of their own, but also excessively simplistic for a world in which each side contains rich and poor (both countries and people) and in which winners and losers on issues are seldom arrayed solely on one side or the other. Finally, virtually all the proposals would require very large increases in central control or direction of international economic activity since only centralization can guarantee that benefits will go to enough developing countries, that real benefits and not merely opportunities will be increased. Proposals at the recent UN Industrial Development Organization (UNIDO) Conference for massive, government-directed, and centrally controlled industrial redeployment to the developing countries are illustrative of the extent of the Group of 77's demands and the problems they raise: a large number of new institutions and funds are advocated to facilitate redeployment, but there is no discussion of whether we can know beforehand which industries to redeploy or of how to determine which developing countries are to receive them.[6] Beyond the technical problems, it should also be noted that the either/or choice implicit in the North-South confrontation may no longer be the best or the only axis of concern. One of the major consequences of the Dialogue, then, is that it tends to force concentration on one bargaining relationship — a concentration that is appropriate in some cases, but simplistic in others — and, consequently, to ignore other North-South relationships or to force them into the province of special relationships or bilateral deals.

The proposals also usually reflect the interests of the richer developing countries, in part because they are most able to grasp the opportunities created by external changes, and in part because they are more aware of their own interests and more able to influence the process of demand formation.[7] They are also usually more able to deflect radical proposals that appear threatening to their own interests into more moderate channels, as with the recent compromises on the debt issue. Finally, since the proposals are so difficult to package, movement away from initial blue sky demands toward genuine compromise with the developed countries is difficult, for there is fear that the whole package will unravel or that the developed countries will seek to use partial concessions to split the Group of 77 apart. Consequently, even the currently much vaunted movement away from a period of direct confrontation to a period of detailed negotiation may be more apparent than real: there is still much stonewalling on critical issues by the rich countries, there is much less than meets the eye in some acclaimed triumphs (e.g., on the Common Fund), and the developing countries still insist that commitment to broad new principles must precede negotiation of specific issues.[8]

THE VIEW FROM HOME

There is persuasive evidence that the dialogue looks considerably different from Lima, Accra, or New Delhi than it does from Geneva or New York.[9] In the majority of developing countries —

---

6. For the extraordinary range of demands presented at the most recent UNIDO Conference, see *Industrialisation for the Year 2000: New Dimensions* (Vienna: UNIDO/IOD 268, May 1979).
7. This indicates why the least developed countries (mostly African) have become an increasingly powerful "single issue" constituency in the bargaining process — especially within the Group of 77, usually demanding support for direct resource transfers as compensation for supporting the rest of the Group's demands.
8. This is one reason why I find assertions that "the North-South dialogue has contributed to a spirit of realism which is leading to a strategy of mutual accommodation" either misleading or premature. The quote is from OECD, *Development Co-operation: 1977 Review*, Paris, 1978, p. 7. Pressing needs always compel the developing countries to make the best immediate deal that they can. But this is only part of the story, for the "spirit of realism" does not reflect a change in goals or strategy or any shared view of what needs to be done. Nor does it reflect resolution of any of the major issues dividing North and South.
9. The material in this section is based on interviews and my own interpretation of a questionnaire sent to a large number of U.S. embassies in the Third World. The questionnaire asked a number of questions about how the North-South Dialogue looked to the governments at home. I was permitted to read the responses, which varied greatly in length and coverage, but of course I cannot quote directly from them. Thus my comments in the text that relate to this survey must be very general and unattributed. But I think the results are worth

for the most part all but the relatively advanced and ideologically committed—the government elites in the capital seem to know very little about the substance of the Dialogue and in some cases are not even aware of the implications for themselves of the proposals in debate. In part, this reflects technical incapacity, but perhaps in greater part it reflects the fact that most of the elites feel that the meaning of the Dialogue is essentially political and symbolic—talking on equal terms with the developed countries symbolizes the new status of the South. For tangible economic returns, however, virtually all the elites surveyed by this author put primary (and in some cases exclusive) emphasis on bilateral relationships with various developed countries. This is hardly surprising, especially given the minimal benefits produced by the Dialogue, but it has certain implications that need to be noted.

The fact that few of the home governments expect major economic benefits from the Dialogue should not be allowed to obscure the fact that there are issues with significant economic costs and benefits under discussion in Geneva and elsewhere. The failure of the home governments to pay early and sufficient attention to these costs and benefits makes it easier to increase the politicization of the issues and harder to devise programs that make economic sense to both sides or that stand a good chance of being effectively implemented. Put differently, the elites at home (for example, development planners or treasury officials) and the elites on the development circuit (diplomats or officials of international institutions) have a number of crucial differences in perspective: the former *tend* to be less ideological, more practical, and more concerned with programs that promise real benefits relatively quickly; the latter are more radical, more concerned with global issues, and relatively more willing to let negotiations drag on until some kind of compromise seems possible. Thus, indifference to the practicality or technical quality of many proposals (except, of course, by the minority that does expect to benefit or lose) means that a useful constraint on the Dialogue's tendency to degenerate into rhetoric is absent or diminished.

Another implication concerns the role of delegates in Geneva, New York, and elsewhere. The evidence seems to indicate that the lack of technical capacity at home and the assumption that the issues are primarily symbolic—joined to the strong emotional commitment to unity—have tended to generate similar patterns of instructions to the delegates in Geneva and elsewhere. For the most part, they have simply been told to support the Group of 77 position. This is one reason why, in some instances, unanimity has been preserved despite the fact that some proposals involve losses for a number of developing countries—and why, as these proposals appear to move closer to agreement, the potential losers band together to block agreement unless they are compensated. But one thing is clear: blind instructions to support the Group position mean that the power and

---

specifying, even within these constraints, since material on how the Dialogue looks from home is very sparse. I should add that an official of an international institution, to whom I described my conclusions, indicated that his institution had conducted a similar exercise — with identical results.

influence of the staff and the small group of leaders who establish that position is considerably enhanced.

CONFLICT IN THE GROUP

If bilateral relationships seem far more critical from the perspective of the home governments — and few governments in the survey indicated that setbacks in the Dialogue, except for a complete break of some sort, would have major significance in bilateral negotiations — it is reasonable to ask why more of these governments have not actually split with the Group of 77. It is obvious, for example, that many conservative, free-market countries in the Third World are hostile to the NIEO demands on both practical and ideological grounds (and are not averse to currying favor with the developed countries) and other countries may find particular proposals directly threatening to their interests. Nevertheless, the Group of 77 has hung together — and not merely for fear of hanging separately. There are both individual and group explanations for this, which we can see more clearly if we examine the motives of the potential dissenters.

Many of the advanced developing countries have little need to protest because they are the primary beneficiaries of most of the items on the agenda and have the capacity and the means to determine and protect their own interests. Conversely, in some cases the poorest developing countries have not been sufficiently aware of the implications for themselves of certain programs — although this is becoming increasingly less true, especially in the later stages of negotiations when practical concerns begin to become more salient. The advanced developing countries, moreover, have other reasons for their support. Many of them are increasingly concerned about achieving and maintaining access to other developing country markets, particularly as they fear exclusion from developed country markets. Thus *pro forma* adherence to essentially rhetorical principles seems a small price to pay for remaining in the good graces of the majority of the Group of 77.[10] The advanced developing countries want it both ways: preferential advantages from the developed countries as a developing country, and preferential advantages (should a Third World preferential arrangement be negotiated) from the other developing countries. This helps to explain why some of them have been so hostile to the notion of developing a new association with the OECD, why they are so fearful of expulsion from the Group of 77, and why they have been among the leading supporters of collective self-reliance.[11]

---

10. A number of NICs (newly industrializing countries) are illustrative in this regard for they have taken a gamble on an open economy, export-oriented strategy and greatly fear increased protectionism by the OECD countries. One has in mind here not only large LDCs like Brazil and Mexico but also smaller LDCs like South Korea, Thailand, and Taiwan.
11. Brazil is illustrative, since it fears exclusion from some Latin American markets and/or competition from neighbors like Argentina and Chile. Brazil also now trades more with other developing countries than it does with the United States. Support for collective self-reliance by the advanced developing countries reflects the fact that they are as dominant in South-South trade as they are in North-South trade: the same small group of NICs earns most of the benefits in both

Some of the "new influentials," like Nigeria, India, Brazil, Mexico, also have leadership aspirations that make it necessary for them to stay in front of their (potential) followers. This is one reason why the Carter administration's effort to concentrate on these countries and to induce them into new forms of cooperation has had so few successes and is so problematic. The desire of these countries for a regional leadership role means that they must support or appear to support the most radical demands, and the developed countries have offered too little in response — and probably can't offer enough — to induce movement away from the Group of 77.

Some of the most critical OPEC countries do not fit into the categories noted thus far and might also be substantial losers from some NIEO programs (e.g., efforts to raise the prices of commodity exports that these countries import). Nevertheless, they maintain the common front primarily because they want to deflect potential verbal attacks from Third World oil importers (and perhaps physical attacks from terrorists) and because they fear developed country efforts to construct a coalition of the poor against them.[12] These fears are far from illusory and public attacks on OPEC from other developing countries are beginning to surface — at some point the fear of OPEC retaliation or the hope of OPEC charity apparently becomes less compelling than the actuality of OPEC's effects.

The potential fissures within the Group of 77 are thus very wide. Currently there are three or possibly four primary fault lines — all of which, of course, are imposed over (although they do not supersede) a staggering variety of local fault lines.

One major and growing fault line falls between OPEC and the non-oil developing countries (this excludes some non-OPEC oil exporters like Mexico and Egypt). A second fault line separates the newly industrializing countries (NICs) from the rest of the developing world; all of the latter want to become NICs, but may be inhibited from doing so by the early start of the NICs. A third fault line is blurred and shifting, but nonetheless significant: on one side, the NICs, some OPEC countries, and a number of others that are doing reasonably well economically, and on the other side, a majority that is not doing well and that probably will not do well for a very long time. Perhaps a fourth fault

---

cases. In addition, NIC exports to the South are more advanced and less labor-intensive, thus permitting movement out of the familiar North-South trading patterns.

12. One observer goes even further and argues that the Arab elites won't support Southern demands because they "need the cooperation of the North in order to maintain their own positions" and that these elites "have perfunctorily gone along with prevailing moods, reflecting at once the low importance of these issues for domestic constituencies and the assumption that the resolutions of these meetings will have no binding effects." See John Waterbury, "The Middle East and the New World Economic Order," in John Waterbury and Ragaei El Mallakh, *The Middle East in the Coming Decade: From Wellhead to Well-Being,* New York 1978, p. 105 and p. 133. While probably true for the recent past, these comments also have to be taken with some caution: in some countries support of the NIEO has been useful domestically and even in the Arab countries, there are elites (and some poor and/or foreign residents) who take the NIEO issues and ties with the rest of the Third World seriously.

line should be mentioned: the radicals versus the moderates. This split is partially implicit in the others, it is frequently unstable because of regime changes, and it is of uncertain importance because even the radicals are willing to (or must) cross ideological lines to achieve national goals. Thus Algeria, despite strong support for the NIEO and for collective self-reliance, has cooperated with Western companies to exploit its oil and gas resources and has attempted to use the revenues from the sale of its resources to build a modern industrial structure — actions that imply integration with the international economy. Still, the radical-moderate split can or has assumed some importance in particular negotiations (for example, the Havana summit of the Non-Aligned Movement). Tactically, each fault line has somewhat different implications and has different effects in different arenas. Strategically, however, an argument might be made that all the fault lines could be collapsed into a single — but not rigid — line of division: Those who are coping and think they will be able to continue to cope with the help of special treatment within the prevailing structure versus those who are not coping and who believe that only radical and immediate restructuring of the international system will provide them with the help they need.

The fault lines indicate broad areas of conflict, but they are less useful in indicating exactly where politically and economically effective coalitions are likely to be established. It should be noted that none of the fault lines correspond very well with the familiar regional splits of the past, especially between Latin America and the Africans (and sometimes the Afro-Asians). Each region has its own oil and non-oil states, its own NICs, its own rich and poor, and its own radicals and conservatives. Nevertheless, practical cooperation across regional lines remains very difficult for a variety of reasons — except for OPEC, such cooperation has been primarily rhetorical — and it is not likely to be any easier if the external environment becomes even more threatening. In such circumstances the need for immediate support will probably overwhelm any efforts to construct broader coalitions. The one obvious potential exception might be a coalition of Muslim states, but — apart from religion — the differences have proved and are likely to continue to prove more powerful than the commonalities.

If the creation of significant transregional coalitions is unlikely (although the commitment to collective self-reliance might produce some genuine results at a later date — perhaps the 1990s), and if regional conflicts continue to make large regional coalitions problematic, what is the most probable outcome? What may emerge, and what may provide the focus for external support, are sub-regional coalitions of like-minded states at more or less the same level of development (Alliance of South East Asian Nations, the Caribbean Group, Organization of Arab Petroleum Exporting Countries, the Andean Pact) and/or a few coalitions between a regional great power and its less developed neighbors. The latter are likely to be less stable than the former, because the Great Power may not have the resources to buy support and because of resentment against its role or against backlash effects. Moreover, the like-minded coalition may be more effective at attracting support from the developed countries.

PRESSURES WITHIN, WITHOUT

The potential fault lines that have just been noted are obviously of primarily economic origin. That might well lead to the charge of "economism," since it is clear that political (and ideological) interests have from time to time dominated or appeared to dominate economic interests and conflicts. It is not my intention to discuss in any direct or detailed fashion the many political issues that affect bargaining within the Third World, since doing so would require a very extensive increase in the scope of this study. This is especially true because the conflicts are so variegated and disparate, which implies that an even minimally satisfactory treatment would require an analysis of a large number of different cases. Nevertheless, it is worth asking very briefly what effect the political issues might have on economic fault lines.

One must begin by noting the obvious: the separation between political and economic concerns is largely artificial, since economic outcomes will surely have a massive effect on political outcomes and since political conflicts and friendships have had and will have a massive effect on what can or cannot be done in economic terms (for example, conflicts impeding regional cooperation and friendship occasionally generating acts of economic charity or sacrifice). Still, a rough separation of the two categories is at least analytically feasible. Precise forecasts about the results of political and economic interactions in individual cases are probably impossible, since there is no effective way of specifying beforehand all the factors that might exercise an important effect. Moreover, influence not only moves in both directions (from political to economic and vice versa) but also can be either beneficial or detrimental or neutral. The key question consequently is whether we can indicate a plausible trend line — around which there will be many variations — for the impact of political issues on economic issues or whether we have no choice but to accept a very large degree of indeterminateness.

Political conflicts within and between Third World countries have had a variety of negative effects on development prospects in the past: regional and sub-regional cooperation has been impeded, national integration (''nation-building'') has been slowed, scarce funds have been diverted to arms spending, domestic inequities between different groups have widened, and so forth. If economic conditions deteriorate (or merely stagnate), an outcome that has been widely forecast for this decade, it surely seems likely that these political conflicts will be exacerbated, at one and the same time making economic cooperation more difficult (thus worsening economic conflicts) and sharply limiting the economic sacrifices that might be made by relatively well-off developing countries for the benefit of their friends and allies in the Third World. This is not to argue, of course, that political factors will be unimportant; rather, it is to suggest that existing political conflicts may exert an even more negative effect on development prospects as the international environment becomes relatively more hostile and that political ties that have induced acts of friendship in the past may not be able to produce much more than rhetorical support as even the richer developing countries must expend more of their own resources in managing their own development programs. There will certainly be much variation around this trend, since community feelings within the Third World are high, since resentments against the developed countries are widely shared, and since in some cases economic desperation might generate some willingness to forget or bypass political conflicts. But it is probably more likely that economic conditions will generate much less cooperation and much more of an effort to steal a march on friends and neighbors. In this sense, one might forecast that the political conflicts will only reinforce the major economic fault lines. Put another way, unless economic conditions improve considerably in the next few years (that is, unless the pessimistic forecasters are wrong), political conflicts may come increasingly to reflect underlying economic difficulties and to be irresolvable without a solution to the major economic conflicts. However, in some cases political conflicts may be so severe or feelings of friendship or community so strong that potential economic fault lines may be obscured or lessened in force. This suggests a mixed and confusing pattern of outcomes with economic fault lines coexisting with very different political (or ideological) fault lines. But even if this is the most likely outcome, it probably will not diminish the long-term significance of economic fault lines that reflect real divergences of interest.

Despite existing and emerging divisions and despite the pressures to break away and seek special arrangements with the developed countries, the Group of 77 has managed to maintain its unity. Calculations of self-interest provide part of the explanation for this, since the poorest countries have nowhere else to go and the richer countries see real or potential advantages in supporting a common position. In any case, the bedrock of unity must be self-interest since poor countries obviously cannot sacrifice real gains for long, no matter how appealing the other forces that sustain unity may be. In addition, of course, even if unity has produced few real gains, the developed countries have not offered enough to make going it alone seem very attractive. As I have indicated, the increasing institutionalization of the Third World coalition has also helped to maintain unity. There are also some very general shared interests that unite virtually all of the developing countries, irrespective of other conflicts: all want to alter the international distribution of power (if not always in the same way), all want more external support of various kinds, and all want the income "gap" narrowed as rapidly as possible. But these goals are too broad to provide much more than rhetorical guidance. Thus the real glue that has kept unity from disintegrating, and that at least delays or dilutes immediate preoccupations with self-interest, may well be an emotional commitment to the idea of a Third World—not so much shared interests, but shared problems, a common interpretation of past and present exploitations, a sense of a shared fate in the future, and consequently a strong desire to stand together and not apart. But in the future, if internal and external pressures on weak governments continue to increase, as appears likely, feelings of solidarity may not be strong enough to preserve unity when or if the developing countries are in sharp competition for scarce resources (food and energy imports, access to markets, aid) — when conflicts of interest are real and immediate, not abstract and long-range. At any rate, for the moment the conflict between the powerful forces that encourage disintegration and the powerful forces that encourage unity has been resolved in favor of unity. More narrowly, the benefits of unity — tangible and intangible — still seem to outweigh the costs. This is a calculation, nevertheless, that will come under constant and increasing pressure.

The North-South Dialogue responds to one pattern of concerns and one set of influences; bilateral North-South relations respond to a different pattern of concerns and a different set of influences. Of course, there is inevitably some overlap, since the two systems are only partially discontinuous. But when they do intersect, usually at grand conferences when ministers from home supplant diplomatic representatives, the concerns of the Dialogue tend to prevail — primarily, as I have noted, because many home ministers do not always take the Dialogue seriously (not expecting many gains from it), because they tend to see it as essentially symbolic (thus making unity important), and because of the strong desire to remain in good standing within the Third World coalition.[13]

The fact that the two levels of North-South interaction are badly integrated is crucially important because *neither* level can function effectively unless a better degree of integration is achieved. For poor, weak, and vulnerable governments, success at one level will always be threatened by failure at the other: the Dialogue will remain a ritual if it is not more closely connected to the domestic pattern of concerns in the developing countries, and domestic (or bilateral) policies are more likely to succeed if supported and supplemented by parallel international policies.[14] This argument also necessarily implies that the reform process must go on at both levels. Tinkering with mechanics in Geneva and New York will not be of much use unless perceptions and policies in Caracas, Nairobi, and New Delhi (not to say Washington, Oslo, and Paris) are also altered. Unfortunately, emerging trends in the international system and

---

13. There is a curious, almost subterranean, aspect to this that ought to be noted. Some of the conservative or moderate countries (for example, Egypt, Morocco, Malaysia, sometimes Brazil and India) indicate their disagreement with particular proposals in private communications with U.S. representatives, but refuse to break publicly with the Group of 77 — as indicated earlier, to maintain access to Third World markets or in hopes of moderating radical demands within the Group of 77's internal negotiations (Brazil and India have done this reasonably well). In a few cases public support of the Group of 77 is also useful domestically or reflects a desire to keep lines open to the radical countries (Morocco and Tunisia are illustrative). But awareness of these "silent defectors" tends to strengthen the feeling of some in the developed countries that the Dialogue is a charade and that real bargaining is unnecessary. And this view is further reinforced when even ostensibly radical countries (like Algeria and Jamaica) also indicate that the state of the Dialogue will have little effect on bilateral relationships.

14. The general theme about the need to more closely integrate domestic and international policies — to pursue reforms at both levels — is virtually a cliché, but the key intellectual question is not the need for integration *per se*, but rather why it has been so difficult to achieve and how it might be done. For an analysis of these questions, see my *The Weak in the World of the Strong: The Developing Countries in the International System*, New York 1977.

in the North-South arena itself hardly suggest that the prospects for successful reform at either level are very high. Indeed, as bad as the North-South relationship has been during the past decade, it may well be even more hostile and unproductive during this very difficult decade. I shall attempt in the next section to indicate, if only very briefly, some of the grounds for this judgment.

THE DIALOGUE IN THE 1980S: RISING PRESSURES AND INSUFFICIENT RESOURCES

External pressures on the developing countries are likely to be especially severe during the next several years. Widespread forecasts of slower growth in the world economy, which will diminish prospects in the trading system and probably limit the amount of resources that can be transferred, are a major part of the problem. The adjustment problems of the developed countries will also exert a significant effect, since these problems may well generate increased inwardness (suggesting not only protectionism but also less concern for the fate of the South) and increased insecurity (suggesting concentration primarily on the relatively few developing countries with key resources). In short, the external environment may be more hostile, less generous, and more unstable. The possibility of external salvation from domestic difficulties will not be high—although periodic. Brandt Commission Reports may sustain the illusion that massive reform is imminent (if only the developed countries exhibit that mystical characteristic called "will").

Internal pressures, which will obviously be exacerbated by external difficulties, may be even more crucial. The central point is that import deficits in food and energy are not being diminished in most cases and that long-term investments to adjust domestic socioeconomic structures to new economic conditions are not being made.[15] And these failures come in the face of declining capacities to earn foreign exchange through trade, stagnant aid levels (in real terms), and increasing doubts about the ability to finance import deficits (commercial bank loans are likely to be both more difficult to get and more onerous in terms). In effect, much more of the current and predicted round of deficits will have to be dealt with by very painful—and very dangerous—forms of domestic austerity. Austerity may become a euphemism for doing without, a result that will surely generate increased instability in the South, major confrontations within the North-South arena, and perhaps a rising concern with issues of justice, fairness, and morality.[16]

An attempt to explore the question of why the developing countries have not made a more concerted effort to adjust to the new developments in food, energy, trade, and the international environment would be eminently appropri-

---

15. These judgments are documented in my study, *The Third World and U.S. Foreign Policy: Cooperation and Conflict in the 1980s* (Boulder, Colorado: Westview Press, 1981). The material in the remainder of this section also draws heavily on the study.

16. Goethe once proclaimed that he preferred injustice to disorder, but in present circumstances injustice (or what is perceived as unjust) guarantees disorder. Unfortunately, even if all concerned could arrive at a common definition of justice, there is no guarantee that a just order (or movement toward it) could be accomplished without disorder.

ate at this point, but it would also take me well beyond my present concern. Nevertheless, a brief comment is imperative, if only because of the connection between domestic failures and emerging patterns in the North-South arena. Part of the failure must of course be attributed to resource constraints: funding imports is very costly, but funding adjustment costs (while import costs still remain high during a period of transition) may be even more problematic. At any rate, available resources have been used, for the most part, 'merely' to stay afloat. In addition, while there is a fairly wide consensus among the experts about the general directions that the developing countries should be following, there is great uncertainty about details, about which specific choice is best, and about future economic and technologic developments. The environment of decision is shifting very rapidly, but the developing countries lack the resources to hedge or to invest in several alternatives until the superiority of one becomes clear. They have no choice but to choose now — because of the dangers of simply permitting existing import deficits to mount — but many of the choices look very risky. The result frequently is ambivalence and procrastination, or "choosing by not choosing."

The hope of "muddling through" is reinforced by another calculation. Most of what the developing countries are being asked to do in terms of increasing domestic food production and productivity and emphasizing less energy-intensive forms of development (and thus also altering traditional industrial development strategies) would require a fundamental restructuring of socio-economic structures and patterns. For the outside expert, looking only at his own area of concern, major reform may not only seem to "stand to reason" but also seem a relatively easy choice (especially if the expert looks *only* at his own problem and not at many other problems). But for governmental elites in weak and poor countries, massive restructuring might seem equivalent to massive instability; it might very well threaten elite perquisites; and — given existing uncertainties and resource limitations — it might not even achieve its intended aims. It is easier to gamble on business-as-usual (and it is a gamble) and to thrust all the blame for domestic failures on the international system. Apart from other considerations, this at least suggests that both external governments and external experts will need to incorporate into their advice and their programs more concern for elite interests and elite incentives to implement programs. There does not seem much point in advocating revolution to elites who will be the revolution's first victims — and who may not even have the solace that the sacrifice was worthwhile, if the revolution flounders in the face of the manifold problems of underdevelopment.

One of the most important implications of this analysis is that the crisis in North-South relations has already begun, if primarily in a latent form — that is, we are now in the midst of a crisis of things not done, but moving all too rapidly toward a crisis of (self-interested, hostile, dangerous) things done. The need to deal with short-run problems — like the recycling of OPEC's surplus funds — is self-evident, but to deal only with these problems is to insure that the crisis will persist and that it might culminate into a massive systemic crisis. Even "resolving" the recycling problem in one or another fashion merely exchanges problems — unless one presumes that the "edifice of credit" need not stand on a very firm base. At the same time, the resources necessary to provide massive support for the developing countries are simply not available and there is very little indication that the developed countries are able or willing to move much beyond incremental reform (or, for that matter, that the developing countries are willing to alter bargaining strategies that emphasize rhetoric more than results). Consequently, the prognosis is grim: permanent low-level crises throughout this decade for most of the non-oil LDCs (and some oil producers), perhaps escalating dangerously as more states feel compelled to protect short-term interests and perhaps generating an international system that turns away from the slow movement toward some kind of shared international social welfare principle.

This forecast might appear, as Keynes once noted in regard to his forecast of the consequences of the 1919 peace settlement, "too bad to be true." But, unfortunately, it is sufficiently plausible to take seriously. What does it suggest about the future of the North-South Dialogue, the subject of this essay? Escalating pressures will strike most directly and most forcefully on individual developing country governments. They will be under immense pressure to secure for themselves as much of a share of available resources as possible in terms of concessional food and energy imports, foreign aid, foreign loans, and preferential market access. This necessarily implies increased competition among the developing countries themselves (and probably between the developing countries and the socialist countries) for access to scarce resources and for special "deals" with particular developed countries. Thus bilateral North-South relations are likely to become even more important than the multilateral relations in the Dialogue, thereby increasing the fragmentation of the international system, enlarging the already large gap *within* the Third World (creating something of a caste system, as distinct from a class system, between the few who gain access and the many who don't), and perhaps increasing the degree of instability and the loss of welfare for the international system as a whole.

It should not be presumed, however, that the Dialogue will disappear. There are too many developing countries that have no other leverage to apply pressure on the developed countries, there are a number of advanced developing countries that will continue to see support of the Group of 77's demands as useful or necessary, and there are several problems that can only (or best) be dealt with in a large setting. As a result, the demands in the Dialogue are likely to become even more extreme as needs become more desperate. But since the "real action" is likely to be concentrated on the bilateral level and since the ability of the developed countries to respond generously may deteriorate, it seems improbable that the Dialogue will be able to be much more than an increasingly acerbic and futile sideshow. In sum, if present policies by both North and South are not altered, and if these grim forecasts should turn to be true or nearly true, what we may see is a more extreme version of the current state of affairs: The Dialogue and bilateral policies will continue to be badly integrated; rhetorical confrontations within the Dialogue will escalate and will contribute to a climate of mistrust and discontent; the bilateral arena will become very competitive and perhaps not very successful; conflict will increase; progress will be minimal; lost opportunities will be great.

It hardly needs emphasis that this forecast might be wrong: a whole range of events, including technological developments, might well intrude to produce an entirely different kind of future. But pessimism is now so widespread that the dangers of a self-fulfilling prophecy are very real. In any case, if present policies seem to have a reasonable prospect of creating a very dangerous system, it would be irresponsible to take the risk that we can somehow "muddle through". It is not my purpose here to comment on what alternative policies seem to make the most sense.[17] But if both North and South seem likely to stumble into successive crises if incrementalism remains the norm, and if demands for immediate and fundamental global restructuring (e.g., the Brandt Commission, the New International Economic Order) are neither politically feasible nor necessarily either wise or equitable (within and between *both* groups), and if a world of "spheres of interest" or selective concentration on a few key relationships (OPEC, the NICs, etc.) is morally and practically problematic, in what direction should we look? It seems to me that both sides — and if only one side joins the quest, success is improbable — should seek an interim bargain that falls well short of global restructuring but moves well beyond the immobility of current policies. A provisional trade-off, the terms of which I cannot discuss here, might aim at an exchange of a commitment to the developing countries of increased and continuing aid (perhaps via licensing and service fees within the international system plus increased funding for the World Bank and the IMF) for a commitment by the developing countries to move away from a negotiating style that emphasizes demands for massive, immediate, and uncertain change. The key point is a guarantee of *permanent* support at an increased level (but below most current demands for a "Marshall Plan") in exchange for commitment to an agreed process that seeks to approach restructuring in careful stages: in effect, a liberal system achieved by moderate steps. This pushes against the limits of what is currently feasible but it does not attempt to leap into a new kind of international order. But the complexities of working out such an interim bargain (which would also have to include an oil agreement) are so vast and the time consumed might be so lengthy that the agreement might be obsolete before it could be implemented. If nothing else, for the developing countries this clearly suggests the wisdom of taking the movement toward collective and regional self-reliance much more seriously than the results achieved thus far imply — while there is still some time.

---

17. I have discussed these for the United States in *The United States and the Third World in the 1980s*, but not for the developing countries — except by implication.

Index

ACDA. See Arms Control and
  Disarmament Administration
Advisors, use of, 38–40
Afghanistan, Soviet invasion of, 14
Africa
  colonial heritage of, 139
  Soviet-Cuban connection in, 39
Arab Fund for Economic and Social
  Development, 114–115
Araripe Macedo, Joelmir Campos de, 32
Argentina
  as nuclear supplier, 71, 86
  and regional nuclear cooperation, 86
Arms
  acquisition of, 35–36
  control, 44–46, 47, 77–83. See also
    Nuclear Non-Proliferation Treaty;
    Peacekeeping
  conventional, 82
  export of, 33
  financing systems, 42
  production, 31(table), 30–33, 34
  sales competition, 30, 82
  transfers, 40–41
  See also Military; Nuclear arms
Arms Control and Disarmament
  Administration (ACDA), 33
ASEAN. See Association of Southeast
  Asian Nations
Asian cultures, 139
Association of Southeast Asian Nations
  (ASEAN), 7, 15
Atoms for Peace, 69–70
Authoritarian regimes, 2
Autonomy, struggle for, 84–87

Balance of payments, 109
Balance of power analysis, 20. See also
  Nuclear Non-Proliferation Treaty

Balance of trade, 102. See also Trade
Bank for International Settlements, 108
Banks
  capital adequacy, 107–108
  international, 104
  petrodollar deposits in, 101. See also
    Petrodollars
  role in LDCs, 98, 102
  United States, 107, 108
Bargaining
  characteristics of, 153–155
  with multinationals, 147
  and political issues, 161–164
Bilateral relations
  assistance from, 100
  and defense treaties, 5–6. See also
    Security arrangements
  importance of, 157, 158, 166
  integration with North-South
    Dialogue, 163
Brandt, Willy, 132
Brandt Commission Report, 112
Brazil
  bargaining style of, 147
  economic growth in, 101
  debt in, 106, 107
  and fear of Group of 77 expulsion,
    158(n 11)
  inequality in, 147
  managerial capability of, 147
  model of multinationals relations,
    130, 144–148
  nuclear policy of, 85, 86
  and oil, 51, 60, 101–102
  political stability in, 147
  and poorer LDCs, 139
Bretton Woods Agreement, 117
  principles abandoned, 128
  See also International Monetary Fund;
    World Bank

Cambodia, 40
Canada
  commodity stockpiling in, 123
  as nuclear supplier, 73
Capital markets
  OPEC funds in, 102
  public-private shift, 97
Carter, Jimmy
  arms transfer restraint of, 82
  foreign policy failures of, 159
  nonproliferation policy of, 90
Caste system, 166
CENTO. See Central Treaty Organization
Central Treaty Organization
  (CENTO), 6
CEPAL. See United Nations Economic
  Commission for Latin America
China, nuclear strategy of, 70, 88
CIEC. See Conference on International
  Economic Cooperation
Cold War, 6, 120, 152
Colonialism, 139–140
Commodity trade
  agreements, 120, 123, 124
  buffer stocks, 122
  exports, 119
  importance of, 121–125
  policy objectives, 122
  price associations, 57
  price fluctuations, 122
  See also Trade
Communications, 141
Conference on International Economic
  Cooperation (CIEC), 11–12
  OPEC role in, 57
Cooperation
  economic, 3, 10–11
  function of, 118
  and nuclear technology, 37–38,
    71–74

169

Cooperation, *cont.*
  role of mutual security needs in, 16
  See also Interdependence
Cuba
  military reach of, 39
  missile crisis, 81
  oil imports, 51–53
Current account deficits, 97

Debt
  burden, 61–62
  co-financing, 113–114
  growth of, 99–104
  of LDCs, 97
Decolonization, 3
Dependency syndrome, 74–76
Deterrence, 87. *See also* Arms, control; National Security; Nuclear Arms; Peacekeeping
Developed countries, 129
Development, 10
  defined, 117
  policies, 2
  relation to political conflict, 2, 161–164
  self-reinforcing, 140–141
  stages theory, 117–118
Direct foreign investment, 143
Disarmament. *See* Arms
Division of labor, international, 119, 130, 131
Domestic market, 126
Dominican Republic, 7

Economic policies, foreign, 9–13
EEC. *See* European Economic Community
Elites
  economic welfare of, 10
  indigenous, 3, 148–150
  and North-South Dialogue, 157
  and reform, 165
Energy
  import deficits, 164
  as national security issue, 76
  See also Nuclear technology; Oil
Engels' Law, 119
Ethiopia, 14
Eurocentric system, 47
Eurocurrency markets
  expansion of, 141
  and LDCs, 97, 102–103
European Economic Community (EEC), 138–139

FDI. *See* Foreign direct investment
Food, import deficits in, 164
Foreign direct investment (FDI)
  attitudes toward, 146
  as exploitation, 149
  global distribution, 133–134
  in Latin America, 135
  in LDCs, 138
  regulation patterns, 145(exhibit)
Foreign interference, 4
Foreign ministries, 17(n 36)
Fund for Economic Cooperation and Structural Adjustment, 111

GATT. *See* General Agreement on Tariffs and Trade
General Agreement on Tariffs and Trade (GATT), 117, 127
Generalized System of Preferences (GSP), 127
Global security system, 47
Government elites. *See* Elites
Group of 77
  cohesion, 139, 158–159, 162–163
  consensus formation process, 153–154
  demands of, 155
  effect of political issues, 161–164
  formation of, 11
  institutionalization of, 153, 162
  and OPEC, 159
  potential split, 156, 159–160
  proposal for buffer stocks, 123
  split between moderates and radicals, 160
  support of, 157–158, 163(n 13), 166
Group system, 153
  proposal characteristics, 155–156
GSP. *See* Generalized System of Preferences
Guest workers, 56

Harvard Comparative Multinational Enterprise Project, 134
Horn of Africa War (1977), 40–41, 43–44

IAEA. *See* International Atomic Energy Agency
IBRD (International Bank for Reconstruction and Development). *See* World Bank
IMF. *See* International Monetary Fund
Imports
  arms, 29(table), 30(table)
  substitution strategy, 10, 126
Independence, 7
India
  nuclear fuels, 76
  nuclear strategy, 70, 85, 88–89
  as nuclear supplier, 71, 86
  and oil, 51–53, 60
  rivalry with Pakistan, 90
  as weapons producer, 32–33
Industrial civilization, 118
Industrialization, 125–129
  complementarity, 130
  momentum, 142
  and oil, 59
  patterns of, 121
  of periphery countries, 125
  structural impediments to, 74
  value of, 120
Industrial redistribution, 129–131
Industrial Revolution, 118
Integrated Programme for Commodities (IPC), 122

170

Index

Inter-American Commission on Human Rights, 16
Inter-American Development Bank
  and co-financing, 113
  resource development assistance, 125
Interdependence
  and arms production, 34
  asymmetries, 1
  complex, 1(n 2)
  economic, 99, 120
  and force, 19–24
  implications of, 148
  of nuclear cooperation, 69
  theses of, 20–21
  between United States and LDCs, 99
  See also Cooperation; Deterrence
International Atomic Energy Agency (IAEA), 69
  safeguards, 78
International Bank for Reconstruction and Development (IBRD). See World Bank
International Centre for Settlement of Investment Disputes, 144
International Coffee Agreement, 123
International Monetary Fund (IMF), 117
  alternative lending mechanisms, 111
  compensatory financing facility, 124
  credit conditions, 109
  criticism of, 110–111
  domination policy, 111
  lending resources, 109
  Saudi Arabian loan to, 109
  Witteveen Facility, 109, 114
International Trade Organization (ITO), 117
International Union of American Republics, 6–7
Interstate conflict, 4
IPC. See Integrated Programme for Commodities
Iran, 105
Israel
  nuclear weapons, 89, 90–91
  as weapons producer, 32
ITO. See International Trade Organization

Jamaica, 109–110

Kenya, 59
Keynes, John Maynard, 117
Kondratieff cycles, 124
Kuwait, 66

Laos, 40
LDCs. See Less developed countries
Legal norms, international, 20
Less developed countries (LDCs)
  alternative financing mechanisms, 109–116
  ambivalence of, 137–138
  and arms control, 78, 83
  balance of payments, 112, 125
  and credit, 103, 108, 115
  debt, 98(table), 103(table), 104
  emotional commitment to, 162
  expectations of, 154
  exports to U.S., 138
  flow of funds to, 108
  foreign direct investment in, 100, 133–137, 143
  and Generalized System of Preferences, 127
  heterogeneity of, 139
  import substitution, 125–126
  at independence, 140
  and industrialized countries, 139
  inequality among, 154
  manufactures exports, 127
  and market access, 127
  and MNCs, 140
  mutual security needs of, 16
  negotiating capacity, 142
  nuclear arms, attitude towards, 92
  nuclear-capable, 68, 79, 84–85, 93–94(table)
  and nuclear cooperation, 85
  and nuclear technology, 70, 75
  nuclear security policies, 88
  and outside input, 149
  peacekeeping role of, 44–46, 47
  per capita income, 154(n 5)
  petroleum import cost, 101(table)
  as raw materials producers, 119
  as single issue constituency, 156(n 7)
  stability in, 142
  and superpower competition, 78
  and U.S. economic interests, 99
  as war terrain, 23
  and world economy, 131
  See also Eurocurrency markets, and LDCs; Interdependence; Multinational corporations; Newly industrialized countries (NICs); Non-Oil Producing and Exporting Countries (NOPEC)
Liquified Petroleum Gas (LPG), 65–66
Literacy rates, 141
Lomé Convention, Stabex system, 124
LPG. See Liquified Petroleum Gas

Manley, Michael, 110
Mexico
  nuclear strategy, 70, 76, 85, 86
  outstanding bank claims, 106
Military
  access issue, 42–44
  deterrent value of, 22. See also Deterrence
  expenditures, 25(table), 26(table), 27–28
  growing reliance on, 19
  hardware for, 28–29
  indexes of power, 24–38
  and prestige, 21
  systems development, 46
  See also Arms; Nuclear Arms
MNCs. See Multinational corporations
MPLA. See Popular Liberation of Angola
"Muddling through," 117, 165, 167

171

Multinational corporations (MNCs), 133
  ambivalence toward, 148
  and bureaucracies, 146
  and elites, 133, 146, 148
  investment location, 134
  and ideology of Brazilian model, 130
  LDCs policy toward, 142–144, 149
  legislation on, 142
  location of, 136
  repatriation of capital, 143
  subcontracting, 130
  suspicions about, 148
  and technology transfer, 150
  tension with governments, 137
  See also Less developed countries (LDCs)

Nationalism
  economic, 10
  role in development, 150
National security
  domestic threats to, 2
  policies, 2, 5–6
  policy instruments, 38
  and weapon production, 33–34
  See also Arms; Deterrence; Military; Nuclear arms
Natural resources, development, 124, 140. See also Oil
New International Economic Order (NIEO), 6, 11, 12, 151, 154
  and nuclear technology, 77, 95
  support of, 159(n 12)
Newly industrialized countries (NICs)
  development problems, 141
  economic strategy of, 158(n 10)
  gap with LDCs, 139
  income distribution, 141
  and international finance, 141
  manufactures exports, 127, 138
  planning capabilities, 141
  See also Less developed countries
NFZ. See Nuclear Weapons Free Zone
Nicaragua, 41

NICs. See Newly industrialized countries
NIEO. See New International Economic Order
Nigeria, 139
Nonaligned movement
  formation of, 6
  and oil prices, 57
Non-Oil Producing and Exporting Countries (NOPEC), 49
  balance of payments, 54
  categories of, 64
  debt, 61–62
  development, 58
  energy demands, 59
  heterogeneity of, 50
  income of, 50, 61
  investment requirements, 65
  oil exploration, 60
  oil imports, 51, 52–53(table), 60–61, 64
  oil production potential, 62–63
  and OPEC, 50–58, 66
  policy instruments, 50
  prospects, 58–63
  See also Less developed countries (LDCs)
NOPEC. See Non-Oil Producing and Exporting Countries
"North-South: A Programme for Survival," 112
North-South Dialogue, 11
  and bilateral relations, 163
  condition of, 151
  consequences of, 156
  delegates, 157
  mutual interests, 131–132
  in 1980s, 164–167
  nuclear issues, 67, 77
  as ritual, 163
  and spirit of realism, 156(n 8)
  survival of, 151–152
NPT. See Nuclear Non-Proliferation Treaty
NSG. See Nuclear Suppliers Group

Nuclear arms, 36–38
  ambiguous policies toward, 88
  availability of, 5
  importance to LDCs, 92
  as mutual deterrence, 87. See also Deterrence
  proliferation, 67
  race, 89
  to strengthen security commitments, 91
  and terrorism, 91–92
  See also Arms; Nuclear technology
Nuclear Non-Proliferation Treaty (NPT), 46, 69
  and balance of power, 46
  inequality of, 79
  interpretations of, 77
  LDCs support of, 78
  as mandate for arms control, 79
  and NSG restraints, 80
  Review Conference, 77, 81
Nuclear Suppliers Group (NSG), 80
Nuclear technology
  appeals of, 68–74
  in bilateral transactions, 85
  and complete independence, 72–73
  and cooperation, 37–38, 71–74
  for economic development, 67
  foreign policy uses of, 68, 70–71, 83–92
  information dissemination, 79
  LDCs commercial opportunities in, 70
  and LDCs dependency problems, 75
  and linkage, 83–84, 93–95
  and NIEO, 77, 95
  in oil-exporting countries, 76
  peaceful applications of, 68–74
  and prestige, 70, 75–76
  prices of, 76
  reprocessing plants, 72
  and security strategies, 87–92
  uranium enrichment, 71–72
Nuclear Weapons Free Zone (NFZ), 81
Nyerere, Julius, 152, 153–154

172

Index

criticism of International Monetary Fund, 110–111

OAS. See Organization of American States
OAU. See Organization of African Unity
OECD. See Organization for Economic Cooperation and Development
Oil
 blackmail, 87
 consumption of, and transportation, 59
 crisis, 76, 80
 exploration, 62(table), 65
 industrialization role of, 59
 prices, 104
 production, 104
 See also Natural resources, development; Organization of the Petroleum Exporting Countries
Oligarchy, 154
OPEC. See Organization of the Petroleum Exporting Countries
Organization for Economic Cooperation and Development (OECD)
 aid, 100
 on co-financing, 113
 Development Assistance Committee (DAC), 49
Organization of African Unity (OAU), 7
 authority of, 14–15
 withholding of recognition, 16
Organization of American States (OAS), 15
 weakness of, 7
Organization of the Petroleum Exporting Countries (OPEC), 49
 aid, 54–56, 55(table), 114, 115
 commitments, 114
 current account surplus, 103, 104
 and Eurocurrency market, 105
 and the Group of 77, 159
 importation of goods, 105

 lending to LDCs, 106
 liquified petroleum gas customers, 66
 Ministerial Committee on Long-Term Strategy, 63
 natural gas production, 65
 and NOPEC, 50–58, 63–66
 and nuclear technology, 76
 Official Development Assistance (ODA), 54
 oil export limits, 58
 oil resources, 58
 oil revenues, 101
 Special Fund, 63–64, 114
 See also Oil

Pakistan
 nuclear technology, 89–90
 rivalry with India, 90
 uranium enrichment program, 76
Pariah states, 35
Peacekeeping, 44–46, 47. See also Arms, control; Deterrence
Peru, 107
Petrodollars
 in private banks, 106
 recycling, 103
 See also Banks
Political conflict and development, 2, 161–164
Political modernization, 74
Popular Liberation of Angola (MPLA), 14
Portugal, 3
Prebisch, Raúl, 118
Prices
 decline in, 119
 fluctuations of, 121, 122
Protectionism, 49, 117, 120
 in developed countries, 128
Public sector, 150

Recession, 102
Reform, 165
 relation to integration, 163(n 14), 163–164

Refugees, 4
Regional organizations
 authority of, 17
 performance of, 8
 proposals for strengthening, 17(n 35)
Resource constraints, 165–166

Saudi Arabia
 loan to International Monetary Fund, 109
 LPG availability, 66
Seaga, Edward, 110
SEATO. See Southeast Asia Treaty Organization
Secession, wars of, 8
Security arrangements
 bilateral, 2
 regional collective, 2, 6
Self-determination, 5
Sino-Soviet split, 40
Society, oligopolization of, 129
South Africa, 91
Southeast Asia Treaty Organization (SEATO), 6
South Korea, 98
South-South
 economic interdependence, 12
 multilateral cooperation, 12
 trade increase, 13
Soviet European bloc, 75
Soviet Union
 invasion of Afghanistan, 14
 strategic parity with U.S., 14
 See also Sino-Soviet split; Superpowers; United States–Soviet Union rivalry
State-nations, 3
Strike fund, 153
Sub-regional coalitions
 damage to, 161
 as unity substitute, 160
Superpowers
 and LDCs, 78

173

nuclear armaments in, 77, 78
struggle of, 40. *See also* United States–
Soviet Union rivalry
See also Soviet Union; United States

Tanzania, 111
Tariff
  effect of, 122
  reductions, 128
Technology
  innovation reduction, 129
  spread of, 141
  See also Nuclear technology
Tecnicos, 146
Terms of trade, deterioration, 49, 119
Terrorism, 44
Third World. *See* Less developed countries
Trade
  balance of, 102
  barriers, 128–129
  deterioration of terms of, 49, 119
  embargo use, 34, 41
  failure in, 164
  free, 117
  in manufactures, 125–129
  See also Commodity trade
"Trade not aid," 118
Transportation and oil consumption, 59. *See also* Oil

Treaty of Tlatelolco, 81
Trickle down theory, 118
Turkey
  bankruptcy potential of, 98
  loan repayment problems, 107

UNCTAD. *See* United Nations Conference on Trade and Development
United Kingdom, overseas direct investment, 135(table)
United Nations, 3, 6, 117
  access to, 84. *See also* Names of organizations and conferences
United Nations Conference on Trade and Development (UNCTAD), 11
  Common Fund, 122, 123, 124
  dislike of, 153
  as North-South Dialogue actor, 154–155
United Nations Economic Commission for Latin America (CEPAL), 118
United States
  aid as percent of GNP, 100
  commodity stockpiling, 123
  imports from LDCs, 138
  and LDCs solvency, 98–99
  as nuclear supplier, 73
  overseas direct investment, 135(table)

See also Superpowers; United States–Soviet Union rivalry
United States–Soviet Union rivalry, 14. *See also* Superpowers
Unity
  concept of, 152
  as emotional commitment, 157
  group system for, 153
  improbability of, 160
  and self-interest, 162

Volcker, Paul, 108
Volunteers, 38–40

Warfare
  accounting of, 23–24
  intraregional, 5
Weapons. *See* Arms; Nuclear Arms
World Bank, 117
  and co-financing, 113, 114
  resource development assistance, 125
  structural-adjustment lending, 112–113
  See also Bretton Woods Agreement
World Development Fund, 112

Zaire, 107
Zambia, import/debt relationship, 54

LIBRARY OF DAVIDSON CO

Books on regular loan may
be presented at the
must
A fine is charged after
Special books are subject to special
the library staff.

NOV. 16, 1982

NOV 17 1989